'And On The 6ᵗʰ Day, God Created Bobby Moore.'

[Revised edition.]

In Loving Memory

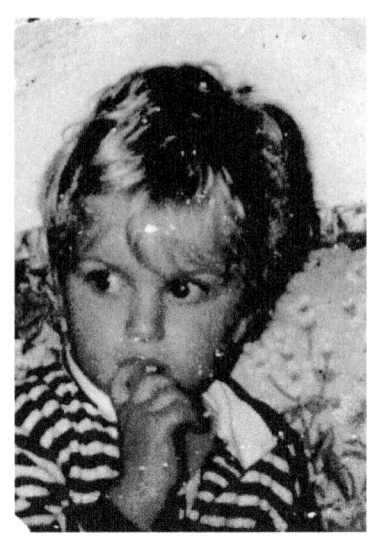

I dedicate this book to my son James Wing; who tragically died just days short of his 23rd birthday.

One of the few things which he was passionate about in his brief life was West Ham United and so I hope that this tome is a fitting tribute to my first-born child.

Rest in Peace, James. Love Dad, Della & Lukas. Xxx

CONTENTS

*

Introduction: May 2012. The Championship Play-off Final: *'I'm Forever Blowing Bubbles.'*

The guy standing next to me at the bar nudged me and grinned, with an incline of the head towards Wembley High Street. "This s***hole makes Newham look like f*****g Monaco, don't it?"

I smiled and resisted the urge to defend my adopted home. I'd been living in Wembley for three years and, well, yes parts of it **are** a s***hole – as he so quaintly pointed out – but hardly any worse than Newham; which can make war-torn Bosnia seem appealing.

I'm a little annoyed by the fact that I've got to drink in this particular pub for this match, as I actually live on the other side of Wembley Stadium. However, the police – in their infinite wisdom – have decreed that my local pub be designated 'for Blackpool fans only' today, and so I abandoned the comfort and camaraderie of my beloved *'Crock of Gold'* – [*that should earn me a few free pints, for the publicity!*] – and travelled to *J.J.Moon's;* comforting myself with the fact that Wetherspoon's pubs are cheaper than their rivals and thus I can get drunk relatively inexpensively.

[*Or, if my Bank Manager's reading this…I can save money towards more useful things, such as electricity bill, gas bill, etc.*

However, if my Bank Manager's **not** *reading this…I heartily recommend Wetherspoon's pubs, as a source of cheap intoxication; saving you enough money to be able to stumble into both McDonald's* **and** *a Chinese restaurant afterwards, and thus finishing the evening – as I did - with a junk-food extravaganza, whilst trying to remember my name and where I lived.*]

Wembley High Road would definitely influence the non-initiated to believe that Wembley consisted of 1,033 Halal chicken shops and a variety of saree wholesalers but this part of North-West London is ethnically very diverse, with a large population of West Indians, Somalian's, Eastern Europeans and the native White British, to accompany the many Asian inhabitants. In fact, it's hardly any different to East London; not even Green Street itself, which these days resembles Bombay in bad weather.

However, the racial make-up of the pub we're in is 99.9% white British and, for once, my wife is the ethnic minority in Wembley; a fact she's acutely aware of and part of the reason that she's decided to wear a blonde wig today. [*Not only is she the only black woman in the pub, she's also the only black woman in a blonde wig!*]

I smile to myself as I look around. My mum had recently criticised my wearing a West Ham zip-up training jacket "at the age of 50"; stating that it was "about time I grew up".

I scan the hundreds of men and women, ranging from teenagers to guys in their eighties, all wearing a shirt, jumper or jacket in the colours of West Ham United.

1950's replica shirts, with button-neck collars; the iconic 1960's / 70's round-neck claret football shirts, with the long sky-blue sleeves; some with MOORE or the number **6** stencilled upon the back and the simple crossed-hammers badge upon the chest; the AVCO TRUST sponsored claret shirts with thin blue horizontal stripes, as worn by the **almost**-triumphant boys of 1985-6; the not-so-fashionable BAC WINDOWS and DAGENHAM MOTORS sponsored shirts, - [*made even worse by the fact that several huge beer bellies are peeping out of the bottom of shirts which were designed*

5

for footballers and not 23-stone lorry-drivers, with their arses hanging attractively out of their River Island jeans; which reminds me, I must throw up my Full-English breakfast!] - the apposite DR MARTEN'S shirts, which arrived a little too late for the heyday of the I.C.F. but were never more suited, as a sponsor to a football club, than to West Ham; through to JOBSERVE and the then-current sponsors SBOBET; incorporating a wide variety of West Ham sloganned T-shirts, sweatshirts, tracksuits and training jackets amidst the replicas. It's a human sea of differing claret and blue combinations and – if there **is** a Heaven – surely this is what I'll be seeing when I get there!

As my mate Dave pointed out; "It's a form of tribalism at a football match. It's about acceptance; it's about being a part of something 'bigger' than you, personally. Once you get to Upton Park you forget about all the other crap in your life. It's not about Dave Garner anymore, it's about **West Ham**! We're not intimidated by anyone; we're all part of 'the one'."

[*He actually said all of that in my previous book, '**Essence of a man: A study in male violence**' but I thought I'd get a plug in early. He hadn't actually turned up in the pub yet.*]

It was extremely frustrating for me, to live in Wembley and yet not have a ticket for the Championship Play-off Final but tickets were prioritised for season-ticket holders and those shmucks willing to pay £150 to the touts and so I compromised by choosing a local pub which would be showing the match on big-screen TV; thus giving me the opportunity to savour the big-match atmosphere and surround myself with Hammers fans, just a stone's throw away from the stadium.

6

The lyrically complicated chant of: *"East, East, East London; East, East, East London"*, was repeated until everybody knew the words and was followed by: *"Chim-chimney, chim-chimney, chim-chim-cheroo, we are the bastards in claret and blue…"*

Ahh, as one of Gershwin's finest ballads floated around the pub, the adrenalin began to rise. Kick-off time was approaching and West Ham were a mere 90 minutes away from a return to the Premiership. Unfortunately so were their opponents Blackpool and a crowd of their tangerine-clad fans – *[Gok Wan would've fainted!]* - passed by the open doors, chanting "Sea-side, sea-siders; **sea-side, sea-siders.**" It made West Ham's response seem positively Shakespearian.

"I'm Forever Blowing Bubbles, Pretty Bubbles in the Air".

The hair on the back of my arms started tingling as the familiar refrain gained momentum.

"They Fly So High, Nearly Reach the Sky. Then Like My Dreams They Fade and Die."

I look across at my wife and she smiles, opening her arms wide in imitation of the hundreds of our like-minded brethren and raising her voice to join the happy throng.

"Fortune's Always Hiding, I've Looked Everywhere."

I balance our drinks and move through the crowd to our table, knowing that it doesn't get any better than this on a Saturday afternoon.

"I'm Forever Blowing Bubbles, Pretty Bubbles in the Air…United" *[Clap, clap, clap]* **"United…"** *[Clap ,clap, clap.]*

*

Carlton Cole squeezes a shot into the corner and the pub erupts. It's been tense but, finally, the West Ham fans have something to sing about. We leap to our feet and I embrace my wife, which is fortunate really, as the almighty slap I receive on my back from a jubilant Hammers fan would probably have propelled me across the table had I not been holding on to her.

The chanting begins anew; to the tune of 'When The Saints Go Marching In':

"Oh, East London...is wonderful. Oh East London is wonderful".

I agree wholeheartedly!

"It's full of tits, pussy and West Ham...Oh East London is wonderful."

Hmmn...that little ditty narrowly missed out on the Ivor Novello Award but, hey, I agree wholeheartedly!

At half-time it becomes a military operation to try and get through to the bar. Everybody is my new best friend, as I'm embraced every few feet by jubilant Hammers fans. This is all very nice but it's been at least 10 minutes since I've had a Guinness and I'm getting withdrawal symptoms.

I finally get served and return to our table just in time to see that bastard Ince – [*not the* **complete bastard** *Ince, who abandoned West Ham when the team were relegated but his apprentice complete-bastard son Ince, who's now trying to prevent our promotion*] – equalise.

The pub goes silent and there's an angry vibe in the air. There are two young women sitting at our table; both very attractive and 'dressed to kill'. As one, they reach below the table and remove trainers from their bags; replacing their high heels with the sportswear. One of them turns to us and states; "If we f*****g lose, we're gonna go out there and kick some f*****g Blackpool heads in."

[*Oh, East London...is wonderful...*]

'*Bubbles*' begins to ring out again, as the nervous fans attempt to lift both the team and their own wavering spirits.

"Why aren't you singing?" asks my wife.

I can't explain that I'm too anxious; expecting the worst now; anticipating bitter defeat.

"You were singing when they were winning", she states.

If she breaks into; *"You Only Sing When You're Winning..."* I may have to put my **own** trainers on!

The noise in the pub is now a strange mixture of anti-Tottenham and Millwall songs; 'tribute' songs to former players – Ludek Miklosko's name repeatedly being chanted – and the now-constant refrain of '*Bubbles*'.

You haven't heard swearing – **really** heard swearing – until you've been to a crowded pub and experienced rabid football fanaticism. The atmosphere is electric and, with the match poised on a knife-edge, could go either way. The immediate Wembley area will experience either euphoria tonight or the largest double-glazing bill in history.

*

Ricardo Vaz Te slams the ball into the roof of the Blackpool net with just minutes remaining and the pub explodes into an orgasm of joy. I am now wearing half-a-dozen pints of Wetherspoon's finest ale, as a tidal wave of alcohol is launched into the air. For minutes afterwards it's a little like Chinese water torture, as droplets of lager drip down from the ceiling onto my head. I don't care. I'm experiencing post-orgasmic euphoria. [*And alcoholism, by this stage.*]

As the final whistle sounds and *"Oh, East London..."* experiences its 97th outing of the afternoon, my wife turns to me and says, with an exhausted expression – [*or maybe p****d?*] – "I can't ever go through that torture again!"

Oh, my dear innocent little Yvonne…welcome to the world of a West Ham United fan.

*

Christmas 1968

Memory is a funny thing. I sometimes struggle to remember important birthdays and major events in my life and yet Christmas 1968 is indelibly etched because of one gift I received that year.

I can even remember the box it was contained within. It was white and sturdy; square, with a green holly pattern running diagonally across it. [Or was it Christmas trees? It was 'Christmassy', I know that much.]

I knew, even as I handled it, that this present would be my favourite. It wasn't even wrapped, just a box with Christmas trees / holly leaves on. That had to mean something significant. No garish wrapping paper with badly-drawn Santa on and reams of Sellotape, designed to frustrate a six-year old child. Just a sturdy box.

I lifted the lid as if the Holy Grail itself would be revealed inside. It was much better than that! It was claret; not red or crimson or scarlet or any other variation of the colour…**claret**…as in the fine wine.

It felt wonderful in my hands; almost as wonderful as it looked to my 6 year old eyes. But wait…it had sky-blue sleeves. Not navy blue or dark blue or any other variety of blue but the **best** blue; the colour of the summer sky.

White shorts and socks. Of course. Who would want any other colour for a pair of shorts or socks. It would be ridiculous to even contemplate shorts and socks which weren't pristine white in colour.

I couldn't wait to try it on; my first West Ham United kit. No item of clothing I've ever worn since has brought me as much joy; not even the hugely expensive Italian wool double-breasted suit I bought in 1988 and which I proudly wore **everywhere**. If it hadn't been so snugly-fitting I'd've worn it as pyjamas.

The West Ham replica kit fit me like a glove. [*I'd rather it had fit me like a football kit but, hey, you can't have everything.*] It would soon be joined by the Away kit; the sky blue one, with two claret hoops around the chest. I was sartorially blessed, age 6!

My first actual memory of football was of sitting in my mother's lap and wondering why my dad was yelling at our little black-and-white TV. It wasn't unusual to hear my father yelling but generally his anger was directed at my mum or I, not at inanimate objects. It was only years later that I realised he'd been watching the 1966 World Cup Final. [*More of which later.*]

Upon commencing school, aged 5, I soon came to realise that there was an entity entitled 'West Ham United'. Oh, there were other entities too, such as Chelsea and Arsenal and Spurs, etc but these were very insignificant creatures if you lived in Hornchurch, Essex. Hornchurch was an extension of East London, being largely populated by re-located East-Enders and West Ham were by far the most important football team in our biased little world.

These were the days when most people still supported their 'local' team; before the 'glory-hunters' started being born. Fickle little fools who supported Manchester United or Liverpool, even though they were on the other side of the country, just because they were always winning. Those poor saps would never know the true joy of watching a team win against the odds; the

11

delights of avoiding relegation by a whisker; the community spirit of following your local heroes; the tribal pride of being a Hammer.

As soon as I actually saw West Ham play on TV my love affair started and I've certainly been more faithful to them than I have to any of the women in my life. [*Though I've also been more faithful to Liverpool and Manchester United than I have to the women in my life; so that's probably not a good example.*]

The Hammers have been my over-riding passion since I first saw the colours and first viewed that magnificent athlete Robert Frederick Chelsea [*unfortunate middle name, I know, but nobody's perfect!*] Moore, striding imperiously up-field; ball seemingly glued to his boot; curly blond hair flowing, as he looked up and measured a precise forty-yard pass to the feet of the galloping war-horse that was Geoff Hurst; whose cannon-ball shot explodes into the netting behind the helpless goalkeeper and brings the Upton Park faithful to their feet.

Nothing can better a West Ham victory; just as there is no worse feeling that a West Ham defeat. This is their soap-opera-like story. Come join me in my passion!

*

Not just a bunch of boring stats. Honest!

My love affair with the Hammers began in the 1960's and has endured ever since. Thus, although I have an interest in the club's history prior to my birth, it is a 'casual' interest. I don't have a passion for pre-Bobby Moore West Ham because there **was no** pre-Bobby Moore West Ham, as far as I was concerned as a child. I lived through the magnificent Moore, Hurst, Peters era and beyond and this is the focus of the book; **my** experience of being a West Ham fan. However, all good

12

stories require a background and so Chapter One will give you everything you need to know about the pre-Moore era.

I have tried to avoid quoting endless statistics, in order that this tome may appeal to the 'casual' fan and not just West Ham die-hards. Obviously there will be **some** significant match facts, player profiles and goal-scoring statistics, etc but I have tried to limit these to a bare minimum, so as to make the book flow as a story. Likewise, I have not been anal and given precise transfer amounts; instead choosing to round them off. Thus, a £253,500 player will be worth £250,000 in **this** book.

There will not be continual references to every player who ever laced on a boot; who the tea-lady was when we won the FA Cup or what the highest attendance was in the 1968-9 season. [*63,274 against Manchester United; in case anyone ever asks!*]

There will, obviously, be an element of personal bias involved and certain players will feature heavily; sometimes at the expense of others whom the reader may think deserving of more type. Tough! Write your own book. [*Or, in the case of Millwall fans; colour in your own Dot-to-Dot pictures.*]

The book will also feature 'background' details which I feel are significant to the West Ham story. This will include an examination of the changing face of the East End of London; commencing with the dire poverty at the time of the club's birth, and the significance of this harsh working-class environment to the Hammers fan-base; as well as the impact of the Second World War upon East London.

With the advent of the modern medias investigative reporting and the proliferation of footballer autobiographies, later chapters will examine the behind-the-scenes machinations and intrigues of the modern game; notably the Harry Redknapp era.

They say that 'you can't know where you're going unless you know where you've come from', so let's go back to the very beginning of this story to try and understand why I'm "West Ham 'til I die".

*

CHAPTER ONE:

'Oh, East London is wonderful...oh, East London is wonderful...deprivation, disease and despair...oh, East London is wonderful!'

Jack the Ripper and cholera epidemics: Why East London wasn't a favourite tourist destination in the 19th Century.

Around the time of West Ham United's 'birth', in the late 19th Century, East London was a place of extreme poverty and deprivation. Over-populated by the chronically disadvantaged and characterised by foul-smelling odours from the industrial plants; sweat-shop clothing factories; grey, depressing living quarters which were barely fit for habitation; rampant disease and crime; it was a downtrodden society within a society.

The awful conditions of the unskilled workers were finally exposed in June 1888 by Annie Besant, who visited the Bryant & May match factory in Bow and discovered girls as young as 13 labouring away for hours each day, for a pittance. Besant went on record and compared the factory to a 'prison' and described the workers as 'white slaves' and 'oppressed'; the girls often being subject to physical abuse from the foremen and injured whilst using the machinery.

The women worked, on average, for 12 hours a day and earned between 4 and 9 shillings per week, dependent upon age and hours worked. Thus, once they'd paid their rent and purchased life's essentials, the girls were forced to subsist upon a bread-and-butter diet each day!

As a result of this expose the working conditions improved for the women of Bryant & May but it soon became apparent that they weren't the only ones suffering from abysmal working conditions.

Unions began to form, representing the 'unskilled' workers and, in 1889, the Gas Workers and General Labourers Union succeeded in getting a standard 8 hour working day introduced. That same year 60,000 Dockers went on strike and brought trade along the River Thames to a standstill for a month.

The Docks offered very poorly paid employment, especially considering that it was such hard manual labour. The employment was 'piece-work' and used casual labour, whereby men would have to turn up early each morning and hope to be picked out from the crowds of waiting Dockers; all desperate to feed their families. This lack of long-term contracts or assurances over their employ caused much depression and anger and the Dockers began to band together and loudly complain.

It was another 'turning-point' in the history of trade unionism, as membership of the unions rapidly increased as a result of this 'worker solidarity'. The working class were finally 'fighting back'.

[Trade Unions weren't even legalised until 1871! Prior to this, it was actually illegal to belong to an organised Union. The Government finally relented and allowed membership to flourish, and this 'organising of Socialist ideals' became the basis of what would develop into the Labour Party.

The first real evidence of this worker solidarity, engendered by the embracing of trade unionism by the working classes, was the General Strike of 1926. The Government's attempts to reduce coal miners' wages led to 1.5 million workers across the country 'walking out' in what was – ultimately – an unsuccessful, mass nine day strike action.]

*

Shipbuilding was big business at the turn of the 19th century and London's Docks were thriving. The West India Docks [built in 1802] imported produce – as the name suggests – from trade routes in the West Indies and was followed by the London Dock in 1805 and East India Dock in 1806, which imported wine and tobacco and stored them in large purpose-built warehouses, from where they were transported around the UK.

Increasing profit and trade required ever-expanding Docks and warehousing and so the St Katherine's Dock, Royal Victoria Dock, Millwall Dock, and the Royal Albert Dock, were all constructed over the following decades, to accommodate the proliferation of differing imports and exports.

[As ships got bigger the King George V Dock was built, in 1921, to handle the vessels which the older Docks could no longer comfortably accommodate.]

The Docks had thus been one of London's principal sources of manual labour work for some time and attracted many unskilled workers, plus Irish and Jewish immigrants to an already poor and over-crowded East London area.

This abundance of unskilled labour based there also led to the opening of many factories in the area, which further exploited the desperate workers. West Ham and East Ham, particularly, experienced a huge increase in hastily-built housing, as the manufacturing industry expanded rapidly, alongside the expansion of the railway network. However, due to the noxious fumes from these factories and the poor sewerage system in East London, only those desperate to earn a living gravitated towards the East End.

Cholera outbreaks occurred in 1832, 1848 and 1854 and the cholera epidemic of 1866 killed 3,000 people in East London. Typhus and tuberculosis were common killers and many orphans were forced to beg on the streets for pennies or accept poorly-paid manual labour jobs in factories, just to survive. As a reaction to this, Barnardo's opened their first 'home for boys' in Stepney, in 1870 but this was no help to orphaned girls and many young women turned to prostitution; especially around the Docks, where visiting sailors would be only too willing to part with some money in return for a young girls 'favours'. [The 'problem' of East End prostitution was highlighted when Jack the Ripper commenced his serial killing of prostitutes in the Whitechapel area.]

As a result of all of the above, the East End became the focal point of the burgeoning Socialist movement, as well as the focus of the suffragettes.

1890 saw the 'official' slum clearance programme commence, as the Government finally accepted that housing conditions in many parts of East London were unacceptably poor. However, because of the continuing expansion of the population, this new housing took the form of unattractive six-storey blocks of flats, rather than new improved houses with gardens. The image of East London being composed of grey, terraced housing and featureless tenements populated by sallow depressed-looking men in cloth caps and work-boots, with wives looking tired and decades older than their tender years, was born around this period of poverty and depression.

*

In this particular case 'Irons' is <u>not</u> Cockney rhyming slang!

The Thames Ironworks was a huge shipbuilding company, stretching across East London and into Essex. Its owner Arnold Hills decided to follow the lead of two other companies who'd created a works football team in order to improve staff morale; joining Woolwich Arsenal – [*later, just plain Arsenal*] – and Millwall Ironworks FC – [*later, just plain Bastards*] – with his Thames Ironworks Football Club, in 1895. This was also the beginning of a bitter rivalry between West Ham and Millwall; a rivalry which initially stemmed from the two companies fighting for the same warship contracts; constantly undercutting each other and striving to keep one step ahead of their competitor and, later, as rival football teams from deprived areas.

Arnold Hills believed that recreation was a positive distraction from the social hardships and poverty of the East End and thus chose Hermit Road, Canning Town, as the site of his team's first home pitch; Canning Town being one of the most destitute sections of East London. The initial kits for Thames Ironworks FC were all blue, reflecting the fact that the university educated Hills had been an Oxford 'Blue'. The club's emblem, in contrast, reflected the working-class makeup of the actual team. The riveters of the ironworks employed a variety of size-and-weight hammers to drive the red-hot rivets into the iron plates of the warships they were assembling and these crossed hammers were proudly displayed on the team's badge and would eventually become the team's nickname; the Hammers, although – initially – the fans would shout "Come on you Irons", when they were still the Thames Ironworks FC.

[Quick Cockney rhyming slang lesson for complete beginners: West Ham are often referred to as 'the Cockney Boys' and so perhaps we should briefly examine this particular area of East London culture before we go further.

The supposed criteria for being a Cockney is to be 'born within the sound of Bow Bells'; the huge church bells of St Mary-le-Bow. However, this is a very vague guide to distance, as the mileage the sound of Bow Bells carried depended upon the prevailing weather conditions. Also – as industry and residential buildings and population expanded – the general noise increased and thus the effect of the church bells decreased.

(Plus, if we're going to be really pedantic – which I occasionally like to be, just to annoy people – the periods when there were no church bells, such as the Great Fire of London and the Blitz, would mean that no Cockneys were born!? Something I'm sure the Scousers would be pleased with.)

The East End of London's borders have changed over the years but can basically be summarised as consisting of Bethnal Green, Whitechapel, Spitalfields, Wapping, Stepney, Poplar, Limehouse, Clerkenwell, Aldgate, Shoreditch, Hackney, Hoxton, Bow, Mile End, East Ham, West Ham, Stratford, Canning Town, Upton Park, Forest Gate and Plaistow.

The actual origin of the word Cockney is uncertain but the term always seemed to imply 'working class East

Ender', to those outside of the area and was often used in a disparaging manner.

Rhyming slang itself is not unique to East London and most areas of the world have their own versions of slang but what is referred to as 'Cockney rhyming slang' is the most prevalent form of bastardisation of the Queen's English and was the patter often used by street traders in the mid-19th century, as they loudly sought to sell their wares and attract the attention of passers-by.

It involves replacing a word with one which rhymes with it or a phrase which is meant to have a humorous connection. There is also some conjecture as to whether the origins of rhyming slang were to hide the actual meaning of phrases from outsiders; thus reinforcing a community feeling in the midst of extreme deprivation.

Rhyming slang can be simple and obvious to an outsider: 'Dog and bone' = telephone. However, if someone says they're going to 'use the dog', as an abbreviation, it becomes harder for an outsider to deduce their meaning.

Sometimes 'specialist' knowledge is required in order to fully understand a reference. Most people realise that 'bottle' means courage but how many know that it derives from 'bottle and glass', meaning 'arse'? (*The reader can use their own imagination to understand why 'arse' may be used to denote a lack of bravery.*)

Other well-known slang words' origins are more obscure. 'On my Tod' means 'on my own' and was a rhyme with a then-well-known jockey named Tod Sloan. 'Having a Ruby' = 'having a curry', after the old singer Ruby Murray, but the most misunderstood is the simple 'Berk'; one of the most inoffensive putdowns, you may think but is actually an abbreviated version of the slang 'Berkeley Hunt'; meaning c**t. [*Ooh, those naughty little Cockneys! They should wash their mouths out with soap.*]

There are also more modern variations. My wife was bemused once when my mate Danny told her he "didn't have a Scooby". I had to explain that he meant that he 'didn't have a clue'. (Scooby Doo = clue.)

Which leads us to the continuing chant of "Come on you Irons", at Upton Park; ironic for thousands of Cockneys to be proudly encouraging, as 'Iron' is usually short for 'iron hoof', meaning 'poof'!]

'Idiot's Guide to Cockney', over!

*

Thames Ironworks FC was actually composed of only a few of the ship-workers and was supplemented by some of the best local amateur footballers. Even back then, there was a desire to win and not just be a leisurely past-time, for Arnold Hills.

A temporary move to a pitch in Browning Road, East Ham was followed, in 1897, by a transition to the Memorial Grounds in Plaistow; now the site of East London Rugby Club.

Originally there had been no thought of Thames Ironworks becoming a professional football team. Hills saw his 'creation' as being a team of enthusiastic amateurs who could boost morale at work via successful performances against other local teams; even after they had won the London Football League, in only their second full season.

Prior to the start of the 1898-9 season though, the decision was taken to turn Thames Ironworks into a professional football team, in order to compete against a higher level of opposition, as the Irons were suffering

21

from a lack of competition in the local league. Thus, they joined the Southern League's 2nd Division.

[In the 19th and early 20th centuries, England's most popular and most prominent sport – football – was divided into Northern and Southern Leagues, due principally to the fact that travel was primitive in those days and so it was easier to compete against teams within easy travelling distance. However, towards the end of the 19th century a selection of Northern and Midlands clubs turned professional and formed the Football League; a league consisting of the very best teams in the country; which, in those days, included the likes of the then-dominant Aston Villa and Blackburn Rovers. This would be the league to which all other clubs later aspired to join.]

Surprisingly, Thames Ironworks won the Southern Leagues 2nd Division title in their inaugural season but found life much harder in the 1st Division; only avoiding instant relegation by defeating Fulham 5-1 in their final game of the season. [*An all-too familiar taste of things to come!*]

[The season also saw its share of tragedy, when captain Tom Bradshaw died on Christmas Day from a football-related injury.]

On 5th July 1900 Thames Ironworks FC was renamed West Ham United Football Club, signifying its need to move away from being perceived as a 'works football team' and to be taken seriously as a professional outfit. At this point only one player actually worked for the Ironworks – local boy Charlie Dove – and the other players had all been purchased from other clubs; again, signalling West Ham's intention to compete with the best.

Charlie Dove's father is often credited with being responsible for the change of kit in 1899, to the iconic claret-and-blue worn today.

The team had already changed from all navy blue to a sky blue shirt, white shorts and claret socks but then came the now-beloved claret shirts with sky blue sleeves, white shorts and white socks.

The reason for this change – *allegedly* – is that William Dove was a sprinter in his youth and when he travelled to the Midlands he engaged in some banter with four Aston Villa players. They challenged him to a race, which he promptly won and – unable to pay the bet they'd not expected to lose – they presented Dove with a full set of Aston Villa kits, which he promptly donated to West Ham, whose players commenced wearing it and used their former kit as their away strip.

[A much simpler version of the kit change was simply that, once they'd decided to take their football seriously and compete against the best, they wanted to **look** like the best and the 'best' – at that period – were Aston Villa. (?)

In 1912 Thames Ironworks closed, unable to contend anymore with the shipyards in the North of England. A dispirited Arnold Hills died in 1927, crippled with arthritis.]

Their first season as 'West Ham United' ended in a respectable 6th place; the following campaign 4th but the next two seasons saw them struggle a little in comparison, finishing in mid-table positions.

The next moment of significance was when the club moved to its current site, the Boleyn Ground, Green Street, Upton Park. [A site which confuses opposing fans to this day, as the club are called West Ham; sited on the edge of East Ham and the nearest tube station is Upton Park!]

The Boleyn Ground is so-called because of the association with Anne Boleyn, who it is believed stayed at Green Street House – sarcastically nicknamed by locals, 'Boleyn Castle' – when she was courting King Henry VIII and a castle was eventually incorporated into the club's badge; set behind the crossed hammers.

[*The pub around the corner was also named 'The Boleyn', in recognition of the eminent visitor to Green Street, but the club thankfully didn't also add pints of bitter to their badge; although many **players** did later add pints of bitter; notably Jimmy 'One-for-my-baby, and-twelve-more-for-the-road' Greaves.*]

Now under the managership of former player Syd King, West Ham finished that 1904-5 season in 11th place and, over the next decade, West Ham neither threatened to win the league nor be relegated; the only happening of any real note being that striker George Webb became West Ham's first player to receive an England cap, in 1911.

In a prophetic foretaste of West Ham's future development of local young talent – and subsequent loss of that talent to 'bigger' clubs – the book '*Association Football*', published in 1905, stated:

"It is the proud boast of the West Ham club that they turn out more local players than any other team in the South. The district has been described as a hot-bed of football and it is so. The raw material is found on the marshlands and open spaces round about; and, after a season or so, the finished player leaves the East End workshop to better himself, as most ambitious young men will do."

Despite the outbreak of World War 1, the 1914-15 season commenced, as scheduled; the authorities believing that it would be 'good for morale' to 'carry on as normal'. West Ham finished in 4th place but football fixtures soon began to assume lesser importance as the 'Great War' claimed an increasing amount of young British lives in the blood-soaked trenches of France; including four West Ham players who had answered the call-to-arms.

Also, the stark reality of warfare was brought closer to home in June 1917, when the first daylight bombing raid over England resulted in 104 people being killed, including 16 schoolchildren, when a German bomb landed near a school in Poplar.

*

Following the end of the Great War, in November 1918, West Ham applied to join the Football League's Second Division. Throughout West Ham's unexceptional Southern League campaigns they had managed some stirring performances and shock victories against Football League opponents in the Football Association [FA] Cup. The biggest ever crowd at the Boleyn Ground – 27,000 – had gathered to witness the 2-1 victory against soon-to-be League Champions Manchester United, in the 1910-11 season. It was purely because of these gutsy performances that West Ham were welcomed into 'the big time'.

20,000 people witnessed West Ham United's opening 2nd Division game against Lincoln City, at Upton Park and a 7th place finish that season was followed by 5th and 4th place finishes in the succeeding campaigns; leading many fans to believe that promotion to the 1st Division was a distinct possibility.

However, in 1922 Hammers fans were infuriated when the club sold striker Syd Puddefoot – [*I know! These were the days before people invented proper names.*] – but manager King had seen great potential in young Cambridge-born Vic Watson, who would go on to become the club's first legendary player and its all-time top goal-scorer; playing a total of 505 games for the Hammers and scoring a remarkable 326 goals.

It was around this period too, that *'I'm Forever Blowing Bubbles'* was adopted by the fans as their 'signature' tune. Once again, there is debate though as to how this came about.

'Bubbles' was written in 1918 and first performed on Broadway the following year, becoming a big British Music Hall favourite by 1920.

Music halls were an extremely popular form of entertainment for East Enders in the mid-19th to early 20th centuries, featuring a mix of music, comedy and novelty acts and one of the most popular music hall singers was East-Ender Marie Lloyd.

In the pre-television age it was traditional for families to sing together around an upright piano for 'entertainment' and this tradition was still going strong into the mid-point of the 20th century and I remember – *with horror!* – hearing *'Any Old Iron'*, *'Boiled Beef and Carrots'*, *'My Old Man Said Follow the Van'*, *'Down At the Old Bull and Bush'*, *'On Mother Kelly's Doorstep'*, *'Knees Up Mother Brown'*, etc, being torturously strangled through a sea of alcohol at family parties in the 'sixties.

[*Oh, how I laughed when Punk Rock came along and I garnered my sweet revenge on unsuspecting aunties. Punk's version of 'Knees Up Mother Brown' had very different lyrical connotations and was extremely painful for said Mrs.Brown!]*

'I'm Forever Blowing Bubbles' began to regularly ring out around the Boleyn Ground stadium and quickly became associated with West Ham United; now being considered the most famous and recognisable football song of them all, alongside Liverpool's anthem *'You'll Never Walk Alone'*, which was also appropriated from a musical.

There have been claims though that West Ham fans 'stole' the song from Swansea! There are accounts which state that Swansea fans were singing the tune for some time and that when they played host to West Ham in the FA Cup of 1921-2, the Hammers fans were so enamoured by the song that they began singing it themselves.

[Regardless, 'Bubbles' is indelibly linked to West Ham and Swansea is a totally unimportant little place in a silly country, with ridiculous road signs that are written in Klingon!]

*

The 'White Horse' was Grey.

1922-3 was one of the most significant seasons in West Ham United's history. They had a decent side, challenging for promotion and they managed to reach the final of the most prestigious tournament in the English game – the Football Association Cup – at the nations' new showpiece stadium Wembley, via defeating fellow 2nd Division side Derby County 5-2 in the semis.

The iconic first-ever Wembley FA Cup Final in 1923 is actually remembered more for the proceedings that transpired outside of the football match, rather than for the game itself, but the events of that day became so well-reported and repeated that that this one game elevated West Ham United to national prominence – merely by association – rather than for any reason their footballing prowess had yet achieved.

A fan's reminiscences of the day which could have ended in tragedy, [especially in light of the later Hillsborough and Heysel tragedies,] from *'The Essential History of West Ham United'* [2000]:

"When we were about two or three miles away from the stadium we suffered a shock. We were told by some coming away from the stadium that it was no good going on because the gates were closed, but we pressed on. The buses finally stopped about three-quarters of a mile away from the stadium, which was about as close as they could get...I saw that the turnstiles had been built into wooden structures that were about 8ft high. The turnstiles themselves were locked and deserted but bodies were climbing over like monkeys and I quickly followed suit. These structures formed an outside perimeter with about 50 yards to go to the steps leading to the entrance gates. These, as we had rightly been told, were all shut. However, I noticed that there was a large bulge of bodies at one spot. Here, the iron gates had been smashed down, unbelievably so because they looked strong enough to withstand anything that might be used on them.

I got behind the crowd and soon was being pushed forward by others who got behind me. I was literally pushed into the ground. I reached the top of the steps to the terrace and had to keep going straight forward because of the pressure behind; then there was another surprise. I could not see the pitch...

Minutes after this the mounted police made their entrance, including the famous Grey. When they started charging at the crowd, there was a stampede for safety.

The stand where I was quickly filled, as did all the other available spaces in the stands. When a space had been made in the centre of the pitch the teams came on. The pitch was finally cleared but only just. The half-circles behind each goal were completely covered by the crowd sitting on the grass. Likewise, the spaces all around the ground beside the touchlines were all filled. In front of them all was a line of policemen with their arms linked to hold the crowd behind them. Play got underway but two or three times in the first few minutes play had to be stopped because in some places on the touchline the police could not bear the strain of the pressure behind them and their blockade broke, with bodies falling over the line. But after a few minutes this was sorted out and play proceeded."

Images of the Grey horse – appearing White in the black-and-white photographs and film of the time – forcing the bulging crowds back off the pitch appeared nationwide, along with stories of the incredible 126,000 fans – [some estimated as many as 200,000 in-and-around the ground at one point] – that had swarmed like ants into an unprepared Wembley Stadium that day.

'The White Horse Final' was thus immortalised but, unfortunately for West Ham, the match itself was a routine 2-0 victory for First Division Bolton Wanderers. There was to be a silver lining though for the Hammers that season. After the Cup Final there were still several league games to complete and West Ham were in with a chance of promotion to the First Division. On the final day of the season three teams were competing for the two automatic promotion places; West Ham, Notts

County and Leicester City. Just to add a bit more tension to the mix, West Ham and County were facing each other at Upton Park!

The capacity 26,000 crowd fell eerily silent as they saw County take the lead but then news filtered through via telephone – [*and not a mobile one, remember!*] – that Leicester had been beaten by Bury. The crowd erupted and were treated to the amusing sight of County player Don Cock – [*he was always making a prick of himself!*] – shaking West Ham captain George Kay's hand and congratulating him on promotion, whilst the match was still going on around them! [*George Kay would go on to manage Liverpool and lead them to the 1st Division Championship in 1946-7 but, hey, he was alright prior to that.*]

West Ham United drew their opening 1st Division fixture, away to Sunderland 0-0 and then defeated neighbours Arsenal 1-0 at home, before settling – for the next nine years – into mid-table cosiness; the fans and the hierarchy seemingly happy just to 'be there', for at no point did the Hammers threaten to loosen the Northern clubs grip upon the First Division title.

Football, in this period, was a much-needed light relief for the working class masses. The General Strike began in 1925, as a dispute between the miners and their employers but, by 1926, The Trade Union Congress had 'called out' all of its workers, including London's Dockers. The Government deployed troops to break through the various picket lines and maintain trade links and, in the end, the TUC accepted defeat; the strike having failed to improve either pay or working conditions.

The 1926-7 season saw West Ham grasp the lofty heights of 6th position in the First Division and, in 1929-

30

30, the Hammers reached 7th place; Vic Watson being the League's top scorer that season with a remarkable 42 goals. [50, in all competitions; a club record.] These were to be the best two seasons of West Ham's near-decade in the top flight.

The following season Arsenal temporarily broke the North's stranglehold on the League title but London compatriots West Ham could only manage a disappointing 18th place. Then disaster struck. West Ham finished rock-bottom in the 1931-2 season and were ignominiously dumped back into the Second Division; a division they would find it much harder to escape from this time around.

*

The Academy of Football is born.

By the early 1930's West Ham United had seven current or former England internationals in their team and yet the inconsistency which would become a hallmark of the side through the following decades was exemplified by the 7-0 thrashing of Liverpool being followed by a 6-1 defeat to Aston Villa, prior to their relegation.

Upon their descent into the 2nd Division the West Ham Board sacked long-serving manager Syd King in controversial circumstances. The gregarious King had developed a drink problem and, after allegedly being 'drunk and insubordinate' during a Board meeting, was suspended pending an investigation into his behaviour.

In January 1933 West Ham finally announced that they were terminating King's employment. King, whose whole life had revolved around West Ham United Football Club for 32 years, as player and then manager, promptly committed suicide. [*Something his team had been doing for years.*]

Charlie Paynter assumed the manager's mantle and this extrovert character would lead both the brass band and the West Ham fans in rousing renditions of '*Bubbles*', prior to their home games. His team though struggled; both with the shocking aftermath of King's suicide and the more physical demands of Second Division football. These were the days when goalkeepers were regularly barged into their own goals by opposing forwards and crunching tackles from behind were the norm. In this period football was a 'man's game,' and the sight of players rolling around the floor, clutching their face and screaming after being gently pushed by an opponent two stone lighter than them – *otherwise known as Didier Drogba Syndrome* – was light years away.

Heavy leather footballs which grew even heavier when it rained and hard – even brutal – challenges were the order of the day and West Ham struggled to adjust to the harsher demands of the less cultured but more physical 2nd Division; narrowly avoiding consecutive relegations and finishing a dismal 20th position. [The disappointment of that league season was only partially alleviated by a good FA Cup run, which saw the Hammers beat several First Division teams on their way to a narrow 2-1 semi-final defeat to Everton.]

The shock of near-relegation to the Third Division coerced the Board into purchasing several new players, such as long-serving goalkeeper Ernie Gregory and inside-forward Len Goulden, who teamed up with Vic Watson and helped revitalise the struggling Hammers. However, promotion remained tantalisingly out of reach. [In 1934-5 they agonisingly **just** missed out on promotion, coming 3rd, behind Bolton on goal difference.]

The following seasons saw the Hammers finish increasingly lower in the League table and this gradual 'decline' brought much criticism from some quarters, as many observers felt that West Ham had the **quality** to gain promotion but lacked the **desire** to 'fight' for the points; a charge which would be levelled at the side again during its heyday of the 1960's.

Indeed, player – and later manager – Ted Fenton recalls punching an irate supporter on the nose, after being accused of 'deliberately losing vital games'! Fenton had been born in nearby Forest Gate and had been on West Ham's 'books' as a youth and so considered such an accusation an outrageous slur on both his character and professionalism.

The 1939-40 season commenced but was then almost immediately abandoned as Hitler invaded Poland and war was declared. [*The swine! Although, decades later, Poland would invade London. You can't go anywhere now without falling over a Polski Sklep!*]

It was considered too dangerous to allow football matches to continue, as the large crowds gathered at the stadiums would make an enticing target for the German bombers.

Nevertheless, despite the abandonment of the League programme, the FA decided to continue with its cup competition. Known as 'the War Cup', these occasional one-off games were used to boost morale.

Unfortunately for West Ham United, nobody later considered this competition to have been a 'genuine' FA Cup tournament and so West Ham's triumph is largely unrecognised outside of East London.

[Just for the record; West Ham defeated Chelsea 5-2, Leicester 4-1, Huddersfield 3-1, Birmingham 4-2 and Fulham 4-3 in the semi-finals before defeating

Blackburn Rovers 1-0 in the Wembley Final, thanks to a Sam Small goal, before a police-restricted crowd of 42,000.]

For the remainder of the war football was marginalised and many players actually took an active role in the conflict. Although no West Ham United players died during the Second World War, many of their careers did, owing to them losing their prime athletic years to the absence of football during the war.

*

In August 1940 a German bomber inflicted the first aerial damage upon London; attacking Stepney, Bow and the City. Britain's RAF retaliated and thus began the aerial bombardments of the Luftwaffe. The German blanket bombing of London, now known as 'the Blitz', commenced in September 1940 and was virtually unrelenting until May 1941; at one point managing 57 consecutive nights of destruction.

Children in London were evacuated to the countryside, whilst London itself gradually disintegrated beneath the German onslaught. Only 'essential workers' – and those who simply refused to leave their homes – remained in the Capital and those who chose to stay built Anderson or Morrison shelters in their gardens; believing that these semi-submerged constructions would be safer than their houses when the bombs dropped. [Eventually the Tube stations would be used as 'mass shelters'.]

The brave 'chirpy' Cockney image originated from this period, when many East-Enders refused to leave their homes; defying the dangers of the Luftwaffe in order to remain where they felt most 'secure'.

[*East Ham born Vera Lynn informed the soldiers separated from their wives and families that 'they'd meet again' and thereby created the template for every* *drunk in history to slur those lyrics at 4:00am, as they trod on the neighbour's cat and fell over the fence…Or was that just **my** family?*]

By the end of the War the East End of London was devastated. Pre-fabricated housing, consisting of steel frames clad with cement panels, were quickly erected around East London in an attempt to re-house the homeless occupants; whilst others simply moved out of East London and into adjacent Essex.

*

Meanwhile, the football season finally resumed in 1945-6. This initial post-war season was divided temporarily into North and South Leagues again, whilst Britain gradually acclimated to peacetime and roads and railways were slowly re-built.

The 1946-7 season saw the return of the First, Second, Third and Fourth Divisions and West Ham United resumed their on-going 2nd Division campaign with another disappointing mid-table finish.

It was the retirement of Charlie Paynter and appointment of former player Ted Fenton as manager, in 1951, which finally heralded a change in West Ham's fortunes. However, this didn't happen overnight. [*And Rome wasn't built in a day, apparently!*]

The famous West Ham youth academy, which concentrated upon developing the younger players and slowly bringing them through into the first team; rather than relying purely upon buying players from outside and constantly replacing them, commenced under Fenton.

Fenton slowly began to reshape the team but – behind the scenes – it was several of the players themselves who provided the true impetus behind this 'revolution', via offering up their own ideas and tactical suggestions.

35

Principal amongst these were outspoken central defender Malcolm Allison and his 'disciples': Ken Brown, John Bond, Dicky Walker, Noel Cantwell, Frank O'Farrell, Dave Sexton and Malcolm Musgrove, who regularly met up in Casettari's café, in nearby Barking Road, after training, and discussed Continental training methods and tactics; recognising that the foreign game was rapidly changing and technically improving but that the English game stubbornly adhered to outdated tactics and training methods, such as running up and down the terraces continuously to build stamina, but which didn't involve using a ball. [!]

Thus, the celebrated 'West Ham Academy of Football' was coming to fruition behind Ted Fenton's back, in an East End café; where salt and pepper mills represented players, as Allison moved the various condiments around in 'patterns of play', espousing his thoughts on the foreign opposition he had seen and how their styles of play differed so dramatically from the English.

[It is significant that it was this group of players who agreed with Allison's principles and eagerly discussed formations and tactics with him; as they would all go on to successful managerial careers when their playing careers finished.

Full-back Cantwell left West Ham in 1960 and captained the successful Manchester United side before becoming manager of Coventry.

Manchester United became a recurring theme for these men, as wing-half O'Farrell went on to manage them – unsuccessfully – aided by his friend Musgrove; inside-forward Sexton also had an unhappy spell there but found managerial success at both Chelsea and QPR.

John Bond and Ken Brown, meanwhile, teamed up again at Norwich, before Bond moved on to manage

Manchester City, leaving Brown as sole manager of Norwich City.]

The positive changes Allison and Co were making didn't immediately transmit themselves to the pitch though. West Ham laboured in mid-table, in Fenton's first four seasons in charge; seemingly destined to be a solid 2nd Division side and no more than that.

Slowly, though, the dominant personality of Malcolm Allison began to exert more influence in training and success slowly beckoned. The old-style British training methods of purely building physical strength and fitness were gradually replaced by ball-skills training and competitive 5-a-side matches.

From Malcolm Allison's autobiography: '*The Colours of My Life*'. [1975.]:

"The facilities were disgraceful. We used to train on a pock-marked, scruffy little track at the back of the ground. We used to have to run in-and-out of a copse of trees. It was impossible for the trainer to keep his eye on all of the players. If he was alert he might spot blue cigarette smoke filtering through the trees.

My relationship with Fenton was...scarcely satisfactory. I did give him some problems but they arose chiefly out of my frustration with the way the club was run. And, eventually, **I** began to run the team, with his tacit agreement. He could see that I was getting results. 'Player power' is a phrase which has become fashionable in modern football. But it was being practised in the West Ham dressing room 20 years ago. I began to draw up my own training schedules and people like Noel Cantwell, John Bond and Frank O'Farrell came in with me."

West Ham again finished the 1955-6 season in a disappointing 16th place but Allison's behind-the-scenes attempts at a quantum change in approach showed signs of bearing fruit as West Ham reached the quarter-finals of the FA Cup via three successive wins over First Division opposition; losing that quarter-final only after a replay against Spurs.

1956-7 saw a much healthier 8th place finish and the last piece of the promotion puzzle was completed when Fenton signed goal-scorer Vic Keeble, from Newcastle for £10,000, prior to the start of the 1957-8 campaign.

West Ham revealed their intentions by thrashing First Division Blackpool 5-1 in the 3rd round of the FA Cup. Although they went out in the 5th round the Hammers played some fantastic football that season, including an amazing 8-0 spanking of Rotherham, as they solidified control of the Second Division's top spot.

Malcolm Allison had assumed the captaincy in the absence of the injured Noel Cantwell but then revealed the shocking news that he had contracted tuberculosis. Allison was taken into hospital and had a lung removed; spending the remainder of the season in a convalescent home; his playing career seemingly over, just as his influence had engendered a remarkable transformation in the West Ham team.

The Hammers clinched the 2nd Division Championship with a final day 3-1 victory away to Middlesbrough and, after a 26 year absence; West Ham United were finally back in the top flight.

[In this season they also inaugurated the 'Hammer of the Year' Award; by which the fans could vote for whoever they considered to be the most influential West Ham player of the season; defender Andy Malcolm becoming the first recipient of this trophy.]

But...could they **stay** in the top Division this time? And, more importantly for their fans, **could they finally**

win something? The 'glory years' of the 1960's were just around the corner!

*

INTERLUDE.
A WEST HAM FANS MEMORIES. NO.1

Name: Doreen Wing. **Age:** 80. **Profession:** Retired.

Born: Canning Town, but raised in East Ham. [Moved to Hornchurch, Essex, during the war.]

Connection to West Ham: Supported them as a child. Dated – and was engaged to – defender Andy Malcolm, in the mid-1950's.

Why did you support West Ham? [Early memories.]

"Well, we lived close to the stadium. You know where 'The Boleyn' pub is? Well, if you went down Green Street and along the High Street, we lived just across the road from there.

I used to go to matches with my dad; as well as to the speedway at West Ham. It was just the thing you did, in those days. West Ham were the local team and so ***everyone*** *around there supported them.*

Even when we moved to Hornchurch, ***that*** *was a West Ham area; all of the people who lived* ***there*** *supported them too.*

Obviously, later on, when I was dating Andy Malcolm, I supported them because I used to go to every single game with him."

Who is your all-time favourite West Ham player and why?

"Needless to say, I've always 'stuck up' for Andy Malcolm, because I was engaged to him and we dated for about 4 years.

It's hard, because I'm obviously biased towards that era. I knew all of the players and got to like quite a few of them.

*Kenny Brown I **really** liked; loved him. He was a great friend of Andy's and we went to his wedding.*

Ernie Gregory, the goalkeeper, was a really nice man too."

Who was your least favourite player of all-time and why?

"Malcolm Allison...God, he was so full of himself!

*And I remember that Andy absolutely **hated** Ted Fenton, the manager."*

What's your strongest single memory of supporting West Ham United?

[Laughs.] *"The players used to call me 'the Queen', because Andy was the only player who had a car. Can you believe that? When you think about how much footballers earn these days and the fancy cars they all drive. When we used to pull-up in the ground's car-park Andy's would be the only car in it! And **that** wasn't even his; it was his dad's car.*

If we played Away anywhere, about half-a-dozen of the other players used to pile into his car."

What was the best game you ever saw, or best experience of supporting West Ham?

"The FA Cup games were always good because the atmosphere in the ground on a Cup night was fantastic.

But, the best game I ever saw was when Andy took me to Wembley to watch England play Russia; who were a good team then, but England were brilliant that night".

[England won 5-0.]

What was the worst game you ever saw / worst experience?

"Worst experience...I suppose – related to West Ham – it would be splitting up with Andy.

There was a testimonial dinner for someone but Andy could be very moody and suddenly, for no apparent

40

reason, he stopped talking to me and went to the dinner-dance on his own.

*I was really upset that he'd gone without me and I told my dad and he said that **he'd** take me there.*

Well, when I arrived I could see why Andy hadn't taken me. He was dancing with this other 'bird' and, even when he saw me, he just ignored me and carried on dancing with her.

I remember Noel Cantwell coming over and asking: 'What's going on with you two?' but I didn't know!

In the end, my dad got so annoyed on my behalf that, the next time Andy danced past us, he threw a pint of beer over Andy! Andy just carried on dancing – beer dripping off him – as if nothing had happened.

That was the end of Andy and I."

Any non-football pitch related anecdotes around supporting West Ham?

"I remember one week, me, my dad, Andy and Andy's uncle were travelling to an Away match at Luton, in Andy's car.

There was no such thing as Sat-Nav's in those days but Andy was quite good at finding his way around, just by using road signs.

On this occasion he asked his uncle to 'look out for the road signs' and direct us there.

We'd been driving for a while and Andy was concerned that we were heading in the wrong direction. He asked his uncle 'where we were' and his uncle replied:

'Near a town called Laybee'.

*'**Where?'** asked Andy.*

'That sign we just passed', insisted his uncle. 'It said l-a-y-b-y 2 miles'. My dad's face was a picture!"

Ever had an affinity for another club and / or hated another club and why?

*"I'll watch **any** football match, but I've never supported another team. If it's a good game, I'll enjoy it!"*

*

Chapter Two: The Holy Trinity: How West Ham United won the World Cup.

A changing of the rear-guard.

It is no exaggeration to state that, without Bobby Moore, West Ham United would never have achieved the level of success or popularity that they achieved from the 1960's onwards. To this day he remains the Hammers' most famous player and is revered by the Upton Park faithful; many of whom are too young to have even seen him play. And yet, his impact upon the club and his iconic blond image can be seen everywhere around the ground and across the spectrum of Hammers memorabilia. But even the legend himself had a debt owed to Malcolm Allison.

In a similar vein to the periods Allison spent in Cassetari's Café with his team-mates, analysing modes of play and dissecting opponents; Allison would also spend extra hours on the training ground, coaching the younger players and local Barking-born Robert Moore became Malcolm's 'special' protégé.

Moore later claimed that Allison had imparted the single best piece of advice he'd ever been given in football, namely; "Always know where you're going to pass the ball, **before** you've received it."

In this way the teenager learnt to be more aware of the movements of his team-mates and how to play 'the killer pass,' with barely a glance upwards.

The imposing Allison also taught Moore to be a 'bigger' physical presence and to 'hold himself high' on the pitch and this gave rise to the image that would burn itself upon millions of memories over the next couple of decades, as the majestic Moore glided across sodden, mud-caked English fields with an almost arrogant gait.

And yet…the willing young protégé who soaked up all of the advice his mentor could impart, was also partly responsible for the sad ending to his dream.

Ever since he'd been diagnosed with tuberculosis and had had a lung removed, Malcolm Allison had been determined to prove all of the doubters wrong and come back for just one last glorious game in the First Division he'd fought so firmly to get West Ham United back into.

Allison trained incredibly hard; pushing his ailing body back to peak fitness and forced himself back into contention for the Hammers defence. Just one game, that's all he wanted; **one game**, to experience the delights of top-class football, in a claret-and-blue shirt.

It was not to be. Manager Ted Fenton – perhaps as a silent revenge, for all of the times the outspoken Allison had over-ruled his decisions and loudly proclaimed, to anyone who would listen, that **he** was the true 'power' behind West Ham's transformation – pinned the team-sheet upon the wall and Malcolm Allison's name was not to be seen. There would be no last moment of emotional triumph at Upton Park for Malcolm. Instead, he gazed at the name 'Bobby Moore', where he believed his own name should have been; walked into the dressing room and – in a moment of pure class - shook his embarrassed understudy's hand and walked out of Upton Park for good.

[The Malcolm Allison story would not end there, of course.

Determined to 'enjoy life to the full' and not allow the 'disability' which had robbed him of his First Division dream to ruin his life; Allison became a larger-than-life extrovert figure, much-loved by the media; whose hard-drinking, cigar-chomping, womanising persona hid the same sharp football brain which had helped formulate the West Ham Academy.

Allison would famously lead – alongside Joe Mercer – Manchester City to the First Division Championship in 1967-8; the FA Cup in '69 and, in 1970, the League and European Cup Winner's Cups.

However, after deposing Mercer and taking sole managerial charge of City, his 'magic touch' deserted him and Allison moved to Crystal Palace, only to preside over successive relegations.

Sadly, a disillusioned 'Big Mal' descended into alcoholism and died aged 83, in 2010, when suffering from dementia. He was one of the last great 'characters' of English football.]

*

The return to the First Division in 1958-9 began with a 2-0 victory away to Portsmouth and a repeat 2-0 win in front of a new-capacity crowd of 37,500 against reigning champions Birmingham; which, in turn, was superseded by an incredible 7-2 triumph against Aston Villa. It was the dawn of a bright new era.

Rock 'n' Roll music was blaring out from transistor radios and the first 'teenagers' were establishing their individual identities; many of them adopting the Teddy Boy personas which would help differentiate their hopes and aspirations from those of their grey-suited parents; still locked in the austerity of post-war London. Britain was changing but West Ham United were basically the same team which had garnered promotion, with the addition of £30,000 inside-right Phil Woosnam

44

from Orient and the emergence of some bright new talent from its 'Academy'.

West Ham finished in a strong 6th position at the end of their first season back; a defender again winning the fans '*Hammer of the Year*' award – this time Dagenham-born Kenny Brown, who would go on to make 455 appearances for the Hammers.

In retrospect, though, that season will always be remembered for the fact that an unassuming young man named Moore slipped the number 6 shirt over his head for the first time and quietly commenced one of the most glorious careers in football history.

*

Welcome to the Greenwood era

West Ham also made a good start to the 1959-60 season and briefly topped the table in November before being thrashed 7-0 by Sheffield Wednesday, a defeat which precipitated a sudden downfall in fortunes, and the Hammers plummeted to an eventual 14th place finish.

When the 1960-61 season looked as though it was going to be a relegation battle, the West Ham Board stepped in and unceremoniously sacked Ted Fenton. There had been a suspicion for some time that Malcolm Allison had been the real instigator of the upturn in the club's playing fortunes and now the Board decided to replace Fenton and his old-fashioned ideas of playing football, with a more modern-thinking manager.

[However, refuting the general belief that attractive football came to West Ham under the reign of Ron Greenwood, Ted Fenton remarked: "Many a time managers would come up to me after matches and say: 'What wonderful football your lads played'. Even when we lost!"]

Thus, the Hammers Board recruited Ron Greenwood, the Arsenal assistant-manager and England Under-23 squad coach. This would produce a marked change in West Ham's style of football, as Greenwood favoured forward momentum and attacking opponents with flair; rather than grinding out 1-0 wins or defending a narrow lead. For Greenwood, football was all about the pursuit of goals and it wouldn't matter if you conceded three, as long as you were capable of scoring four!

It would make for some of the best years of flowing attractive football ever seen at Upton Park, and would firmly establish West Ham United's reputation as one of the most entertaining teams to watch in Britain, **but** it would also make for much frustration and 'what if's', over the following decade, as many would be critical of Greenwood's defensive and tactical naivety.

After eventually finishing that campaign in mid-table, Greenwood commenced his first full season in charge by making his intentions clear. He was going to build the team around the player he saw as being the most talented; the fast-emerging young defender Bobby Moore, with whom he shared his 'football vision'.

However, this vision wasn't always appreciated by everyone; as related by Moore himself in *'Bobby Moore: The Life and Times of a Sporting Hero'* [1993]:

"I couldn't deny his brilliance. The man is the encyclopaedia of football. At international level, with international players, he was fantastic. In his prime, without question, he would have made a tremendous England manager. Perhaps an even better manager than Alf Ramsey.

...On a World Cup level every player in the squad understood him and benefited from him...He sees things in football which are beyond the comprehension of many players and coaches in the game.

That was one of the problems at West Ham. Ron talked about the game at such a high level that sometimes it went straight over the head of the average player.

…Some days I believe there were only a couple of us who understood a word he was on about. He never seemed to realise that he should have been 'talking down' to more than half the team."

Bobby Moore finished that '61-2 season by joining Walter Winterbottom's – [*Look, I've already explained that many people weren't allowed to have **real** names in those days; they had to have silly ones, if they were working class*] – England World Cup squad. Although he didn't actually play in the tournament, it was testament to the 21 year olds advances and, just a year later – when Alf Ramsey assumed the manager's role for England – Moore was named his England captain; Ramsey following in Greenwood's footsteps here by building his national side around the assured young defender.

In the season which saw 'little' Ipswich Town guided to the First Division Championship by Alf Ramsey, West Ham finished a creditable 8th place.

It was a time of great change in English football. An un-fancied team such as Ipswich could replace the previously all-conquering Double-winners Spurs via clever tactics from an inspiring mind such as Ramsey's, and Greenwood, too, instigated some much-needed changes in the Hammers' training routines.

The emphasis moved away from sprinting, distance-running and strength-developing exercises and moved towards even more training with a ball – something

Malcolm Allison had first attempted to instigate – and one-touch passing was vigorously encouraged.

A bitter Ted Fenton had complained, after his dismissal, that 'no money had been made available' for him to buy players to strengthen the team and yet Greenwood managed to convince the Board to part with £15,000, to buy England striker Johnny Byrne from Crystal Palace and then smashed the club's transfer record when he purchased Chelsea winger Peter Brabrook for £35,000.

Nicknamed 'Budgie' because of his inability to keep quiet – [*and not because he always crapped on the floor!*] – the irrepressible Byrne would prove to be an exciting new asset and a fan favourite.

As many of the 'old guard' who had helped West Ham achieve promotion were sold, new young talents came into the side; such as local lad Ronnie Boyce, a combative midfielder, who was under-rated by the fans but much appreciated by Greenwood for his work ethic and who reached his peak as a player in the mid-sixties. Boyce would spend a remarkable 13 seasons at Upton Park and go on to become a coach under several different managers.

Plaistow-born, Dagenham-based Martin Peters finally established himself in the team, after having endured one of the most remarkable debut months at the tail-end of the previous season.

Peters had been played in various positions in the reserves – a fact which would both help and hinder his reputation in later years and be a source of annoyance to Peters himself – but debuted for the first team at right-half. Against Arsenal, goalkeeper Lawrie Leslie broke his hand and – in the days before multiple substitutions – left-back John Lyall had to replace him in goal; with Peters switching to left-back and the injured Leslie

48

playing on at right-half! [*Back in the days when 'men were men' and Didier Drogba hadn't been invented.*]

Incredibly, West Ham drew that match 3-3 after trailing 3-1 before the injury and, in his next game, a bemused Peters found **himself** playing goalkeeper, after Leslie's deputy Brian Rhodes broke his collar-bone after falling heavily.

The biggest 'breakthrough' of the new 1962-3 season though was the metamorphosis of Geoff Hurst; who had been toiling away unsuccessfully as a central defender. One thing which Ron Greenwood quickly realised was that, as a centre-half, Geoffrey Hurst made a good carpenter!

The Manchester born but Chelmsford, Essex-raised Hurst had made sporadic appearances for the Hammers under Ted Fenton's reign but had failed to impress. However, Ron Greenwood had been a centre-half himself and one thing he knew for sure was that Geoff Hurst wasn't a 'natural' defender. Nevertheless, Greenwood was impressed with Hurst's enthusiasm and ability to run all day and impose himself upon opponents and so he wanted to try something radical.

From Hurst's autobiography *"1966 And All That"* [2001]:

"One Monday morning I feared the worst when I was told to report to Ron's office after training. Two days earlier I'd played an appalling game in the reserve team against Shrewsbury. Nothing went right for me that day. I suspected that, having read the match report, the manager was about to give me a serious lecture – or worse.

I knew that some months earlier Ron had considered letting me go to Crystal Palace...Anyway, my fears were unjustified. What Ron said in his office that day

49

surprised me. 'I gather you were terrible on Saturday', he said. 'We can't go on like this. I want to do something about it. I want you to play in an attacking role. I want you to play up front against Liverpool tonight. I won't hold it against you if it doesn't work...' He convinced me that, if I had any future in football, it wouldn't be as a half-back."

The 'gamble', of course, paid off spectacularly. Hurst scored 15 goals in 27 games that season; one more than West Ham's England international centre-forward Johnny Byrne! The tall, well-built Hurst was the perfect 'target man'; someone who could 'worry' opposing defenders with his strength and physical presence and allow other 'nippier' players to feed off his lay-offs and score goals. Plus, he also possessed a thunderbolt of a shot, in his powerful left boot. The number 10 shirt would be his for the next decade.

West Ham finished a disappointing 12th place that campaign but it was a season of 'bedding in' the new players and refining Greenwood's attacking system of play.

Aside from the emergence of Hurst and Peters that season, 1962-3 is remembered for the first example of football violence at Upton Park.

In later years West Ham United would gain a reputation for having one of the most notorious football hooligan 'firms' in Britain – the Inter City Firm – but, on this occasion, the Hammers fans were 'innocent'.

In the days when dads still stood on the terraces with their young sons, clad in chunky claret-and-blue woollen scarves their mum had knitted for them and armed only with those annoying bloody wooden rattles; organised hooliganism was light years away.

Terrace songs of the time were reflective of the simple working class musical taste. To the tune of 'Me And My Girl', Hammers fans would innocently sing:
"The bells are ringing, for the Claret and Blue,
The South Bank's singing, for the Claret and Blue.
When the Hammers are scoring..." etc.
Compare this with a typical little Simon and Garfunkel-like ditty from the 1970's:
"Oh, we hate Bill Shankly and we hate the Kop,
We'll fight Man United until we drop,
We don't give a willy and we don't give a wank,
We are the West Ham boot boys".
[I bet **their** scarves weren't knitted by their mums!]
Liverpool and Everton fans were the first to attract widespread publicity for the misbehaviour of their fans, at the tail-end of the 1950's and it was the visit of soon-to-be League champions Everton that season which 'introduced' football violence to Upton Park. [*Years later Leeds United would introduce it regularly; only their violence was on the pitch!*]
Drunken and annoyed Everton fans reacted to Johnny Byrne's goal against their team by throwing bottles of beer onto the pitch and then attacking police who attempted to restore order. By the end of the decade these scenes would become all-too familiar across the nation.

*

The 'Glory Years'

It seems a contradiction to state that a season in which West Ham could only manage 14th position in the League was one of their 'best ever' but the fact is that 1963-4 saw the Greenwood formula begin to gel and many of West Ham's players would experience their peaks over the following seasons, both at club and international level.

A home-and-away win double over the eventual champions Liverpool was followed by an away win against Manchester United. Oh, it doesn't get any better than that. *In fact, literally... it **didn't!***

Their league form suddenly became erratic and the most significant single result of the season was the 8-2 home defeat by Blackburn Rovers. As a result of this humiliation Greenwood dropped the attack-minded right-half Martin Peters and replaced him with 'hard man' defender Eddie Bovington.

Peters was distraught and angry; feeling it unfair that only one man should be singled out for blame after such a heavy defeat. However, Greenwood's decision seemed to be vindicated when the Hammers travelled to Blackburn for the away fixture and amazingly beat the side which had only just thrashed them, 3-1.

[Another who missed out – but for much longer than the remainder of the season – was full-back John Lyall, whose career ended prematurely due to a serious knee injury. A sympathetic Greenwood gave him the role of youth team coach and, over the succeeding years, Lyall became more-and-more visible at Greenwood's side; eventually succeeding him as manager in 1974.]

Meanwhile, Bovington would retain his place in the side, at Martin's expense, for the rest of the season and this would be the team which would eventually experience FA Cup triumph.

[Standen, Bond, Birkett, Bovington, Brown, Moore (captain), Brabrook, Boyce, Byrne, Hurst, Sissons.]

(On reflection, it seems obvious where West Ham later went wrong. There simply weren't enough surnames beginning with B in the team. Now, if Greenwood had

only have gotten rid of Moore and Hurst and replaced them with players beginning with B, West Ham may have become unstoppable! Just a thought...)

In the 3rd round of the FA Cup West Ham defeated Charlton 3-0; Brabrook, Sissons and Hurst scoring the goals. Hurst bagged a couple and Byrne one in the 3-0 victory against Orient and the two players repeated this feat in the 5th round against 2nd Division Swindon. The quarter-final win against fellow claret-and-bluers Burnley – [*the imposters!*] – was achieved via a brace from Byrne this time and another from Sissons. This set up a semi-final with the 'ultimate' opponents, Manchester United.

United – who had their own version of the 'Golden Trio'; Denis Law, George Best and Bobby Charlton – were heavy favourites to win and yet West Ham produced what Bobby Moore later described as their "best-ever team performance" that day, to stun United by 3 goals to 1.

Boyce scored twice and Hurst notched the third in what many observers described as 'the game of the season'.

Surprisingly, the Final victory itself was remembered with very little affection by any of West Ham United's 'Holy Trinity'.

Martin Peters had been silently sulking ever since his demotion after the Blackburn debacle and finally decided to confront Greenwood, just prior to the Final.

Greenwood reassured Peters that he'd have "many more opportunities to play at Wembley" but the young man wasn't as confident about that as his manager seemed.

From Peter's autobiography, *'The Ghost of '66'* [2006]:

"Missing the FA Cup Final of 1964 was the biggest disappointment of my career...after our 3-2 win I stood self-consciously on the edge of the pitch as Bobby

Moore and the others paraded the Cup. I tried to join in the merry-making but it didn't come naturally. The consolation that day was that our win ensured we'd be playing in the European Cup Winner's Cup the following season – an arena in which Greenwood's style of football would really blossom…First though, I had to get my place back in the team."

One can understand Peters's frustrations. Strangely, though, neither Hurst nor Moore, who **both** played in the Final, remembered it with any real affection either. Hurst described it as 'an anti-climax' after the glorious semi-final victory over the supremely talented Manchester United side and the perfectionist Moore was unhappy at how poorly West Ham played on the day, against Second Division opposition.

[Although Moore's reflections may well have been coloured by the fact that he'd witnessed the first signs of a crack in his previously positive relationship with his manager.

Bobby had been voted the First Division's '*Player of the Year*' and he was delighted to receive this accolade from his peers. The presentation dinner though, took place a couple of nights prior to the Cup Final and Greenwood refused to allow any of the other players to attend; believing that it would 'affect their rest and mental preparations' for the Final. This was bad enough but, when Moore stepped up to receive his award, there wasn't a single member of the West Ham United backroom staff or Board there to 'support him' and applaud his achievement.

Bobby was annoyed; believing that the Hammers had become complacent about having the England football team's captain in their ranks.]

Regardless of the fact that it wasn't a pleasing footballing spectacle, West Ham United's 3-2 victory over their opponents Preston North End was an amazing moment for their multitude of fans; who'd been waiting for a moment of significance – such as this – for decades; ever since West Ham had appeared in the first-ever Wembley Final in 1923.

In the match itself a listless Hammers trailed 2-1 at half-time; John Sissons providing the solitary moment of success for the East Londoners.

Hurst equalised early in the second period and, with just a couple of minutes remaining, a Ronnie Boyce header sealed the 3-2 victory.

Most of the Hammers players that day – and presumably the manager – believed that this was the start of a new era of success for West Ham, as they had also reached the semi-finals of the League Cup that season; losing 6-3 on aggregate over the home-and-away legs to the eventual winners Leicester City.

The 1964-5 season did indeed provide an improved League campaign – 9th place – but their defence of the FA Cup ended in the 4th round, when they were defeated by Chelsea. All hopes for success that season then lay only with the European Cup Winner's Cup competition.

An uninspiring 2-1 aggregate win over Belgian part-timers La Gantoise resulted in the West Ham players being booed off the Upton Park pitch by their own embarrassed fans; who believed that their team should have beaten their obviously less-skilled opponents far more emphatically.

Sparta Prague, of Czechoslovakia, battered West Ham physically, with challenges which would never have been allowed in modern football but still lost 3-2 on aggregate, thanks to goals from veteran defender John Bond and wingers Sealey and Sissons, before the Hammers defeated Lausanne, of Switzerland, 6-4 over the two legs; the goals coming this time from Byrne, Peters, an own goal and three from young striker Brian Dear.

The semi-final provided the best pure football of the tournament when West Ham beat the skilful Spaniards of Real Zaragoza 3-2; via strikes from Dear, Byrne and Sissons; thus reaching their second consecutive Wembley Final.

The one-off Final match was against the Germans TSV Munchen 1860 and was a prophetic taste of events to transpire there a year later.

Brian Dear again replaced the injured first-choice centre-forward Johnny Byrne for the Final and enjoyed his best run of form for West Ham that season; as did bustling midfielder Ronnie Boyce.

Martin Peters had been reinstated, earlier in the campaign; Greenwood deciding that he preferred the more technically skilled Peters to the hard-tackling Eddie Bovington.

However, Peters was unhappy with the fact that Greenwood seemed to use Martin as a 'trouble-shooter'; playing him wherever an injured player needed replacing and – by the end of his time at Upton Park – Peters had, remarkably, played in all 11 positions!

A disenchanted Peters demanded to know from Greenwood 'what he considered his best position to be' and to **'play him there!'** Unfortunately, Greenwood wasn't even certain himself.

Eventually, Greenwood decided that the answer was to allow the versatile Peters to 'roam'; drifting across the midfield from wing to wing and ghosting in behind the main strikers. It was this flexible attacking-midfielder role which was to gain Peters England international recognition.

The unheralded winger Alan Sealey scored both the West Ham goals in their glorious 2-0 Final victory but this was to be the highlight of his all-too-brief career. In a freak training ground accident, whereby he fell over a wooden bench chasing a ball, Sealey broke his leg, just before the start of the following season and never managed to recover his previous form; drifting forlornly out of football and dying at the ridiculously early age of 54.

[Fellow winger Johnny Sissons had been a revelation in these early seasons of his career but his form then seemed to inexplicably tail-off and both Hurst and Moore felt that Sissons was a potentially world-class winger, who never managed to live up to early expectations.]

A rampant Hammers side dominated the Final, against decent German opposition, in what Ron Greenwood described as; "Bobby Moore's greatest game for West Ham United. It was technical perfection."

It was certainly an improvement upon West Ham's performance in the previous years' FA Cup Final and was a magnificent game of football to watch for the neutrals.

But it was also the end of a brief false dawn for the Hammers. There would be no 'building on their triumphs' and making a run at the League title; only a pattern of cup defeats against lower-level opposition and constant relegation battles. The reasons for this would be much debated by both fans and players alike.

From *'Bobby Moore: The Life and Times of a Sporting Hero'*:

'Like a delicate cobweb, glistening in the sunlight, West Ham were beautiful to behold but inspired no feeling of permanence.

On so many days they spun a silken web of delightful football, only to be blown into tatters by a storm of old-fashioned British sporting aggression.

"It was well known," said Moore, "that everyone enjoyed playing against West Ham as much as they enjoyed watching them. We had endless discussions about what went wrong but nobody seemed able to put their finger on it…

It's been loosely talked about as needing to add steel to the West Ham team but that's too simple…I look on tackling as a skill. Any time I see a defender just whacking through the back of a forward's legs to get at a ball, that to me is ignorance. You can't win the ball if you've got a body in front of you. You don't have to go around kicking people up in the air to be a good tackler. The art is to deny a forward space and force him to knock the ball away."'

Geoff Hurst's conclusion was blunter! From *'1966 And All That'*:

"Our one-touch football was pure and simple and our movement off the ball ensured there was always space to move in to. But there was a downside. When we lost possession of the ball we had almost always created space for the opposition to exploit.

This was our Achilles heel. This was what made West Ham vulnerable and unsuited to grinding out 1-0 wins or goalless draws away from home; results that form the backbone of any successful league championship bid. The football West Ham played was conducive to six-goal thrillers. The crowds appreciated the entertainment and, most of the time, the lads loved to play 'the West Ham way'.

The trouble was, lots of our opponents loved the West Ham way, too! They considered us a soft touch and I have to admit that there were times when we were muscled out of games by opponents whose values were totally different from ours."

Despite all of the hopes of both supporters and players that West Ham United may finally contest the League title, the 1965-6 season brought only disappointment, in yet another mid-table finish. There were again some good cup results but, this time, no silverware to show at the end of a season which had promised so much.

The Hammers got off to a flying start in defence of their European Cup Winner's Cup trophy; destroying Olympiakos of Greece 6-2 on aggregate; Hurst and Peters both scoring twice, with Byrne and Brabrook the other contributors.

Magdeburg, of East Germany, proved tougher to get past and West Ham had to settle for a 2-1 aggregate victory; Byrne and Sissons the scorers.

The West Germans, Borussia Dortmund though, comfortably defeated the Hammers 5-2 over the two legs and West Ham were left with only the League Cup for possible compensation.

The Hammers were blessed with a dream draw throughout their route to the Final; constantly facing lower-league opposition and yet struggling to dispatch their inferior foes. [*And, for your information, I'm not biased; that's just a fact! Well, obviously I **am** biased…but it's **still** a fact.*]

Finally, West Ham United played like the superior team they were, when they demolished Cardiff City 10-3 over the two-legged semi-final before meeting their first Division One opposition in the Final; West Bromwich Albion.

This would be the last season that the League Cup Final was contested over a home-and-away basis. The following year it would be akin to the FA Cup Final and played as a one-off match at Wembley Stadium. It wouldn't have mattered anyway, as West Ham lost both legs and 5-3 on aggregate.

However, the most significant moment of the entire season for West Ham United was the shocking announcement, as the campaign moved towards a close, that their outstanding player Bobby Moore wanted a transfer!

Moore's friend Jimmy Greaves was believed to have alerted the West Ham captain and England colleague that Spurs manager Bill Nicholson was a big admirer of Moore. Realising, at this point, that West Ham were not going to be winning the title any time soon, - [or, even ever] - Bobby decided that cup competitions were all well-and-good but – if he wanted to achieve **all** of his ambitions as a footballer – he would probably need to move to a 'bigger' club.

[Tottenham Hotspur had won the League and FA Cup 'double' in the 1960-61 season and were still one of the top sides in the country; boasting a talented selection of footballers.]

A disappointed Greenwood stripped Moore of the captaincy; believing that his star performer had lost mental focus on helping West Ham to finish the season on a high, and the captain's armband was handed to the gregarious Johnny Byrne; who was a motivator in the dressing room, with his non-stop banter.

Despite Bobby's previous belief that West Ham United had 'taken him for granted' and didn't truly value his worth, he was wrong! Greenwood and the Board had no intention of letting their most valuable asset leave and the various parties involved all began to 'dig in their heels'; refusing to compromise.

As the 1966 World Cup loomed the situation began to worry England manager Alf Ramsey, who didn't want his captain's concentration affected by such distractions. In the end, Ramsey acted as intermediary between Moore and Greenwood and the two men finally reconciled. Moore agreed to sign a new contract; he would be staying at West Ham for the foreseeable future **and** regaining the captaincy. Now, all he had to worry about, was football's single most prestigious competition and England's assault upon the Holy Grail; the Jules Rimet World Cup.

*

'One World Cup and Two World Wars!'

England had long been considered one of the premier footballing nations in the world – *after all, we'd invented the game! Clever little sausages* – but had failed to actually prove it in major tournaments. Now, with the World Cup being hosted by England, there would be no better time to prove our worth.

Alf Ramsey was a dour little man; Dagenham born but with a precise, practised cut-glass accent which caused some derision behind-his-back, but he had initiated positive changes in the national set-up; being the first manager who was actually allowed to pick the team! Previously an international committee, consisting of a group of old guys wearing blazers and sipping port whilst discussing how the Empire 'wasn't what it used to be', had chosen the players.

61

Ramsey had also realised that the game itself was changing and that England's tactics needed to be able to negate or surpass those of the Continentals and South Americans; whose ball-skills and all-round technical ability was beginning to move them onto another level.

Ramsey instilled a fierce pride in wearing the white England shirt with the three blue lions adorning the chest and encouraged a togetherness in his players which made the disparate characters seem like a club team.

Of Ramsey's first-choice eleven, there were four players whom you could have described as definitely 'world-class'; goalkeeper Gordon Banks, of Leicester; captain and central defender Bobby Moore – *who just happened to play for West Ham United, in case you hadn't noticed!* – midfield maestro Bobby Charlton of Manchester United and centre-forward Jimmy Greaves of Spurs. These players were the central fulcrum of the team, which the other 'less blessed' players would work around. It all depended upon how much Ramsey's know-how and motivational skills could inspire the less gifted players to shine.

The opening group match was a boring 0-0 draw with Uruguay, in which England looked anything but world-beaters. However, a Bobby Charlton thunderbolt of a shot and a second goal from Liverpool striker Roger Hunt, against Mexico, put England in a strong position to qualify for the knockout stages and, sure enough, two more goals from Hunt against France saw England into the quarter-finals. Nevertheless, one man paid a huge price for this victory.

Jimmy Greaves was badly injured in the game and wouldn't be fit to face Argentina. And so, Alf Ramsey drafted in West Ham's Geoff Hurst as his replacement.

[Can you feel history about to be written? Oh, come on...I can!]

It was a remarkable turnaround. Just a few years earlier Geoffrey Hurst had been a God-awful central defender, about to be released by his club. By the 1965-6 season, Geoff Hurst was one of the most dangerous strikers in the country and bagged an incredible 40 goals for West Ham United that season.

Now, he would score the most important goal of his career so far; the header which put England into the semi-finals. A header from a near-post cross provided by...Martin Peters.

If Hurst's rise to prominence was incredible, then it was probably eclipsed by that of Martin Peters. Dropped from the West Ham United team in the 1963-4 season, it had taken Peters years to establish himself as a regular for his club. And yet, once Greenwood had settled upon a role for Peters within the side, Martin had rapidly blossomed and attracted the attention of Alf Ramsey; who decided that he could use Peters in a similar 'roaming' role for the national side. Nonetheless, Martin was still shocked to get the call-up, just weeks before the tournament commenced.

Initially just pleased to be part of the squad, Peters was delighted when he was selected to play against Mexico and would be an ever-present for Ramsey for years afterwards; who described Peters as being: "10 years ahead of his time". *[Which made it difficult for him to follow bus timetables.]*

However, the quarter-final victory was overshadowed by the fact that it was an incredibly bad-tempered match and Alf Ramsey was incensed by the Argentine's aggressive tactics and blatant fouling; as well as their spitting!

In his post-match interview a shaken Ramsey famously referred to the Argentinians as: "like animals" and the animosity between the two countries intensified thereafter.

From *'Bobby Moore: The Life and Times of a Sporting Hero'*:

'Even during the heat of the battle Moore retained his composure and held the rhythm and the temper of his team together. Moore's splendid form had done much to get England that far without conceding a goal and the captain wasn't about to let his men throw it all away because of Argentinian intimidation.

"Animals? I don't know. The South Americans play the game by a different code. They were sure as hell not very pleasant to play against. They did do some nasty things. They'd tug your hair; spit at you; poke you in the eyes and kick you when the ball was miles away and no-one was looking.

It wasn't nice but it wasn't worth losing the game over. I managed not to get involved. Around and about me I could see lads like Alan Ball, Nobby Stiles and big Jack Charlton getting steamed up and finding it difficult to get on with the game.

I just said to them that the only way to deal with them was to beat the bastards! That was what would hurt them. Because their attitude was to simply not lose".'

The Argentinians weren't the only ones dishing out 'dirty' tactics. Portugal – not usually known for being an aggressive team – kicked the pre-tournament favourites Brazil out of the competition. Literally! And now, they would face England in the semi-finals.

Fortunately, it was nothing like either of the team's quarter-finals and was a pleasing spectacle for the fans.

England finally found their best form and dispatched Portugal 2-1, thanks to two Bobby Charlton goals.

England were to face West Germany in the World Cup Final but who would be leading the attack? Geoff Hurst had played well but first-choice centre-forward Jimmy Greaves was now fit again. Perhaps unsurprisingly, Alf Ramsey decided not to mess with a winning formula and retained Hurst. Many people claimed that this was the beginning of Greaves's slow 'descent' into alcoholism but this is a theory denied by the man himself.

From *'Greavsie: The Autobiography'* [2003]:

"Of course I was disappointed. Of course I was upset. Who wouldn't be? But the truth of the matter is, my decline into alcoholism came not in the immediate aftermath of England's success of '66, but in the early seventies, following my retirement from professional football…

I have to say that while I was 99% certain that Alf wouldn't change a winning team for the final, the remaining 1% harboured the hope that he **would** and include me.

On the morning of the final Alf was very distant and I sensed that he had made up his mind to pick an unchanged team. After breakfast I went back to my room and started packing my bags. Bobby Moore asked me 'what on earth I was doing'.

'It's all over for me, mate', I told him. 'I'm just getting ready for a quick getaway once the final is over'.

…Throughout my nine years as a professional footballer I had dreamed of playing in a World Cup Final. I had missed out on the match of a lifetime and it hurt."

Jimmy's omission was also recalled from his friend Moore's perspective, in Jeff Powell's biography, *'Bobby Moore: The Life and Times, etc…':*

'The happenings at Wembley on July 30th, 1966, have long been copiously treated with purple prose, dissected by expert analysis and replayed into the memory banks of the English people…

It wasn't enough to be dismissive of the working man's obsession. For, in its way, that afternoon's sport changed the society in which we live.

The emotional magnitude of the occasion broke through the barriers of class and culture to harvest thousands of wealthy and influential converts to the muddied arts of the round-ball game…

Just one of the many economic spin-offs was the beginning of the boom in colour television. England awoke that day to countless early-morning deliveries from rent-a-set.

It was less public knowledge that the man who was about to be acclaimed as the world's paramount footballer started his day of coronation trying to console a friend.

Bobby Moore woke that Saturday morning to find his room-mate Jimmy Greaves packing his bags. Greaves was fretting for the place he had lost to injury and Geoff Hurst. Moore, the 'ice man', suffered with his friend:

"Jimmy was hurt. I don't care what people say about Jimmy; about how he didn't work and he didn't care; how his attitude was all wrong. I knew the man and I knew what he was going through. All he wanted was to play in the World Cup Final. He believed that he could get the goals to win it for England. He believed that he was 'something special' and it broke his heart not to have the chance to prove it.

That moment began Jimmy's disenchantment with football".'

And, finally, Geoff Hurst's own reminiscences on Ramsey's selection of himself over Greaves for the Final; from *'1966 And All That'*:

"Jimmy Greaves was fit again and, having scored 43 goals in his previous 54 matches for England, had every right to expect a recall. Jim even said at the time that he couldn't imagine himself not playing in the World Cup final. In fact, no-one could imagine him not playing!...he was world-class and no-one admired him more than I did...He was a genius at getting into the penalty box and scoring goals. He was also a really nice guy...

You can imagine my elation then, when Alf drifted over to me casually after a training session the day before the final and said; 'I want you to know that you'll be playing tomorrow'."

[Regardless of the truth of his feelings, Greaves and Ramsey never reconciled and the man who should stand miles ahead of everyone in the goal-scoring table for his country, only played for England on three more occasions, finishing with 44 goals from 57 games.]

England took to the Wembley pitch wearing their 'away' shirts of red, with white shorts and because of the significance of the victory, this shirt remains the most iconic England strip.

Aside from the importance of it being the World Cup Final, this was never 'just a football match'. Twenty years after the end of the Second World War there was still a very raw hatred amongst many English towards the Germans. Many supporters still had clear memories of losing loved ones during the conflict; of being bombed out of their homes; or, of being a prisoner-of-war in the harsh German camps. Worse still, many remembered – with horror – the atrocities of the concentration camps, and anti-German feelings were rife.

Commented Geoff Hurst: "There was a lingering bitterness towards the Germans that, in my opinion, helped create the atmosphere in which the match was played. My wife's father had been a paratrooper and was in tears at the end of the game. Most of the players had had relations who had fought in the war.

It may be difficult for young people today to appreciate that this feeling still existed in this country in the mid-'60's."

The imperious Robert Moore proudly led his men out and then promptly watched them concede an early goal to the Germans. Hurst then equalised from – of course – a Bobby Moore cross.

'1966 And All That':

"My first goal, after 19 minutes, was a typical piece of West Ham opportunism; the sort of thing that Bobby, Martin and I had worked on over the years under Ron Greenwood, at Upton Park...I knew where Bobby would put the ball and he knew that I'd be running into that space. It was the sort of thing that had worked dozens of times for West Ham.

Sure enough, the pass from Bobby was perfection. I ran in from the right, met the ball with my head and steered it past Hans Tilkowski, the German goalkeeper."

The West Ham connection came up trumps again, when Martin Peters put England ahead, with a volley, in a goalmouth scramble. From *The Ghost of '66':*

"For a second I couldn't take it all in. I'd just scored a goal in the World Cup Final! Suddenly, the roar from the crowd was rolling down the terraces. I wheeled away, running back up the field, Geoff and Roger sprinting towards me. I saw Banksie running towards me form the opposite end of the field. It was the most extraordinary moment; like being struck by lightning. My fingers were tingling with the excitement. My head was spinning.

As we lined up to restart, I must confess that the thought crossed my mind that we had just won the World Cup and we'd won it with a Martin Peters goal."

Agonisingly, though, the Germans equalised in the final minute. [*B*****ds! They bombed our chip shop, you know? Well, obviously not the football team, but people like them…**other** German b*****ds.*]

From '*1966 And All That*':

"I was exhausted in the period just before the final whistle and suddenly to be faced with another 30 minutes was a daunting prospect. As we prepared for extra time Alf told us not to lie down on the pitch. That's what the Germans were doing. 'Look at them', he said. 'They're finished. They're flat out on their backs'. He told us; 'You've won it once. Now go on and win it again'. So we did!

After ten minutes of extra time Nobby Stiles hit a terrific ball from midfield out to the right. He had a reputation as a hard man but I'd played with him in the England Youth team and knew that he had far more skill than most people acknowledged…Alan Ball – my personal 'man of the match' – was running along the right flank. Alan said later that he didn't think he was going to reach it. 'I was finished', he said. But he did reach it, looked up and hit a first-time cross to the near post.

If anything I made my run a little too soon. This meant that instead of moving on to the ball, it was falling slightly behind me. I needed to adjust my body and take a couple of touches to get the ball into a shooting position. To get the power required to strike it properly, I had to fall back. As it turned out, I connected beautifully with the ball but, in so doing, toppled over. I therefore probably had the worst view in the ground when the ball struck the underside of the bar and bounced down on the line.

…At that moment, with the jubilation of the crowd pouring down upon us from the terraces, I had no doubt that it was a goal. But within seconds the German team were appealing to the referee."

It seems incredible, in light of the controversy which surrounded this third England goal, that goal-line technology was still being debated in 2012. Regardless, the referee and linesman conferred and decided that it **was** over the line and a weary England had regained the lead. Now they had to withstand a late German onslaught as the minutes ticked away.

With just seconds remaining, yet another cross came in to the England penalty area.

'1966 And All That':

"Bobby Moore, untroubled and completely in control as usual, chested the ball down, played a short pass to Alan Ball, received the return and looked upfield to see where to play it next. I remember Jack Charlton screaming at him; 'Kick the f*****g thing out of the ground!'

Instead, 'Mooro' turned back into the penalty box, with the ball at his feet. Jack was going mad at him. The Germans were frantically trying to regain possession but Mooro was a picture of composure. He looked up, carried the ball forward and then hit the killer pass upfield to me. It was the perfect ball.

My first thought was not to give it away. We had to keep possession. I sensed that Overath was chasing me as I headed towards the German goal. Then I was aware of Schnellinger, having deserted Alan Ball for the first time in the match, coming at me from the side.

By this time I was about ten yards outside their box. I can't imagine where I got the strength from to make that run. I was exhausted…

The match was practically over. Kenneth Wolstenholme was telling a nation glued to their TV sets; 'Some people are on the pitch…they think it's all over'. It was at this point that I decided to hit the ball with every last ounce of strength I had and it flew into the net. Wolstenholme continued his famous piece of commentary: '**It is now!**'"

From *'Bobby Moore:…etc':*

"It was another West Ham job. I couldn't count how many times I'd knocked that same pass into that same space for Geoff to make that same run. They were shattered and it split them wide open. Geoff was exhausted too but he was stronger than them."

Geoff Hurst's hat-trick guaranteed his place in sporting history and he remains the only player ever to have scored three goals in a World Cup Final. In today's' transfer market it would have made Hurst unaffordable.

Bobby Moore was voted 'Player of the Tournament' and became, alongside Brazil's Pele, the most famous footballer in the world. Perhaps because of all the plaudits the two men gained, there was the merest hint of bitterness from the third member of West Ham's 'Holy Trinity', when he spoke of the event years later, and his ego ensured that the reader understood his own worth.

From Martin Peters autobiography, *'The Ghost of '66':*

71

"I guess I was always considered the third man. Even Ron Greenwood, in his book *Yours Sincerely*, treads carefully when discussing the three of us. He starts one chapter with the words: 'Hurst, Moore and Peters – no order of merit, that, just alphabetical'.

Normally, when the three of us are clumped together, the names appear in this order: Moore, Hurst and Peters. I can't argue with that. I didn't in 1966 or in the years immediately afterwards and I don't now.

Bobby Moore was an iconic figure in the 'sixties. The captain of England, he stood astride the game, alongside Pele. Unlike David Beckham today, his fame was based solely on his ability to play football superbly well...He was clearly number one in the pecking order and I'm sure Geoff Hurst would agree with that.

Geoff is second because he uniquely scored three goals in a World Cup Final...I'm happy to be in Bronze medal position. Only two English footballers have scored goals in a World Cup Final and I'm one of them! Had it not been for my goal against West Germany, England would probably have lost 2-1.

Geoff says – as Bobby did when he was alive – that of the three of us, I was the best footballer. Naturally, I wouldn't argue with that! Coming from two footballers of their stature, it's a great accolade. I was proud to be the third man in that trio.

The three of us had been friends for some time but it was the 1966 World Cup that made us a 'trio' in the eyes of the public. Before that, we were just three players from the same club...

I can't remember the three of us ever having a serious row or 'falling out'. Our friendship survived the years and when we were on the pitch together we had an uncanny understanding. It's amazing that three young players should develop together at the same club and then play such a pivotal role at international level.

Ron Greenwood used to tell anyone who'd listen how lucky he was to have inherited three such players. The fact that we all contributed to three distinct parts of the team – defence, midfield and attack – was a considerable bonus for West Ham **and** England."

It is no exaggeration to state that winning the World Cup changed the face of English football. Suddenly, footballers were high-profile celebrities and the days when First Division players could be seen in their local pubs, drinking amongst their fans, were numbered. Soon, footballers – especially in 'Swinging London' – would be frequenting swank nightclubs and VIP areas in 'Members Only' drinking establishments; photographed with glamorous models and movie stars and paving the way for the future mega-celebrity - and excesses – of the likes of David Beckham and Paul Gascoigne. [Manchester United's George Best becoming the first football 'superstar'; as the handsome young Irishman embraced the burgeoning nightclub scene, and became the most high-profile example of 'wasted talent'; succumbing to the lure of 'celebrity' and neglecting his supreme talent; retiring far too early and sinking into alcoholism.]

Players as level-headed as Moore and Hurst managed to avoid these pitfalls but this sudden fame could be hard to handle for a young man; as evidenced by the more introverted Martin Peters:

"At first, I found it difficult to cope with fame. I was used to the fans at West Ham asking for my autograph but nothing had prepared me for the level of adulation that followed England's World Cup victory. Strangers stopped me in the street, on the train, in shops and restaurants. I found it embarrassing. It wasn't what I wanted. Being a professional footballer was simply a job I enjoyed doing. I didn't feel like a star or a celebrity. I just wanted to be left alone, to lead my life the way I had been doing. I didn't want the fame."

*

'Swinging London'.

Many **did** desire fame though. The 1960's was the era when 'celebrity' became a goal. Even the notorious East End gangsters the Kray twins pursued fame not through their violent killings of fellow underworld characters – [Ronnie Kray's blatant shooting of George Cornell took place just before the World Cup, in Whitechapels' *'Blind Beggar'* pub] – but through opening nightclubs and then inviting movie stars and singers to gala events, where the brothers would ensure that photos were taken of themselves with the likes of Judy Garland. Even top fashion photographer David Bailey took the now famous black-and-white portraits of the menacing siblings.

It would not be until their arrest in 1968 and subsequent conviction in '69 that the true brutality of the Kray's reign of violence in East London would be revealed; including brutal protection rackets and Reggie's vicious knife murder of fellow villain Jack McVitie, and yet their notoriety increased over the subsequent decades, as they developed an almost cult-like following, and the Bethnal Green area would forever be associated with Ronnie and Reggie.

East End gangster Henry 'Buller' Ward remembered, in his autobiography, [2008]:

"I went with Ronnie once to collect some protection money from a club. Once he was back in the motor he suddenly started crying his eyes out. I thought; 'What the f**k?' I said: 'What's wrong, Ron?'

'Oh, nothing', he said. 'I just get a bit depressed sometimes'.

Another time, a bloke called Ginger Cooper came up to Ron in a nightclub and said: 'Hello Ron, how are you? The last time I saw you, you were in the nuthouse'.

Ronnie just pushed his glass straight in the bloke's face, cutting it badly and then walked away without a care in the world, saying; 'Do us a favour, Buller. Take him to the hospital'.

I took him to hospital and on the way Ginger asked me: 'What's the matter with that bastard? I **did** see him in the nuthouse!'

I just shrugged and told him to be careful what he said to the Twins. Obviously my advice fell on deaf ears because they later shot him in the leg.

Same with a bloke called Ernie Isaacs; I warned him to keep his mouth shut but he wouldn't and **he** took a bullet in the leg as well. You couldn't afford to 'mouth off' about the Twins.

I knew Ronnie was a bit of a loose cannon but, to be honest, I was always more wary around Reggie. At least you knew where you stood with Ron. He was a nutter and so you chose your words carefully but Reggie could be all smiles and handshakes one day and screaming abuse at you the next. I always had the feeling that Reggie could smile 'hello' and then stab you when your back was turned."

Meanwhile, Britain was 'invading' the world's music charts and 'Swinging London' was leading the way. [*'Swinging' as in the hip / fashionable sense of the word and not as in throwing your car keys onto the table and ending up with the fat bird from next door.*]

British fashion, music and culture in the mid-'60's was largely centred upon the Capital.

Soho's Carnaby Street became famous for its youth fashion shops and exclusive clothing boutiques, catering – specifically – for the young Mods and the blossoming Hippy scene.

Mod – derived from Modernist – had actually reached its peak and sharp-suited young men with Vespa's and Lambrettas' were beginning to morph into their more visually intimidating successor, the Skinhead.

[One of the most popular Mods was the East End-born Steve Marriott; who enjoyed incredible success in the late sixties and through the seventies with his bands, The Small Faces and Humble Pie.

In many ways, the Mods and Rockers conflicts, throughout the early to mid-sixties, would be a forerunner of the emerging organised football violence.]

Many of the Skinhead's clothes remained the same; retaining the classic Ben Sherman and Fred Perry shirts and Sta-Prest trousers but Dr.Martens work-boots and braces were added and carefully coiffured hair removed until only stubble remained. It was now an openly working-class image; perhaps reflective of the new Labour Government in power; which sought to consolidate its unexpected success by allying itself with the increasingly powerful Trade Unions.

Those who didn't follow the abrasive sounds of Jamaican ska and early reggae, favoured by the skinheads, followed the emerging psychedelic scene, as rock / hippy culture began to flourish.

Times were changing. A London 'working class', or Cockney accent was no longer considered something to be ashamed of and, exemplifying this, Cockney accents would increasingly be heard in movies and TV

76

programmes of the time; and **not** in a derogatory way. Finally; a 'cut-glass' English accent was no prerequisite for success.

With the triumph and interest engendered by the World Cup, fashion icons and pop music stars were now rubbing shoulders at glamorous parties with footballers and Bobby Moore – with his blond good looks and sharp dress sense – fitted into this thriving celebrity scene perfectly.

And yet, whilst the 'beautiful people' adored each other and West London buzzed with money-laden creativity and aspiration, East London continued to experience relative poverty and a very basic lifestyle.

Children played in rubble-strewn derelict bomb sites; still not developed since the war. Rag-and-bone men continued to ply their trade in horse-drawn carts. People waited anxiously for the coalmen to arrive and refill their coal bunkers, in order that they could replenish their open fires and warm their houses. It was all far removed from the fashionistas of Chelsea's Kings Road.

Transport and hospitals were fast improving, at this point, but this was largely because of encouraged immigration.

Since the 2nd World War and the resultant losses of life, Britain had been inviting Caribbean's, Africans and Asians to come to England and help to 're-build' the country. The 1960's saw a huge surge in these immigrations and the consequence was racial tension.

[Brick Lane, in East London, became the biggest Bengali community outside of Bangladesh itself!]

But this 'build it quick and everything will be fine' attitude was thrown into turmoil when Ronan Point – a 23-storey tower block in Newham – collapsed due to a gas explosion. It was remarkable that only 4 people died but this frightening design fault led – thankfully - to the demise of the high-rise council flats which had typified 1960's architecture for the working classes.

Regardless of these 'social issues'; the England football team's success ignited a massive increase in interest in British football generally and the BBC's highlights package, *'Match of the Day'* became essential male viewing on a Saturday evening; as did ITV's rival Sunday afternoon live show *'The Big Match'*, as TV companies sought to satisfy the cravings of a suddenly soccer-hungry nation, which looked forward to the new 1966-7 season with huge anticipation.

*

'Holy Crap, Batman!' The Trinity becomes the Dynamic Duo.

Bobby Moore, Geoff Hurst and Martin Peters walked out on to the pitch ahead of all of the other players, prior to West Ham United's opening home and away fixtures of the 1966-7 season and received a tumultuous standing ovation from the crowds. Then, West Ham promptly lost both matches and the Holy Trinity were brought crashing back to reality.

Interestingly, in John Lyall's autobiography, he recalled that there were occasions – immediately after the World Cup – when the trio allowed their burgeoning fame to expand their egos a little. From *'Just Like My Dreams'* [1989]:

"We were preparing for a difficult game at Leeds and I felt I needed to bring them down to earth a little bit.

Ron had left me in charge of training that day and I devised a routine that was difficult but, probably, just within their capabilities. If they failed to do it I would have made a little point – none of us are perfect, lads –

78

but, if they succeeded, I would have to hold my hands up in admiration.

I used the entire length of the training pitch at Chadwell Heath, with a goalkeeper at one end and Hurst, Moore and Peters strung across the width of the pitch, at the other end. They had to pass the ball between them, as they worked the ball the length of the field and then score. The catch was that the ball wasn't allowed to touch the ground at any stage and each player, on receiving, had only one touch. In other words, they had to volley or head their passes between them from one goal to the other; using the entire width of the pitch.

Most of the other team members were on the side-lines, speculating about the degree of difficulty and who was most likely to fail among these three great players. **None did,** and I held my hands up in admiration."

It seems incredible that a team which included the three World Cup winners and the likes of the talented Johnny Byrne couldn't have achieved more success but the reality was that Ron Greenwood's 'pretty' football just wasn't likely to succeed against the more cynical approaches of some of the other First Division sides; who simply physically battered the Hammers into submission.

West Ham could beat Arsenal 3-1 at Highbury and Leeds by 7-0 but they were also capable of losing 6-1 to eventual Champions Manchester United and 4-0 to the likes of West Brom. This inconsistency saw them slump to 16th place, in a season in which their fans had expected so much from 'the conquering heroes' of the World Cup.

In 1967 I discovered two things for which I would retain an enduring affection for the rest of my life. The TV series 'Batman', provided me with endless

79

excitement and drama, as the Caped Crusader ran around in his underpants chasing villains, such as the nefarious Joker.

Meanwhile, West Ham United ran around in their pristine white shorts, being chased around muddy pitches by disreputable villains, such as Don Revie's Leeds United [*Otherwise known as; "those dirty b******s!"*]

My impressionable 5 year-old self was hooked and the Dark Knight and the Golden Boy of British football became my first heroes.

[*My first crush was on Catwoman. I had similar feelings for Bobby Moore but in a heterosexual way.*]

*

The 1967-8 season was the first one in which I actively followed the Hammers, via gossip at school from fellow West Ham fans and the teleprompter which churned out the results on a Saturday afternoon. [I was too young to be allowed to stay up and watch '*Match of the Day*' but I pored over photos of my heroes and longed – enviously – for a West Ham United kit of my own; as worn by several of my school-friends. *Christmas 1968 would satisfy this particular craving.*]

In a season in which ex-West Ham Svengali Malcolm Allison would lead Manchester City to the League title, there were a series of changes to the West Ham team, as Ron Greenwood attempted to find a consistently winning formula.

The popular Johnny Byrne was sold back to his previous club Crystal Palace, as Greenwood lined up Brian Dear as Hurst's regular strike partner. [*A partnership which would last just the one season before Ron looked at other options; such as a headless chicken and Geoff Hurst. Oh no, that **was** Brian Dear!*]

Local boys Trevor Brooking, Harry Redknapp and Frank Lampard established themselves in the side, on left midfield, right wing and left back respectively and their names would become deeply etched into West Ham's history.

Redknapp had actually been wanted by Spurs and Chelsea but chose West Ham instead and debuted for them in '66. By the time he'd become a regular feature, the sight of the flame-haired winger – *[polite for 'ginger']* - setting off on another mazy run in front of the 'chicken run' stand – [a corrugated iron and timber construction, which had been at the Boleyn Ground since its earliest days and would last until the late 20th century] – inspired the classic recitation from the Upton Park fans, to the tune of the Boy Scout's 'anthem', Ging Gang Gooley:

"We've got 'Arry, 'Arry, 'Arry, 'Arry Redknapp,
On the wing, On the wing."

[These were the quaint, pre-ICF days, you'll understand? In later years it would be superseded by the far more aggressive chant:

'Arry Redknapp's Claret and Blue Army!' *But more of that later.]*

In his 1998 autobiography – [*imaginatively titled;* '*Arry*'] - Redknapp recalls those late '60's years at Upton Park:

"West Ham was a fantastic place to be in the 1960's. There was a great set of lads at the club and we could all bask in the reflected glory of Bobby Moore, Geoff Hurst and Martin Peters.

Mooro was a God; there are no two ways about it. When I broke into the first team Bobby was 'top man' at Upton Park. Everybody looked up to him. You'd have thought – given his stature - that he would be aloof

81

with the new kids coming into the side but, from day one, he looked after me. He took me under his wing and really made sure that I was okay. We got on great but he treated **everyone** that way.

Bobby was also a natural-born leader. When he did something, everyone followed suit."

In the later version of his autobiography *'Always Managing'* [2013] Harry Redknapp reflected some more on his friend and former captain Moore:

"What a man. I mean it. What a man! The straightest, most honest bloke you could ever meet in your life. Not an ounce of aggression in him, not a hint of nastiness. Won the World Cup and even the German opposition loved him. The Brazilians idolised him. Not just Pele, but all of them. People say the 1970 Brazil team was the greatest football team of all time, and Bob would have walked into it. In fact, I think he would have made the 'team of the tournament' at any World Cup throughout history.

Everyone wanted to meet Bobby; everyone wanted a night out with him. And Bobby loved the social side of the game. He captained the England football team, but he would have captained an England drinking team, too, if we'd had one. Gin and tonic or lagers were Bob's drinks, and he could really put them away. We used to travel to away matches by train a lot in those days, and when we got on board after the game he would make a point of asking how many lagers they had in the buffet car.

'We've got four cases Mr Moore', he might be told. 'Right', Bob would say, 'bring them all down here'. And he'd roll off the cash needed for every last drop of beer in the place and get stuck in.

About ten minutes from Euston, Bob would nip into the toilet, have a shave, change his clothes, put a clean shirt on and reappear looking immaculate. Not a hair out of place. And then he'd go out drinking for the rest of the night!

They were different times and football wasn't as professional in its outlook as it is these days. Even so, Bobby was probably the most diligent player in making amends for his sins the next day. He might have been out every Saturday night, but he was in every Sunday morning without fail, to run it off. He would get to the training ground at 9:00am in an old tracksuit, put on a plastic bin liner beneath it, and run a dozen laps to get a sweat going. The rest of us would still be in bed but Bob would be out, pounding around the field at Chadwell Heath, rain, wind or snow.

Sometimes you wondered how he did it. You would leave places so drunk you could barely stand up, and Bobby looked like he'd just walked in from having a dinner suit fitted. He was like that as a player too. He looked a million dollars as he led the team out. We all tried to copy him but nobody pulled that perfectly-groomed appearance off quite like Bob...

I think, deep down, Bobby was a shy person and had to have a good drink to 'let go'. Once he'd had a few, he would open up and be good company. George Best, Mike Summerbee, Alan Ball, Norman Hunter, they all liked a night out with Mooro. As far as those lads were concerned he was the best character around; a lovely man and great company. I think most footballers back then wanted to be like Bobby.

Did we really know him though? I'm not sure any of us did. Bob was a very private person. He must have had trouble in his life – and I was as close to him as anybody – but I can never remember Bobby volunteering anything about his problems. Even when he was seriously ill he kept it to himself".

Apart from the emerging home-grown talent of Redknapp, Brooking and Lampard, Ron Greenwood also dipped into the transfer market in 1967 and purchased right-back Billy Bonds, from Charlton, for £49,500 and goalkeeper Bobby Ferguson, from Kilmarnock, for £65,000.

Born in Woolwich, Bonds had been a Charlton fan as a boy and ended up making his professional football debut for them, aged 18. Upon moving to Upton Park though, Billy soon realised that the football at West Ham wasn't necessarily about winning; it was all about 'entertaining the fans'; even if it meant losing games they should've won, simply because they kept chasing more goals instead of sitting back and defending their lead. Indeed, one of Bond's most vivid memories of his first season there was when West Ham lost 4-3 to Stoke, after leading 3-0!

Nevertheless, despite all of Greenwood's positive changes, this new-look West Ham side could only manage yet another mid-table finish.

Despite Greenwood's modern thinking when it came to tactics and flowing attractive football, the actual training methods at West Ham remained rooted in the past.

Harry Redknapp recalls in *'Always Managing'*:

"In Ron Greenwood we had the most forward-thinking coach in the country. We all had great respect for him yet, when compared to today's sports science ideas, our training was prehistoric.

Everybody would board a coach, nearly fifty of us – first team, youth team, three to a seat, some standing up in the aisle – and off we'd go to Epping Forest. There, Ron would lead us on a little walk and then off we'd trot up a hill, running to where Ernie Gregory, the first team coach, would give us our directions.

We'd have a little jog and then run down Epping New Road, the whole team in single file, lorries flying past us, until we reached the next checkpoint in the forest. After about half an hour of this we would be strung out like washing. Bobby Moore was always near the back, Brian Dear always last, and on we'd run for another three miles, ending up at a point called Mott Hill. By then it wasn't unusual to see Brian riding past us on a milk float, shouting: 'Come on, you lot'.

He'd jump off about a hundred yards from the end of the run and join the rest of us, staggering to the finish. Then it was back on the coach and to our training ground. If Ron thought we hadn't worked hard enough, another run would be scheduled. By the time we'd finished we'd run and run and run, often in boiling hot sun. And then, after lunch, it would be time for the afternoon session at Chadwell Heath!"

Redknapp describes this period as 'the dirtiest era in the game's history', and singles out sides such as Leeds United as being particularly guilty of unnecessarily brutal fouling. Unsurprisingly, many players – particularly the attack-minded ones, who were targeted by opposition defenders – spent a lot of time in the treatment room. But, here too, Harry recalls how primitive sports medical treatment was at the time:

"Back then there was no equivalent of modern physiotherapy and medical science. Our physio, Bill Jenkins, was one of the most terrifying men I've ever met. And it wasn't just me – the whole team was petrified of Bill. He was a Welshman, one of the first into the Auschwitz concentration camp in the war, and had clearly seen some terrible sights. Not that this gave him a more enlightened or caring attitude towards humanity. He would torture you by turning the electric treatment machines up to full and punch you in the chest if you complained! He would regularly have Budgie Byrne in tears or screaming in pain.

He'd put all of these sucker pads on you and then run an electric current through them, to make the muscles tense and then relax. Then he'd start getting angrier and angrier if it didn't seem to be doing any good, and turn them up so high it felt like the inside of your leg was being ripped out.

That's why West ham had so many injury problems. The last place anyone wanted to go was the physio's office!

Unless the injured player brought him half-a-dozen lagers he'd tell you to f**k off. Bobby Moore, the captain of England came in, and he told **him** to f**k off!'""

*

The 1968-9 season proved better, as the new signings and emergent young talent began to settle and understand each other. Martin Peters managed his highest-ever goal tally for the Hammers – 24 – second only to Geoff Hurst's 31.

West Ham finished 8th and the highlight of the season was the fantastic 8-0 demolition of Sunderland; in which Geoff Hurst scored a remarkable 6 goals!

However, 1969-70 saw the Hammers drop back down to a paltry 17th place, and early exits in both cup competitions. It was the most disappointing season yet under Ron Greenwood's management and the final straw for Martin Peters.

In October '69 Greenwood shocked the football community by dropping Peters; claiming that Martin was 'saving his best performances for England' – [an accusation he'd also levelled against Moore] - and that Peters 'clearly wanted to leave'. And he was right!

However, Greenwood soon reinstated Peters to the side and, after a long heart-to-heart discussion with Martin, agreed that he could leave at the end of the season. For Greenwood, there could be no lingering bad feeling towards his protégé.

From Greenwood's autobiography *Yours Sincerely':*

"Martin Peters was not a typical English player and the terraces didn't relate to him. In a way, his ability went above their heads. But I had no reservations about him. He was the answer to a manager's prayer. He was a football connoisseur's dream. His understanding of time and space was delightful. He knew when to move and where to move…He did everything so perfectly he made it look **too** easy."

Recalls John Lyall:

"I remember one Friday morning, at Upton Park, watching Martin Peters and Harry Redknapp playing about together. Harry was crossing from the corner flag and Martin was almost lazily volleying the ball into the back of the net. It was something that came so naturally to him.

As I watched them I heard Martin shout to Harry; 'Chip one in and I'll hit the crossbar'. Harry centred the ball and Martin drove his shot, first time, smack against the crossbar.

'Lucky!' Harry shouted.

Martin just smiled.

'I bet you five-to-one you can't do it again', cried Harry, who enjoyed a little wager.

Martin accepted and, when the ball came over – a perfect centre, to be fair to Harry – Martin drove it, first-time again, against the crossbar.

By this time Harry was a little perplexed; not to mention concerned about his money.

'Double or nothing', he shouted. Again, Martin accepted. The ball came across, falling nicely in front of him, waist-high and Martin volleyed it straight against the crossbar.

He was a very special player, with a very special talent."

Like Bobby Moore before him, Peters was hankering for the one thing he now believed he'd never win if he stayed at Upton Park; a League Championship winner's medal. Martin acknowledged that he wanted to move to a 'bigger' club, who might help him to achieve this ambition and Tottenham Hotspur [?] made their interest known.

The West Ham Board held out for a lucrative remuneration, which they felt was applicable to a World Cup star and, in the end, the two clubs compromised with a British-record £200,000 fee, **plus** Jimmy Greaves.

[Which goes to show how far Greaves's career had plummeted since the disappointment of the World Cup! Jimmy was now the plastic gift within the cereal box.

As it turned out, the swap benefited neither man. Clearly past his prime, Greaves would retire at the end of the following season; disillusionment and a worsening alcohol problem eroding his love for the game.

Peters, meanwhile, could never replace the talismanic Jimmy in the hearts of the Tottenham fans and – considering that he'd gone there to 'win the League' –

left virtually empty-handed, when they sold him to 2nd Division Norwich in 1975, for just £50,000; for Tottenham – like their hero Greaves - were past their prime by the time Martin joined them.

Ex-Hammers John Bond and Ken Brown were managing Norwich and were trying to play football 'the Greenwood way'; attractive and attack-minded. They saw the out-of-favour Peters as the last piece of their puzzle; named him captain and were immediately promoted to the First Division. Martin visibly enjoyed the last few years of his football career; finally hailed as a 'fan favourite' by the worshipping Canaries supporters.]

Interestingly, in contrast to the feeling of unfulfillment which Moore and Peters harboured at different parts of their West Ham careers, Geoff Hurst never felt inclined to leave. [*Bless him!*]

Manchester United boss Matt Busby bid £200,000 for Hurst, immediately after the World Cup – an enormous sum in those days – but Greenwood turned him down. Geoff was unaware of this at the time but, when told years later, was completely unperturbed at the fact that he'd missed out on the chance to play for England's first European club champions.

Here is Hurst's explanation for his happiness at Upton Park and some reminiscences of highs and lows from those erratic final seasons of the 1960's. From *'1966 And All That'*:

"Mansfield were among the most notable conquerors of West Ham in the days when the scalps of Moore, Hurst and Peters were highly prized. They provided the biggest FA Cup upset of season 1968-9 when they beat us 3-0 in the fifth round on a damp February day. At the time they were a Third Division club, just avoiding

89

relegation that season, while we were in fourth place in the First Division.

Three months earlier we had beaten Bolton 7-2 in the League Cup and Sunderland 8-0 in a league match at Upton Park. I scored three against Bolton but I really hit the jackpot against Sunderland with six goals; equalling the club's individual goal-scoring record set by Vic Watson in 1929.

We were playing so well at that time that few defences could have withstood our attacking momentum for long. Even so, I have to admit that I helped the first goal in with my hand. I confessed to the media after the match and, in the newspapers the next morning they made more fuss of the one I handled than the other five I scored legitimately!

…It annoyed me that some people thought we were pushovers. We worked as hard as anyone, both in matches and on the training ground but most of our efforts went into developing the skills of the game. Ron was a purist with high ideals. He encouraged us to enjoy the game.

I think, deep down, most of us realised that we were never likely to win the league championship; something Ron conceded publicly only after he stepped down as West Ham's manager.

I accepted that was the reality of the situation and I was happy with that because I loved playing for West Ham. Initially, most of my team-mates felt the same but I think a time came when Martin Peters, for instance, felt that he would have to move to another club if he was to have any chance of winning the major prizes in club football.

From time to time we registered an outstanding victory that provoked a lot of soul-searching among the players.

90

'Why can't we play like this every week?' was a familiar complaint from within the dressing-room.

One of our most memorable triumphs came in the League Cup in November 1966. West Ham won 7-0 and, remarkably, our victims that day were Leeds United, one of the great club sides of that era.

We had already brushed aside Tottenham and Arsenal when Don Revie's mighty team came to Upton Park on a chilly autumn evening for the fourth-round tie. Revie's squad read like a who's-who of international football; Bremner, Giles, Lorimer, Gray, Jack Charlton, Cooper, Madeley, Reaney and Norman Hunter.

Unlike Ron though, Revie favoured a more cynical, tactical approach to the game and would turn a blind eye to the kind of physical excesses that Ron abhorred. Nonetheless, Leeds United were one of the most talented teams in Europe. This made our victory all the more astonishing.

Budgie Byrne played one of his greatest games of his career that night and had a part in all three of my goals...I heard later, from Jack Charlton, that Revie kept his players up until the early hours of the morning, discussing the biggest defeat of his managerial career. Leeds were not used to losing; certainly not by seven goals!

...When you're playing for a team that can score seven goals one day and four the next, it's really quite good fun. When your 'job satisfaction' is that high, why should you want to play for anyone else? I think most of us were quite happy to play for Ron and the beliefs that he cherished."

As the 1969-70 season drew to a close, England prepared for their defence of the World Cup and Messrs' Moore, Hurst and Peters put aside their

91

respective disappointments of the League season and readied themselves for battle once more against the world's finest footballers. It would be a tournament Bobby Moore, for one, would never forget **but** for all the wrong reasons!

*

INTERLUDE
A WEST HAM FAN'S MEMORIES.　NO.2

Name: Jeff Ives. **Age**: 67. **Profession**: Retired Journalist. **Born**: Loughborough, Leicestershire, but raised in Dagenham, Essex. [Now lives in Hornchurch.]

Connection to West Ham: Fan; plus, he often covered their games and met many of their players, when working as a sports journalist for *'The Express'*.

Why do you support West Ham? [Early memories.]

"Well, locality, for one thing. The first game of football I ever went to was West Ham against Blackpool, in 1958. It was an FA Cup game and West Ham were a 2ⁿᵈ Division side against the 'mighty Blackpool' side that included Stanley Matthews, Stan Mortenson, Jimmy Armfield; all those great players, and West Ham came from behind to win 5-1.

It was a typical, wet, windy, January cup tie and the pitch was a mud-bath, but I just got gripped by it all. The floodlights; the roar of the crowd; the sight of Stanley Matthews running up-and-down the wing, right where we were standing; the white shorts and socks, with those lovely claret-and-blue shirts of West Ham – **everything** *about that game just 'took me over'.*

I was lucky enough – years later – as a journalist, to interview Jimmy Armfield and I asked him if he remembered that game.

*'Yes, I remember. **I** was the one who began the West Ham fight-back! I tried to knock a back-pass to our*

92

goalkeeper but it got stuck in the mud. Johnny Dick ran on to it and 'crack', it was 1-1. West Ham never looked back and it was a fantastic result for them.'

It's funny what players can remember. I also spoke to Vic Keeble, many years later, when he was an old man, and I asked him if *he* remembered that game.

'Of course I do', he relied in an instant. 'I scored a hat-trick!'

I went to that game with my brother, a couple of cousins and my uncle. I was about 12 years old and I remember being swept in to the ground; everybody literally pushing each other through the turnstiles. It wouldn't be allowed today, for safety reasons.

It was an incredible atmosphere; well, it still is today but now that I've got to that old, cynical age, it doesn't match how it used to feel. In those days you needed to get there about an hour before the game, as the stadium would already be nearly full. I think the gates used to open about 1:30pm and you'd be in the queue, soaked from the rain but excited.

And the **roar** that you heard when the players came out on to the pitch was unbelievable!

Nowadays, people are strolling into the ground five minutes before kick-off. The atmosphere's just not the same and the players walk out to what's best described as 'polite applause'.

I don't get as excited as I used to but I think that's a lot to do with age. When I was a boy I was looking up at all these big, grown men and they were my heroes but, now, the players are younger than my own son and it's harder to get emotionally attached to some of these kids."

Who is your all-time favourite West Ham player and why?

93

"Martin Peters! When I first started watching the game, you knew where the number 4 played; he played in front of the number 2, and the number 7 played out wide on the wing; the inside-right – number 8 – played in-between him and the centre-forward, etc.

Suddenly, this skinny kid came along, wearing number 4 but running down the left wing, where the number 11 should be running. We were all like: 'What's going on here'?

He'd then turn up in the inside-left position, heading in crosses. He was the first player to have this kind of over-lapping, roaming role and he was just phenomenal. [Credit must go to Ron Greenwood too, for allowing him that freedom.]

I was devastated when they sold him to Spurs for £200,000 plus Jimmy Greaves. Jimmy had been a great player in his time but, at that point in his career, he was on the decline with his alcohol problem.

A few years ago I got very excited at a young kid I saw coming through, who I thought was going to be 'the next Martin Peters'. Michael Carrick was the same build; had the same confidence on the ball; could play right-or-left footed; had good vision but, for me, never fully lived up to his potential. He seemed to settle into this defensive-midfielder role, when I felt he should have been encouraged to come forward more and be more of an attacking-midfielder. Still, I can't speak higher than that of him; the fact that I think he's the nearest thing I've seen to Martin Peters.

I read on-line the other day that John Bond's been admitted to a hospice. In my opinion John Bond was the best right-back never to have been capped for England.

I recently wrote a piece for 'Knees Up Mother Brown', an on-line West Ham fan forum; which was a tribute to

*John Bond basically. He was 'Mr.Cool'; the first player I saw with 'cut-down' boots and **short** shorts. He had a kick like a mule and was known as 'Muffin the Mule'"* – [laughs] – "*but, for other reasons, I'm led to believe.*

He would always test the goalkeeper, even from 35 yards, and he was an exceptionally good right-back.

There was one season when Vic Keeble was injured and they played Bond at centre-forward. He scored some cracking goals, including a hat-trick against Chelsea.

'Bondy' was a fantastic player and I was very sad when I heard the news about his illness".

[John Bond died, shortly after this interview, in September 2012.]

Who was your least-favourite player of all-time and why?

*"Oh, they come-and-go, don't they? **Lots** of players, in recent years, but they go 'off your radar' once they leave.*

To be honest, there have been plenty of players – over the years – who haven't been good enough, but you can't hold that against them, can you? As long as they try their hardest".

What's your strongest single memory of supporting West Ham United?

"Realising that – as much as I loved them – there were a lot better teams out there!

*When Ron Greenwood became manager he used to bring over these foreign teams – teams from places like South America; Costa Rica, Brazil, those sort of countries – to play us in pre-season friendlies and these were **very** competitive games, not 'friendlies' like you see them played now, and the ball-skills these foreign teams showed made you realise how much English teams needed to improve.*

95

I particularly remember a more recent game, against Dynamo Tbilisi, in the Cup Winner's Cup and West Ham were absolutely played off the park. Al this stuff about 'Fortress Upton Park' was disproven that night."

What was the best game you ever saw, or best experience supporting West Ham?

*"Oh, I don't know; there've been so many great games over the years. Beating Manchester United **whenever** is always good; likewise with Spurs."*

[Pause.] *"Do you know what, Dave? I find that so difficult to answer."* [Laughs.] *"And the way my memory is these days, I'd probably have to say: 'This May, at Wembley'."*

[The Play-off Final win against Blackpool.]

What was the worst game you ever saw / worst experience?

"Worst experience would be the whole season under Avram Grant. Some of the performances that season were dreadful and the players were going out there not knowing what to do.

I subsequently found out that the manager wasn't giving them any kind of direction at all and they used to go out there expecting to get beaten.

I'm glad they got relegated that season, quite honestly, as at least it meant we got rid of Grant!"

[**Author:** Although that somewhat spoils the suspense for the reader, in that later chapter, but hey!]

Any non-football pitch related anecdotes around supporting West Ham?

"Funnily enough, I was thinking about this earlier today.

It was FA Cup 3rd round day, 1969-70 season and we were playing Middlesbrough away. It was snowing heavily that day; freezing cold and I didn't actually go to the game, as I was playing football myself for a local amateur team called the 'Old Barkabbeyans'; a group of ex-Barking Abbey School students.

We were a decent side and often, after our games, we'd hold a disco - £2.00 to get in and you could eat and drink as much as you liked – and West Ham players would often come down, after their own game.

The disco was held in an old clubhouse behind Barking bus garage and, that night, some of the West Ham players came down straight from the Middlesbrough game. This was back in the day when everyone still wore suits and the players would still travel on public transport and mix with the fans socially.

There was Geoff Hurst, Brian Dear, Bobby Ferguson, Frank Lampard, Harry Redknapp and a couple of other players there and everyone was having a great time.

At one o'clock in the morning there was a knock on the door. Now, I expected it to be the police and we didn't have a licence to sell alcohol but, when I opened the door, it was two of my mates.

They stood there in the snow, freezing cold, having only just got back to London from Middlesbrough. They informed me that West Ham – who had lost 2-1 – had been 'awful', and so my mates were less than pleased when they stepped in and saw Geoff Hurst on the dance- floor, stamping his feet to the old Dave Clark Five tune and singing: 'And I'm Feeling' –stomp-stomp – 'Glad All Over'.

*My mate was fuming. 'F*****g 'glad all over'? The way **you've** f*****g played today?!'"*

[Laughs.] *"That was it, for my mate. That destroyed his admiration for Geoff Hurst.*

Another memory is of when West Ham played Leyton Orient, in the FA Cup, in the late 1980's. We drew that

97

game 1-1 and went on to win the replay 4-1 but, in the first game, we were awful.

I was in the press-box, working for 'The Express' and at half-time there was the usual gaggle of reporters, standing together discussing the game and I looked over into the corner and – sitting there all alone – was Bobby Moore.

*He was silently drinking tea from a cardboard cup and I just thought it was so sad that no-one had approached him and asked for **his** opinion on the game. Here was one of England's greatest-ever footballers and he was being ignored!*

I walked over to him, introduced myself and shook his hand. I sat down next to him and we chatted about the game and about his time at West Ham, and then the second half started. As I stood up to go back to my seat, he shook my hand and said: 'Jeff, thank you very much for coming over and talking to me'.

He was an absolute gentleman and it was so sad that he died just a few years later".

Ever had an affinity for another club and / or hated another club, and why?

"I read these fan forums and see all these 'I hate Spurs' type comments, and all of the hatred and name-calling. I don't give a damn about hating other teams; I appreciate good football and good teams, and all I hope is that these good teams come over to West Ham and lose!" [Laughs.]

"Funnily enough, when I was working as a journalist, I used to cover Spurs quite regularly and they used to play some lovely football, in the 1970's.

Also, because I was born in Leicestershire, I've always had a soft spot for Leicester City." [Laughs.] *"Not that I'd ever actually **pay** to watch them!"*

Chapter Three: *Congratulations: You have just met Billy Bonds*

Bobby, Brazil and the Bogota Bracelet.

The England squad which prepared for the 1970 World Cup in Mexico is generally conceded to be far stronger than the one which had won the tournament in 1966. There was competition for every position in the team and the only players who seemed guaranteed a starting place were Gordon Banks in goal, Bobby Moore in defence and Bobby Charlton in midfield. The other positions were pretty much interchangeable, although the likes of Alan Ball and Martin Peters seemed likely to be first-choice players.

Brazil were, once again, the pre-tournament favourites but defending champions England were considered to be one of their strongest competitors. Drawn in the same qualifying group, the consensus was that both teams may actually go on to meet each other again in the Final.

The England squad flew into Bogota, Columbia, for their pre-tournament warm-up games and Bobby's - Moore and Charlton - wandered into their hotel jewellery store; killing time by browsing the glass display cases.

Sometime later there were vague accusations being voiced about a 'missing bracelet' but nobody paid too much attention. Several days passed before Moore was shockingly arrested; accused of stealing a gold and emerald bracelet from a display case. The whole football world was in shock and the England captain was detained in custody whilst the rest of the squad flew out to Mexico and prepared for their first group game.

As both a shaken Alf Ramsey and everybody back home in England tried to absorb what the Hell was happening, Bobby was kept under armed guard for five days, before finally being released; the victim of a clumsy attempt to 'frame' a famous celebrity; a forlorn effort to blackmail 'compensation money' from a wealthy sports figure.

Ramsey's own personal belief, however, was that it was a Latin-American plot to unsettle the reigning World Champs by removing their iconic figurehead. [Alf had never forgotten the Argentinians tactics in the previous tournament.]

This belief helped unite England's players even more and strengthen their already marvellous team spirit. There was a perfect mix of experience and emerging young talent and when Bobby Moore finally re-joined his team-mates, the atmosphere was electric, but Moore was far from happy.

From *'Bobby Moore:...'*

"It was all very well getting a letter saying the case had been dropped for lack of evidence but that wasn't good enough. It wasn't what I was looking for. I wanted my name cleared.

People kept advising me that I should let it drop but I didn't like the feeling that whenever I walked into a jewellers to buy a present I had to keep my hands behind my back and point to the goods with my nose. I also didn't like being told it would be dodgy for me to go to a certain part of the world in case they arrested me all over again.

I was innocent and I wanted the world to know that I was innocent. It made me sick to my stomach that some people thought I still had that damn bracelet."

England beat Romania 1-0 in their opening game, thanks to a goal from Geoff Hurst but England-Brazil was the game that everyone wanted to see; the defending champions versus the ultra-talented former champions and tournament favourites.

Bobby Moore produced the performance of his career that day, under the stifling Mexican heat; a textbook display of perfect unruffled defending, against the most talented attacking side in world football. [*Apart from West Ham, of course!*]

It's not often that a defensive tackle becomes one of the most-repeated highlights of a football match, but Moore's perfectly-timed intercession upon a flying goal-bound Jairzinho became legendary footage over the succeeding years.

Gordon Banks made the save of the century from a goal-bound Pele header and the team, as a whole, played splendidly but it wasn't enough to prevent a 1-0 defeat at the hands of the brilliant Brazilians, who included such legends as Gerson, Rivelino, Tostao, Jairzinho and Cesar.

Some moments in football history have been magically captured on camera for posterity. [*A modern example being that cultured egotist Vinnie Jones squeezing the life out of Gazza's testicles.*]

In complete contrast however, to this example of modern football thuggery is the image of an exhausted Bobby Moore – the finest defender in world football – and Pele - the finest **player** in world football, exchanging their sweat-soaked shirts at the final whistle and placing a hand gently on the other's cheek, in smiling camaraderie.

England's subsequent 1-0 victory over Czechoslovakia set up a quarter-final date with their arch-enemies West Germany. 2-0 up with 20 minutes remaining, Alf Ramsey made the most awful mistake of his storied career. Believing the game to be won, he substituted the talisman Bobby Charlton and Martin Peters, in order to rest them both for the semi-final.

Crushingly, the Germans scored twice in that final 20 minutes, to take the match into extra-time. On this occasion there would be no Hurst-inspired dramatic finale. The now-dominant Germans defeated a tired and demoralised England and all we could hope for was that they didn't go on to win the competition. [*They bombed my nan's house, you know? She'd only just finished cleaning the front door-step; bless her!*]

Brazil deservedly won the tournament but many observers were left to wonder; 'What if...?' regarding Ramsey's tactical misjudgement. Although much blame was also attached to goalkeeper Peter Bonnetti, who replaced an ill Gordon Banks, and was at fault for two of the three goals; playing as if he'd never seen a football before in his life. *The Chelsea wan-* [**The following has been edited by the publisher, for legal reasons.**]

*

Bobby's little Blackpool incident. [The beginning of the end.]

As if the disappointment of the World Cup exit wasn't bad enough – coupled with the Bogota bracelet fiasco – Moore faced the 'downside' of fame, closer to home.

A kidnap threat was made against his wife and children and it was taken seriously enough to warrant a police guard around his family for the following weeks.

Then, just as that threat had evaporated, Bobby's wife received a 'phone call, informing her that her husband would be shot, at Upton Park that afternoon! Police raced to the ground and escorted Moore home from the stadium. It appeared that not everybody loved the Golden Boy of British football.

Despite Harold Wilson also being a generally popular Leader, he too faced a shock, when his Labour Government was defeated in the 1970 General Election. Much of the Conservative's success was attributed to MP Enoch Powell's anti-immigration rants at the time; which played upon white working-class and middle-class fears of the various ethnicities settling in Britain during this period.

East London, particularly, was rapidly becoming multi-cultural and the white housewives of Canning Town, Plaistow and Bethnal Green, who sauntered around the popular Roman Road market, in their ubiquitous headscarves and pinafores, soon found themselves sharing poorly paid employ in the 'Rag Trade' with their Asian counterparts in brightly coloured sarees. Racial tension was ever-simmering, as counter-cultures clashed.

Popular TV programmes of the time, such as *'Til Death Do Us Part',* also highlighted the working-class fears / hatred of the 'foreigner' but via humour, laced with the 'anger' of caricature East End racist Alf Garnett.

However, Conservative Leader Edward Heath then unpopularly took Britain into the European Economic Community [Common Market] and thereby began his own descent into political unrest. [*Not realising that it*

103

wasn't just the Asians and the Afro-Caribbean's many Briton's didn't like; it was also the French, the Germans, the Italians...pretty much everybody really. Hell; they didn't even like each other, that much!]

*

Meanwhile, back at Upton Park; as a reaction to the decline of the preceding couple of years, Ron Greenwood promoted former full-back and reserve team coach John Lyall to the assistant manager's position, prior to the 1970-71 season; recognising that he needed help to continue pursuing his dream of attractive, fluent football in the cynical modern game.

They purchased centre-half Tommy Taylor from Orient for £80,000 and he immediately looked to be the perfect ball-playing partner for Bobby Moore; even sharing a physical likeness!

However, West Ham's form again began to slump and when the Hammers travelled north to Blackpool, in the 3rd round of the FA Cup, they badly needed a boost in confidence.

This was in the days before global warming; when the seasons were recognisably different and summers were warm and winter's **bloody freezing**. Thus, when the team surveyed the Blackpool pitch the day before the fixture and saw nothing but snow and ice, they quite reasonably assumed that they'd be travelling back down the motorway the following day; waiting for the game to be rescheduled.

With this mind-set, Bobby Moore, Jimmy Greaves, Brian Dear and young Bermudan forward Clyde Best – [then just establishing himself in the team and becoming West Ham's second black player, after defender John Charles] – headed off into the Blackpool nightlife. They were more than a little upset then when,

104

on arising Saturday morning, they were informed that the game was **on.**

West Ham were unceremoniously thrashed 4-0 by the lower division side and the brown stuff really hit the fan when a disgruntled supporter contacted the club and informed Ron Greenwood that he'd seen half of the West Ham team in a nightclub, the evening before this dispiriting defeat. [*Hey, no-one likes a grass!*]

Greenwood was apoplectic and the repercussions were huge. Best successfully argued that he hadn't actually had an alcoholic drink but Moore and Greaves were both dropped and fined. [Brian Dear suffered the most. He never played for West Ham again. *So some good came out of it!*]

Bobby Moore remained bitter about this punishment for years and it proved to be the final nail in the coffin of his relationship with Ron Greenwood. The two men, who had once been so close, barely spoke throughout the remainder of Moore's time at Upton Park.

Greenwood was quoted as saying: "Bobby was one of the few truly great players who could make the game look simple. For a long time I rated him the best player in the world.

Ask me to tell you about Bobby Moore the footballer and I will talk for days. Ask me about Bobby Moore the man and I will dry up in a minute."

In turn, Moore commented: "I know very little of Ron as a man. We are different people. I have a lot of enjoyment outside of the game but I don't know if Ron has much of a life outside of football."

Moore always angrily claimed that he'd only had a couple of drinks and that the rest of that evening had been spent simply chatting to fans and friends. Perhaps

Jimmy Greaves's version though was more honest. From *Greavsie'*:

"I consumed about a dozen lagers in the club. It says much about my alcohol consumption at the time that I wasn't drunk. Bobby and Brian Dear drank about five pints each, while Clyde Best had spent the entire evening with a single Coke."

*

For my 9th birthday my dad finally took me to see my first live game, in that 1970-71 season, against Derby County. Why then did it have to be the one where my idol Bobby Moore had been dropped by Greenwood?

The anticipation was electric. I'd never been so excited; *not even when Catwoman had bent over once.* As we stepped out of Upton Park tube station my senses were assaulted. I had never experienced such a crush of humanity; waves of claret-and-blue scarfed men flooding along a crowded Green Street.

The bustling Queen's Market was a cacophony of noise; the traders shouting above the hubbub, in order to attract punters; that wonderful smell of roasted peanuts; the not-so-wonderful smell of horse-shit from the huge police horses, indifferently surveying the throng; the pie-and-mash shops bursting with patrons; my dad attracted to the Hulk-snot that is jellied eels; the vendors waving programmes and selling shiny scarves with writing on - ?! - and not knitted ones like my nan had made for me.

It was almost too much to take, the constant rendering of *'I'm Forever Blowing Bubbles'*, every few yards; the guttural yelling of "Come on you Irons!" Then, there it was, the Boleyn Ground itself. As we edged closer my heart prepared to explode from my chest. Through the turnstiles...climbing concrete steps...that green pitch –

so green! – and so close that I could touch it...the chanting, singing hordes...the opposition fans trying to raise their voices but immediately being drowned out by the Upton Park faithful...the swearing; **God,** the swearing! I'd never heard so much bad language and, worryingly, most of it was coming from my dad!...the banners which pleaded for the return of Bobby Moore...the abuse directed towards Greenwood for dropping the heroic one...the beautiful sight of **West Ham United** walking out onto the pitch...the crescendo of noise...the orgasmic thrill of watching beautiful football in the company of people who expected and appreciated it.

It all made the 4-1 defeat unimportant. If I'd thought that I was hooked before this; my first experience of Upton Park made me a helpless addict. It was – as Billy Bonds had surmised – unimportant that we'd lost. It was all about the thrill of the football played. And no team thrilled its fans the way West Ham United did.

A season later, Derby manager Brian Clough; sensing blood like a shark, contacted Bobby Moore and enquired whether he'd be interested in joining his soon-to-be League Champions. Moore was intrigued. Working under the abrasive Clough wasn't everyone's cup of tea but Bobby saw through the bluster and recognised that Clough could help him achieve his one remaining ambition; a League Championship winner's medal. Thus, Moore agreed to leave West Ham.

Unfortunately for him, the West Ham Board – despite Greenwood's annoyance with Moore and the deterioration of their relationship - refused the transfer. He was simply too valuable an asset for the Hammers to lose. And so, there would be no Championship medal for Bobby.

[As it turned out, the refusal was probably a blessing in disguise. Shortly afterwards, Clough left Derby County, and so Bobby may well have found himself stranded in the Midlands, without the charismatic Clough to massage his ego.]

As a child I was largely unaware of these behind-the-scenes machinations and it was upsetting to discover – years later – the extent of Moore's discontent at Upton Park. Sometimes you're better off not knowing such things, as it can taint otherwise perfect memories.

*[I was similarly shocked to discover that Warren Mitchell, who played the Johnny Speight-created oafish Alf Garnett so brilliantly in the TV satirical comedy 'Til Death Us Do Part' [1965-75], was **not** in fact a West Ham fan; as portrayed. I couldn't understand why anybody who supported another club – (Spurs, in Mitchell's case) – could force themselves to pretend to support another. Even more confusing was the fact that Mitchell had been **born** in West Ham. It just wasn't right. These things can affect the balance of nature, you know!*

Moore actually made a cameo appearance in the series, in '72, in an episode in which Alf wanted his grandson to grow up to be 'like Bobby Moore'.

West Ham fan and 'professional Cockney' Danny Dyer later played a Chelsea hooligan in 'The Football Factory'; which was even more un-natural. You can't live in the I.C.F. area and make-believe that another team have 'hard' supporters. It's like being the Queen and pretending that Prince Phillip is important.

I know I'm whingeing here but…actor Perry Fenwick is a West Ham fan and portrays Hammers fan Billy Mitchell, in the TV soap 'EastEnders'. All is well with that, and yet; Canning Town-born West Ham fan David

108

*Essex played a Leyton Orient fan in the same series. It's just not right, people! It **must** stop now! This is how people like Hitler and Thatcher get in power...people pretending they haven't noticed.*

Can you imagine what Adolf and Margaret's love-child may have been like? John Terry, would be my guess.]

Meanwhile, in the equally unhappy world of Ron Greenwood, desperate measures were called for in order to avoid relegation, as the campaign wound to a close.

Striker Bryan 'Pop' Robson was bought from Newcastle for £120,000, as the Hammers desperately sought goals to dig them out of the hole they found themselves in.

In the season which saw London rivals Arsenal win the League and FA Cup 'double', West Ham United barely escaped relegation.

At the end of a dismal campaign, Britain had gone decimal but Brian Dear was still only worth two-bob; the misfiring formerly-lethal Jimmy Greaves retired and sunk into full-blown alcoholism, and young Trevor Brooking was put up for sale. Thank God no-one rated him, back then; for Brooking was about to blossom into one of the Hammers greatest-ever players!

Remembers Brooking:

"The day I had to think seriously about whether I should continue in football came in 1971, when I was out of the side and earning only a small amount of money in the reserves. It came home to me just how badly off we were when the window cleaner cleaned the windows in our semi-detached house and my wife had to hide in the bathroom because she didn't have enough money to pay him! As it was, she had to work for the first five years of our married life, because we were so short of money…

At the end of the '70-71 season I went on the transfer list. I began to think more deeply about my game and why it wasn't progressing, and I accepted Ron Greenwood's criticism that I should be more aggressive and more involved in matches.

Playing in front of just two or three hundred people in reserve matches is soul destroying, and you reach the stage where you are secretly hoping that a first-team player will get injured or lose form, so that you can win your place back. That doesn't help team spirit...

In one of our talks, Ron Greenwood once asked me why I kept falling over in matches. 'It is a bad habit, that you need to get out of your system', he said. 'For someone of your height and weight, you shouldn't be knocked off the ball so easily'.

The only explanation that I could offer was that I had a long stride at the time and perhaps I was off-balance more than I should have been. I worked on it in training and conquered it. Afterwards I didn't go down so easily, and was more able to ride tackles from the side".

Billy Bonds, meanwhile, had firmly established himself as a fan-favourite at Upton Park, with his tough-tackling, committed displays. When Billy went in for a tackle it wasn't for the faint-hearted to watch and often came rated with an X-certificate. Bonzo's 'steel' was what many observers felt had been missing from West Ham for years and, prior to the 1971-2 campaign, Greenwood decided to move Bonds forward, into midfield, where his tenacity could provide a ball-winner to complement the smooth creativity of Brooking.

John McDowell was drafted in at right-back; Brooking finally found consistency with his form and – when things were going well – the forward line of Hurst, Robson and Best could terrorise any defence. The

110

muscular, power-shooting Best was the Hammers top scorer that season but my particular favourite was 'Pop' Robson; so called because his thinning wispy hair made him look much older than his years. He was Greaves-like in his ability to dart into the penalty area and slam the loose ball into the net and he too became a hugely popular character with the supporters.

League form remained as erratic as ever that season, despite the changes and the flowering of Trevor Brooking but I was now a regular at Upton Park and – win, lose or draw – was never less than delighted at the football I saw. In my own personal opinion, the football I watched at West Ham in the early to mid-'70's, was the finest display of pure attacking football that I've ever seen.

[*Even if the defence were like a group of hung-over strangers, doing unwanted Community Service together, on some days! It was that horrible feeling of knowing that you can score at will but realising, also, that you're going to concede bucket-loads. The talent of Bobby Moore alone was not enough to compensate for our other defensive frailties.*]

A 14th place finish wasn't anything to get excited about, but the League Cup run that season certainly was and this cup campaign remains vivid in my memory today.

After beating 2nd Division Cardiff 3-2 on aggregate, thanks to two goals from Hurst and one from Bonds, they were extremely unlucky not to defeat the mighty Leeds, at Upton Park. However, a Clyde Best header surprisingly won the replay at Elland Road.

West Ham certainly weren't going to be doing it the easy way, as they were then drawn against Liverpool! The omens looked good when the Hammers defeated them 2-1, courtesy of Hurst and Robson and followed

111

this win with an emphatic 5-0 thrashing of Sheffield United. [A Robson hat-trick and a brace from Best.]

The two-legged semi-final against Stoke City then produced a season's worth of drama. West Ham won the away leg 2-1, with goals from Hurst and Best but then agonisingly lost at Upton Park 1-0, to take the sides into a third meeting.

It could all have been so very different though. With just minutes to go West Ham were awarded a penalty, which could take them to their first Wembley Final in years. Hurst – usually so lethal from the spot – saw his pile-driver brilliantly saved by his England team-mate Gordon Banks.

The Hillsborough replay ended 0-0 and so to the fourth amazing encounter, at Old Trafford. Despite watching thousands of football matches since, this game is etched upon my memory because of its sheer drama. It would be over thirty years before there was another match quite like it involving West Ham and that one too would end sadly.

Goalkeeper Bobby Ferguson was badly injured, after colliding with a Stoke forward. In the days before goalkeeper substitutes became the norm, Bobby Moore had to don the keeper's gloves and take over in goal.

[My neighbour Jeff was a journalist and he used to bring me photographs of the West Ham games, which his newspaper hadn't used. Like a complete shmuck I threw them all away, years later but – if I could have retained just one of them – then the one I will always regret ditching was a poignant black-and-white shot of a rain-lashed Moore; head bowed; forlornly trudging towards the goal.]

Almost immediately, Stoke won a penalty. Incredibly, Bobby saved it but couldn't keep out the follow-up

112

strike. [*That doesn't really count, does it? Needing two attempts to squeeze a penalty past a guy who wasn't even the goalkeeper? Who'd celebrate that? That Stoke b*****d did, actually.*]

Billy Bonds equalised for the Hammers and then a clearly dazed Ferguson returned to the field after 15 minutes of treatment; which had consisted of back-room staff firing balls at him, in order to test just how badly concussed he was! [*If he'd been American he'd've sued them for assault.*]

Trevor Brooking put West Ham ahead, in this incredibly exciting end-to-end see-saw of a game but Stoke equalised and this amazing match went into extra-time; Stoke scoring the decisive goal and my little 10 year old heart was broken. [*'And Like My Dreams...etc.'*]

Ironically, this would be one of Geoff Hurst's final games for West Ham United. At the end of the season Stoke manager Tony Waddington decided to bolster his attack, prior to their assault upon Europe – [*having beaten Chelsea in the League Cup Final; so **some** good came out of it!*] – and when Ron Greenwood informed Hurst that Waddington had made an offer, he realised that the fact his manager had actually **told** him this time meant that he was willing to sell Geoff. 13 wonderful years at Upton Park were over.

[Vic Watson is West Ham United's all-time top goal-scorer but Hurst comes a strong second, with 248 goals in 499 appearances.

Hurst quietly played out his career and, upon retiring, was offered the role of first-team coach, under Danny Blanchflower, at Chelsea. When Blanchflower then quit, Hurst was promoted to manager. However, several seasons spent ineffectively trying to get Chelsea

113

promoted back to the First Division, resulted in Hurst being sacked in 1981. *I thought that he did a marvellous job there, myself! Lol.*

Nevertheless, he would go on to enjoy some last success, when reunited with his old mentor Greenwood, in the England set-up.]

West Ham also released Harry Redknapp that season, after an altercation with Ron Greenwood, in which the abrasive Harry threw a bottle of lager at him.

Hurst's replacement for the '72-3 season was Ted MacDougall; who'd been a revelation at lower-division Bournemouth but had proved a bust at Manchester United. He would go on to become an even bigger flop at Upton Park! An unpopular character in the dressing-room, MacDougall wouldn't last the season; although, to be fair, Geoff Hurst was going to be a hard act for anyone to follow!

From Lyall's *'Just Like My Dreams':*

"Determination and aggression were the qualities that underpinned Geoff Hurst's game. He developed into an outstanding, very coachable striker; who Ron, in later years as England manager, used to demonstrate skills and tactics to his international stars.

There are few players of 6ft who can be both physically commanding and possess superb technique. Geoff had both qualities...

He was **the** outstanding all-round striker of his era and would be priceless in the modern age, when strikers are basically pigeon-holed in two categories. They are either the target man or the goal-scorer who feeds off him. Geoff could fill both roles."

Adds Greenwood:

"Hurst had a lot to learn but he was a coach's dream. Nobody could have worked harder. He listened and

114

practised and kept on practising and the improvement in his game was remarkable. He learnt to take the ball coming at him from behind and worked on his heading and shooting from all distances and angles. His control improved 100%; his mobility acquired a new edge and he quickly grasped the principles of making and using space…

A partnership that was very special developed between Hurst and Johnny Byrne…Between them they had everything to undermine opposing defences. Hurst, with his late angled runs, his controlled power and aggression, his persistence and selflessness, posed one sort of problem; whilst Byrne, with his deft touches, instant control, ability to beat his man and quickness presented another. Both, too, knew exactly where the net was.

I cherish our association. Geoff Hurst was a loyal club man, a brilliant team man and a great player. Can any manager ask for more?"

[*Well, obviously, yes; because you sold him, you silly old sod!*]

For whatever reason – considering we'd had many better individual players and teams, in previous seasons but had flirted with relegation – West Ham United finally found consistency in the 1972-3 season and finished in a lofty 6th place; via some solid all-round team performances. The blend of youth and experience; home-grown and purchased talent, **finally** seemed to be gelling. It was West Ham's misfortune that only the top 5 teams qualified for Europe that season.

The always-dangerous Pop Robson was their top scorer and Brooking was now firing on all cylinders; his silky skills being well-matched by the tenacious tackling of Bonds in midfield. Originally criticised by Greenwood

115

for being lazy and too easy to knock off the ball, Trevor Brooking began to show why Bobby Moore declared him; "A luxury West Ham need."

A two-footed midfielder - [*I know smart-arse; they've* **all** *got two feet. I mean, as in being able to kick the ball equally well with either foot!*] - Brooking preferred to play on the left and would bamboozle defenders by either quickly whipping a left-footed cross over or by cutting inside, on to his right foot and curling a pass onto a striker's head with pinpoint accuracy.

Also, that season, left-back Frank Lampard was capped for England; whilst his club and country captain Bobby Moore broke the West Ham appearance record **and** received his 100th England cap. However, Bobby's days were numbered internationally. [*108 actually.*]

[This was the beginning of the end for England, as a major force in world football. Defeat against Poland, in a World Cup qualifier, was blamed largely on a rare defensive mistake by Moore. Thus, for the return fixture at Wembley, Alf Ramsey replaced Bobby with Leeds's Norman Hunter; who promptly made exactly the same mistake and cost England victory!

Failure to even qualify for the 1974 World Cup led to the sacking of Alf Ramsey; who had controversially dropped his long-time captain Moore from his stuttering England side, in an effort to introduce new players to halt the inexorable decline. It was a sad ending to two great international careers.]

*

It wasn't only our football team which seemed in decline; England itself was falling apart in this period. During Ted Heath's reign as Prime Minister he had declared a 'national State of Emergency' an incredible 5 times; something only usually seen during times of warfare! But, in a way, Britain **was** 'at war'; the working classes fighting extreme dissatisfaction with Government policies.

In 1972, the Dockers had called for a national strike, in the attempt to safeguard jobs which were being threatened by the increase in containerisation.

The lowest point though came in 1973-4, when Britain was reduced to a 3 day working week and the Provisional IRA commenced its bombing campaign in England; as a response to the refusal of British troops to leave Northern Ireland.

The Tories had introduced a 'cap' on pay rises but the unions weren't happy, as working-class wages didn't match the constant rise in inflation. The coal-miners subsequent 'work to rule' led to lowering supplies of coal and, thus, blackouts and power-cuts.

As intended, the miners' strike caused chaos but the Conservatives had commenced closing coal mines anyway, as the need for coal decreased with the increasing usage of North Sea oil, gas and even nuclear energy, to produce electricity.

In response to the potential loss of their livelihoods the miners stopped working altogether and the resultant loss of power hit every household in Britain. Heath announced that industry would have to reduce to a 3 day working week, in order to save remaining electricity supplies.

Candles morphed from romantic symbols to essential methods of survival and, soon, petrol was rationed and food supplies in shops dwindled, as deliveries ground to a halt. It was the worst period of austerity since the War and already poor areas, such as East London, were hit doubly-hard.

Whilst the likes of Hackney's Marc Bolan, David Bowie – [born in Stepney] -and everyone's favourite paedophile Gary Glitter lit up the nation's colour TV screens with their Glam Rock; the rest of the time Britain sat in grey, depressing darkness.

[Can you have a 'favourite paedophile'? I suppose, if you can, then Michael Jackson would probably be the world's favourite. Allegedly!

'I'm Forever Blowing Bubbles' takes on a whole new meaning when you think of a typical evening at Wacko Jacko's crib.

(Bubbles was his pet monkey; for those of you who didn't get that joke...although, once you've broken a joke down and explained it, it kind of sucks.)]

*

The pattern of being a West Ham United supporter had now been indelibly set. A stunning success would almost certainly be followed by a massive failure, and listless defeats against the likes of Stoke would be followed by thumping victories against teams such as Chelsea. There was simply no rhyme or reason to West Ham's form.

'That c**t MacDougall', as he was affectionately referred to by Billy Bonds, went to Norwich in a swap that saw cultured midfielder Graham Paddon move to Upton Park. However, West Ham failed to build on the promise of the previous campaign and finished 1973-4 in a lowly 18th position, in the season which saw three teams relegated and promoted, instead of the previous two; which the football authorities hoped would make things 'more exciting' for the fans and rectify rapidly falling attendances. [Similarly, three points for a win was later introduced, in order to stimulate more adventurous football and deter sides from 'playing for the draw'.]

However, declining attendances was probably more to do with the steadily worsening epidemic of football hooliganism that was stopping families attending matches together and scaring many supporters away.

*

'ICF, ICF, ICF!'

No history of West Ham United would be complete without accepting that their infamous hooligan 'firm' became more newsworthy than the team itself, in the late 1970's / early '80's.

Most football teams had unwittingly attracted hooligan gangs by the late 1960's; largely made up of local working-class lads, who followed the age-old territorial imperative of 'defending their turf' against rival visiting supporters. In the 1970's though, the 'violence bar' was raised when larger numbers of these fans began travelling to away games; no longer content in merely defending their own territory but set upon humiliating the opposition support by 'taking their ends'; meaning, claiming the areas which the hard-core home support considered its own.

[*And not 'taking their ends' in the prison or George Michael sense.*]

West Ham's hooligans were originally a disparate bunch of hard-men and local lads who drank and fought together and principal amongst these were the Mile End Mob.

Cass Pennant explains, from '*Congratulations: You Have Just Met The I.C.F.*' [2003]:

"The Mile End Mob had emerged as a firm as early as 1968, when white working-class skinheads began to congregate behind the popular goal end on match days.

Our home end was The North Bank; the largest end in Upton Park…

Like gypsy families, they were an extremely tight-knit firm and the main characters were all related – many of them were brothers. To be part of this firm you had to come from the Mile End area of London. They trusted no-one and picked fights with everyone else at West Ham. Now and again they fought amongst themselves; nobody dared do anything to intervene.

By the early 1970's they had earned a fearsome reputation throughout London and had separated themselves entirely from West Ham's other firms by taking up residence behind the goal the opposite end to The North Bank. Their status had reached hero-worship proportions among the West Ham bovver-boy following; although our own supporters had every reason to fear them the most. Yet, when it came to fighting our rivals, particularly other London clubs, they were often our saviours…

The District Line train picks up more of us as it stops at East London tube stations. Eventually it reached Mile End station. The mighty Mile End gang swarm on from the platform, shoving anyone not Mile End from their carriage.

The rest of us are buzzing; the excitement reaches a crescendo. Now the Mile End are on board, we feel f*****g invincible."

By the mid-1970's there were several main 'firms' amongst West Ham's support; the Mile End Gang, the Teddy Bunter Firm, Steve Morgan's South Bank Crew and the Essex and East London Firm.

One of the main 'faces' who helped to unify these various gangs was the terrace legend Bill Gardner. A truly 'hard' man, Gardner started off in the Mile End

120

Gang but then joined with Teddy Bunter's Firm as their 'main man'. Regardless of your affiliation, no-one doubted that Bill Gardner was anything less than dangerous.

From *'Congratulations:..'*

"As Gardner nears the top, Chelsea; who've been standing there with their fists clenched, start to back away until he is on top of those stairs with them. I'm close enough to hear him utter that by now familiar introduction line: 'Afternoon gentlemen, the name's Bill Gardner'.

As soon as Bill announces himself a big gap opens up around us. Bewildered looks all round, sort of saying; 'Look, we're not Chelsea anymore; in fact, we're nobody at all'.

Such is the aura and presence of West Ham's terrace legend. The Chelsea lot know that when you'd found Gardner you'd found West Ham's top boys and all their main firm. It's now an altogether different proposition for the faint-hearted among the Chelsea Shed boys."

The unification though of the various firms can be largely credited to the likes of Andy Swallow, Grant Fleming and Micky Ramsgate.

Many of the younger West Ham hooligans would meet up in the *'Denmark Arms'* pub, in East Ham and discuss strategy for forthcoming 'rucks'. Annoyed at being dismissed as 'boys' by the older West Ham hooligans, they plotted ever more adventurous escapades and attracted more-and-more members; eventually christening themselves 'the Inter-City Firm', in consideration of the fact that – instead of travelling the time-honoured routes to opposing grounds – they were using the high-speed inter-city trains to circumvent both opposing fans, waiting at the stations and the police.

121

These 15 to 18 year olds made their statement to their older peers on Boxing Day 1977, when around 50 of them 'took' the home supporters Holte End at Aston Villa.

The older terrace legends were forced to sit up and take notice and, eventually, the different groups bonded into one unstoppable force; the Inter-City Firm; the I.C.F.

Micky Ramsgate reinforced their burgeoning reputation with a method of humiliating fallen victims. He had a set of business cards printed with *'Congratulations: You have just met the ICF,'* typed across them; to be dropped casually onto the unconscious bodies of beaten opposing supporters.

The simple chant they used, as they surged into action, was chillingly effective too; 'I.C.F, I.C.F, **I.C.F., I.C.F.!!'**, building in volume as it was spat aggressively at the terrified onlookers.

The I.C.F also spawned its offshoot; the 'Under 5's'; a mocking name for the youngest followers of the Inter-City Firm. These teenagers specialised in thieving from away teams local stores and 'taxing' opposing supporters; ie; robbing them of clothes or money.

This was the beginning of extreme football violence!

Another West Ham terrace legend Carlton Leach remembers, in his autobiography *'Rise of the Footsoldier'*: "I was about six years old when my dad first took me to Upton Park to watch West Ham play; perched on his shoulders, cheering the lads on for all I was worth. Marvellous, innocent childhood entertainment. Never did I dream that ten years later I'd be running amok on the terraces as one of the most feared football hooligans in Britain, targeted by the police, hated by rival fans, dreaded at every ground country-wide…

My schoolboy passion for the team grew into an all-consuming obsession. I lived, breathed and dreamed West Ham United. I started to bunk off school to watch them. Then, at 13 or 14 I joined up with a crowd who went to **every** game, home or away. I got to know the real hard-core supporters, including Vic Dark, who became a well-known bank robber, and loads of other mates who shared not only a fixation for the Hammers, but also a passion for violence…

I deliberately set out to become one of the guv'nors of the rowdiest bunch of soccer hooligans of all time, the ICF.

It was a name that sent a shudder through any club we were visiting and through the local constabulary. I wanted to be respected. I wanted to be feared. I wasn't a violent kid away from football grounds, but put me at a West Ham game and I became an animal. I was a soldier, out there fighting for my team. I wanted the adulation of the fans. I wanted to be a top name on the terraces."

*

Final[ly]

Regardless of England's problems under the Conservatives; for West Ham United there were only two moments of real importance in the 1973-4 season; plus some minor controversy.

In the midst of the Hammer's poor run of form, which saw them hurtling down the table, goalkeeper Bobby Ferguson was dropped, after publicly stating that there were 'too many gutless men in the team'. He was immediately replaced by the young Mervyn Day, as Greenwood sought to maintain the team's fragile morale.

On the plus side: Leeds United had been decimating all opposition, on their way to the League title and could quite reasonably have been expected to trample all over the Hammers. My dad couldn't get us a ticket for this game, as it was a sell-out. Nevertheless, we went and he 'tipped' the guy at the turnstiles to let us through. I sat on the cold stone steps and embraced the most fantastic atmosphere I've ever experienced at Upton Park.

38,500 fans squeezed into the Boleyn Ground that day and roared the Hammers on to an incredible 3-1 victory. Best, Robson and Brooking scored, on a day when West Ham United could have beaten any team on earth.

The other moment of significance was the sad departure of Robert Moore. After 16 years and 642 appearances Ron Greenwood finally allowed his captain to leave. Surprisingly, although First Division clubs were interested, Moore chose to join his friend and fellow ex-England international Alan Mullery at 2nd Division Fulham.

[Trevor Brooking – having made his England debut that year - was also linked with a move away; this time to Spurs but elected to stay. A West Ham United fan since he was a boy; Barking-born Trevor would remain incredibly loyal to 'his club'.]

My little self was gutted but, many years later when I read various biographies, I realised just how unhappy Bobby had been at West Ham.

From John Lyall's autobiography *Just Like My Dreams':*

"As a player Bobby Moore had immense foresight, vision and knowledge. He had an enquiring mind and what he learned, particularly from Ron, helped make him one of the greatest international captains ever and he led both England and West Ham by example.

He could see and interpret correctly everything that was happening on the pitch. That's what gave him such wonderful vision. He was always looking for space to play the ball into. If he couldn't see it in front of him or on the wings, he was happy to play the ball back to his own goalkeeper; knowing this would draw the opposition out of their defensive positions and create space for West Ham's attackers.

He was also a great interceptor; one of the best I have ever seen in the game. He didn't have to tackle very often because he invariably knew where the ball was going and he would be there first.

…Despite world-wide fame Bobby was an unassuming man. Those who didn't know him have suggested that he was aloof but nothing could be further from the truth. As a player, at West Ham, he wanted to be treated like all the others and would often put his team-mates before himself."

Ron Greenwood's reflections were more personal and slightly contradicted Lyall's glowing assessment of Moore the man:

"Our relationship became unhappy and strained. There was an icy corridor between us…In 1966 I had taken the club captaincy from Moore. His attitude clearly meant that he was less than 100% committed to the club and so I gave the job to Johnny Byrne, who bubbled with enthusiasm. It wasn't a difficult decision because it made the point that no player was bigger than the club.

Moore didn't show a flicker of emotion when I told him; I am not sure that he ever did show any…

Off the field, we had a problem. I felt he became very aloof; locked in a world of his own and although his cold detachment was a strength on the field and even a shield in situations like the one in Bogota, it was an attitude which made things very difficult in the small, everyday world of a football club.

Moore even started to give the impression that he was ignoring me at team-talks. He would glance around with a blasé look on his face, eyes glazed, in a way that suggested he had nothing new to learn...

It was impossible to get close to Moore. There was a big corner of himself that he would not or could not give. To begin with I think it was a sort of protective act but, eventually, the act became reality. He seemed to step inside an image from which he couldn't escape. It worried me because I knew what a nice person he was at heart. I remembered him as a lad, full of enthusiasm and determination, and the way we had shared our passion for the game...

I suppose it was a case of different personalities not gelling and this was as much my fault as his. I tried to bridge the gap between us, once or twice but it never worked. The lowest point of all was the Blackpool affair in January 1971. I felt so let down but Moore even said that he thought I'd let **him** down by not denying the story to the press. There is a right time for a drink and a wrong time. A nightclub in Blackpool a few hours before an important cup tie is the wrong time!

Moore the player would have improved any team in the world...In all his years with us, a side without Moore seemed inconceivable. Even in his last year with us, I would get threats of bomb damage to my house if I dared let him go. I received them by 'phone and by letter and, far from worrying me, I used to think; 'Good, it shows people care'. Moore **was** West Ham but not even a man like him lasts forever. I felt the time had come when we could let him go."

*

Britain also felt that the time had come to let that bumbling fool Ted Heath go and Harold Wilson's Labour Government resumed power in 1974. Heath's reign had been blighted by an almost constant series of strikes; from council workers, through the miners, to the Dockers and Wilson immediately set out to try and placate the ever more powerful unions.

Before the start of the 1974-5 season it was announced that Ron Greenwood would be assuming a more 'advisory' role, as General Manager and that his assistant John Lyall was being promoted to full manager. It was as if the sale of Bobby Moore had a psychological effect upon Greenwood; as though he had indeed 'released' West Ham.

When questioned as to why West Ham United had never lived up to their full potential and won the League Championship; despite fielding so many terrific players over the years; Greenwood was honest:

"I accept much of the blame for this myself. Perhaps I was too idealistic. Certainly, I wasn't ruthless enough. My conscience sometimes got in the way and loyalty was occasionally a handicap. But I was not a dreamer. I believed in our attacking style and was quite convinced that it was the right way to play football. I honestly thought it could win the Championship for us. At the same time, I also recognised that it would be necessary for us to sweat and battle and, over the years, this was what let us down."

Ironically, the ultimate 'sweaty battler', Billy Bonds was named the new West Ham captain and this was a popular choice amongst both fans and his peers; as Bonzo wore his commitment on his sleeve and never gave less than 100% for the Hammers; whilst Mick

McGiven had the unfortunate role of attempting to replace the legend Moore.

Disappointingly, Lyall chose to sell Pop Robson to Sunderland but purchased his midfielder namesake Keith, from Newcastle and two strikers in replacement; Billy Jennings from Watford and the un-known quantity that was Alan Taylor, from lowly 4th Division Rochdale.

After a great start to the season, which included two of the best games I ever witnessed at Upton Park – *even though I was in pre-teen mourning for my beloved Bobby Moore, and wanted my nan to knit me black arm-bands, instead of those bloody tank-tops. [**See back cover photo**]* – a 6-2 victory over Leicester and a 5-2 win over Wolves; West Ham flopped dismally over the second half of the campaign, falling from 5th to an eventual 13th place.

Nevertheless, the FA Cup would prove to be the saviour of West Ham's season and provided John Lyall with a perfect start to his management career. Ten years on from the last occasion West Ham had stepped out onto the Wembley turf, Bobby Moore was once again striding, head held high, onto the fabled pitch. This time, however, he was wearing the white shirt and black shorts of Fulham FC and it was Billy Bonds who wore the captain's armband over the claret-and-blue of West Ham.

In the third round the Hammers had beaten Southampton 2-1, with goals from defender Lampard and striker Bobby Gould. Billy Jennings had proven to be an astute buy and would become West Ham's top scorer that season; his goal earning a 1-1 draw with 3rd Division Swindon. Goals from Brooking and midfielder / winger Pat Holland won the replay; Holland scoring

128

again, along with Keith Robson in the 2-1 victory over QPR.

Some players make their reputations over a period of many years, whilst others briefly burn brightly before fizzling out. Such was the case with former Cup hero Alan Sealey in the '60's and this was again the scenario with Alan Taylor in 1975 and '76. Outside of these two seasons, Taylor produced absolutely nothing of note but will be remembered by Hammers fans forever for his contribution in those two years.

Picked by Lyall to replace Bobby Gould, in the quarter-final against Arsenal; basically because of the frail-looking, angular Taylor's raw whippet speed against the stubborn Gunners defence; Alan sensationally scored twice at Highbury to put the Hammers through to a semi-final showdown with Ipswich.

The Villa Park match-up ended goal-less but the Stamford Bridge replay saw another brace from Taylor send West Ham to Wembley and guarantee him a place in the starting line-up ahead of the veteran Gould.

In one of those strange twists of fate which seem to happen so often in the sporting arena, 34 year old Bobby Moore would be waiting there for his former team-mates. 2nd Division Fulham had enjoyed a remarkable cup run and now stood between John Lyall's boys and FA Cup glory.

If ever I'd felt emotionally torn in my 13 years on this planet, it was here! Akin to Benn versus Eubank and Tyson against Bruno; I wanted my idol Moore to play well but, ultimately, for the claret and blue ribbons to be tied around the iconic cup's handles. Like those ribbons, my blood ran claret-and-blue and a West Ham victory would always be the imperative. [*That's not strictly true. I got punched on the nose a lot at school and it only ever bled red!]*

0-0 at half-time and I was getting worried. This was such a big day in my household and I was allowed to have a can of beer, whilst watching the game with my dad on TV. [*The **game** was on TV; not my dad. The closest he came to TV was when he dressed as a woman for a bet.*]

In the second half, Billy Jennings shoots; the keeper palms it out, only for Alan Taylor to knock it back past him and into the net. I was delirious!

Shortly afterwards, Graham Paddon's shot was spilled by the keeper at Taylor's feet and he clipped it over him. Game over!

Taylor may have made the headlines but Lampard and Brooking were actually West Ham's best players on the day. In a wonderful moment, towards the end, Lampard chased the ball, deep in Fulham's half. Moore stood over the ball; waited for Lampard to commit himself and then smilingly lifted the ball over his friend and former team-mate's head.

[It was a last moment of unruffled class from Bobby. After continuing with Fulham for a while, he ended his career in the burgeoning American 'soccer' scene; playing with the likes of fellow aging-legends Pele and Franz Beckenbaur.]

In a weird echo of Bobby Moore's feeling of dissatisfaction after the Final of 1964, Billy Bonds felt strangely deflated afterwards; disappointed that the Hammers had struggled to break down their lower division opponents and that the game itself hadn't been a great spectacle for the fans. Bonds had been at Upton Park long enough by now to know that entertaining the fans would always be the paramount priority for West Ham United.

*

The 1975-6 season promised to match the drama and success of its predecessor but only matched the drama part of it.

A virtual carbon-copy of the previous campaign saw West Ham start strongly and then fade badly into an eventual 18th place in the League; although a three-month absence due to injury, to influential skipper Bonds proved disruptive; the Hammers looking disorganised in Bill's absence.

The defence of the FA Cup lasted a whole 90 minutes; those Scouse looters Liverpool winning 2-0 at Upton Park. [*Which, if it had been on wheels, would've been left propped up on bricks before their train headed back North. Not that I'm stereotyping.*]

The European Cup-Winner's Cup in '76 was where the real excitement lay and it would prove to be an incredible series of encounters.

From Billy Bonds's autobiography, *'Bonzo'* [1988]:

"It is commonplace for players to praise their own fans as 'the best in the country', but I am quite sure that ours played a big part in helping us to reach the European Cup Winner's Cup Final.

We had fortune with us in that campaign, since in every round the first leg tie was away from home. In fact, we never won on foreign soil. But we did enough to always have a shout in the return game at Upton Park. And our supporters on those memorable nights were worth a goal start to us, in my view!

The atmosphere they generated was tremendous; even better than for the FA Cup. Playing in our tight, compact ground, a cauldron of noise, with leather-lunged East-Enders breathing down their necks, was a totally new experience for most of the visitors. Some clearly bottled it!"

Finnish part-timers Lahden Reipas somehow managed to hold West Ham to a 2-2 draw in Helsinki – [Brooking and Bonds being the Hammers goal-scorers] – but West Ham comfortably won the 2nd leg 3-0; thanks to Robson, Holland and Jennings. This set the pattern for inauspicious away performances, followed by dominant home showings.

Ararat Erevan of Russia salvaged a 1-1 draw, in a game which the Hammers should have won – [Taylor scoring] – before falling 3-1 in the return. [Paddon, Robson and Taylor again.]

Dutchmen Den Haag raced into a 4-0 lead before half-time and West Ham were thankful for the two Billy Jennings goals in the second half, which gave them hope for the return leg.

On a raucous night at Upton Park, West Ham won 3-1, thanks to Taylor, Lampard, Bonds and the incredible deafening support of their fans. With the aggregate score thus tied at 5-5, the Hammers went through to the semi-finals on the 'away goals' rule.

Germans Eintracht Frankfurt took a 2-1 lead to Upton Park – [Paddon] – and were clearly the best technical side West Ham had yet faced. Nevertheless, West Ham triumphed yet again, via 2 goals from Brooking and a third from Robson and they had thus repeated their 1964/5 schedule of successive cup finals.

This time, however, it would be their opponents who would enjoy 'home advantage'. West Ham had had the good fortune of playing at Wembley in '65 and now Anderlecht had managed to reach the Final; to be held in the Belgian club's home stadium, in Brussels.

132

*[Bloody unfair, if you ask me!...Go on; ask me...Thank you. Well, in my humble opinion, I feel that; 'It was **bloody unfair'**.]*

Unfortunately, as well as West Ham played that evening, they couldn't match their opponents and a skilful Anderlecht side ran out comfortable 4-2 winners. [Holland and Robson scoring the Hammers consolations.] This time there would be no glorious return leg at intimidating Upton Park. The dream was over for another year. *[Or four.]*

*

1976 saw England experience a heatwave, which resulted in a drought. Water supplies ran critically low and I've never experienced heat like it in England since. *[Except that vindaloo I ate in '82. And it wasn't the outside of my body which experienced the burning sensation!]*

The football at Upton Park remained exactly the same though; as did the football violence.

By 1976 the ICF were untouchable in London and had repeatedly defeated their closest neighbours Spurs, Arsenal and Chelsea, in pitched battles. However, it was a confrontation with lower-league Millwall which really cemented their reputation for 'ultra-violence'.

The East London and Millwall areas had endured a rivalry ever since the South Londoners had competed for the same shipping contracts, back in the early 20th Century, and continued when the Millwall Dockers failed to come out on strike, in support of the East London Dockers, in the early 1970's.

However, the actual football rivalry didn't really surface until 1972. The two teams had rarely played each other, due to Millwall always being in a lower division – *[the sad losers!]* - but, just as West Ham fans

133

were establishing their reputation for violence; so too were Millwall's, in the lower leagues. Finally, a testimonial match, in '72, brought the two teams together at Millwall's Den and the Mile End Mob infiltrated the home fans Cold Blow Lane End, prior to kick-off. The rest of the match became a constant battle between the Millwall fans trying to reclaim it and the West Ham hooligans aiming to retain it.

As the match finished, the violence moved up to another level.

From *'Congratulations: etc...'* Cass Pennant remembers:

"When we came out at the end of the game, we came out early, with all the Mile End Gang and we stood waiting. There were two gate exits; they only had two gates to get out. And we stood at both gates...

Then I witnessed something I wouldn't like to see again. Out came these biggest – well, f*****g hell – do you know these great big spanners you see, used by railway workers? They must have been something like the length of your arm. They just battered these c***s as they came out of these gates. They didn't care who they f*****g were; they just battered everybody that came out...it was frightening to watch, purely because I wasn't really into that level of violence."

Thus began the extreme violence between the two teams' fans, which resulted in the death of a Millwall follower in 1976. In a skirmish between the two sets of supporters at New Cross railway station, a Millwall fan was flung to his death beneath a train; which inspired the ICF chant; *"We're all mad; We're insane; We throw Millwall under trains."* The die was cast!

[In later years there would be a petrol bomb thrown by West Ham fans at their Millwall rivals and, incredibly,

134

a live hand grenade was thrown by a West Ham-supporting soldier!]

The worst mass violence though, that season, was probably against Liverpool away. Micky Ramsgate remembers:

"After we'd parked we started walking to the ground, when a little kid with 'L.F.C.' tattooed on his knuckles latched on to us.

He couldn't have been older than thirteen. He just looked at us and said; 'You're going to get f****d'. I thought, f*****g hell, this is a rough place!"

The battles with the Scousers were bloody and painful but, the simple fact remained, that West Ham's I.C.F. were willing to travel in numbers to any location in England and battle the best the home club had to offer. This was rarely the case when the situation was reversed and the opposition travelled to East London. Upton Park remained 'a step too far' for even the hardest Northerners.

Season 1976-7 saw Graham Paddon return to Norwich but the popular – *no pun intended* - Bryan 'Pop' Robson returned to Upton Park. Pop hadn't forgotten his shooting boots – [*his mum packed them for him*] - and, by season's end, would be top scorer for the Hammers once more.

Another lower-profile transfer would prove to be a gem over the succeeding years; for the scrawny Alan Devonshire was plucked from non-league football and a part-time job as a forklift truck driver and thrust into the First Division limelight; where his virtuoso displays of running at defenders at break-neck pace and dribbling across the pitch, with the ball seemingly glued to his boots, delighted the Upton Park fans.

[The season also saw the emergence of two local lads in midfield; with very contrasting styles of play; the playmaker Alan Curbishley and the bustling, energetic Geoff Pike.]

John Lyall had claimed that West Ham's involvement in the FA and Cup Winners Cups had affected their League performances over the two previous seasons. He could have no such excuses this campaign, as the Hammers went out in the early rounds of both domestic cup competitions and yet still couldn't find any consistency in their League form.

The strikers weren't providing the requisite goals and so, in desperation, Lyall played centre-half Tommy Taylor in attack. This would be no Geoff Hurst-like transformation. Taylor was 'pants' as a striker and soon returned to defensive duties.

In a reversal of previous seasons, West Ham started poorly and were immediately sucked into the relegation battle but finished strongly and a 0-0 draw with champions Liverpool; followed by a marvellous 4-2 victory over Manchester United in the final game of the season confirmed our survival. This kind of luck just couldn't last though.

Two really bad things happened in my life in the 1977-8 season. Elvis Presley died and West Ham United were relegated. I wasn't sure which one hurt the most. [*Although Elvis had an inclination!*]

Prior to the season commencing, Keith Robson was sold – [*Lyall finding it too difficult to have a team with two men named Robson in*] – and striker David Cross was purchased, from West Brom. The tall, lanky Cross quickly established himself as a fan-favourite with his non-stop running and harassing of defenders but neither his goals nor Pop Robson's were enough to save the Hammers.

Billy Bonds expressed his shock that a team which included Trevor Brooking, Frank Lampard, Alan Devonshire, Pop Robson – and himself – should even be in a relegation battle but, the truth was it wasn't as if we hadn't all seen it coming. You can only put your hand in the mouth of a Great White shark so many times before you're going to be known as 'Stumpy' in your local. The reality was; despite the Hammers lack of enough regular goal-scorers in the team, it was the defence that were letting us down and Mervyn Day, particularly, had a nightmare season; leaking goals like a human sieve.

Once again, a miracle escape was needed. If West Ham couldn't beat Liverpool in their final game of the season, they were down.

Surprise! They were down; brushed aside by those arrogant Scousers, who didn't care that they were robbing the First Division of attractive football.

20 years of First Division adventures was over and even non-West Ham fans were saddened. They may not have been 'title contenders' but they had always been consistently entertaining and the Hammers were often cited as most peoples 'second favourite club'; after whichever was their local or 'glory-hunting' choice of team; as well as the side which the 'neutrals' most enjoyed watching on TV. But now, it was over and even the ever-loyal Trevor Brooking wondered whether 2nd Division football would kill his burgeoning England career.

Reassured by Ron Greenwood that; as long as he continued to play well, the lower-calibre opposition wouldn't affect his international career, Brooking

137

elected to stay and help West Ham battle their way out of the Second Division. [This, unfortunately, wouldn't happen for several frustrating seasons.]

Midway through the '78-9 campaign John Lyall decided that Mervyn Day was never going to live up to his early potential and spent a record £565,000 fee on purchasing the QPR goalkeeper Phil Parkes, in order to stem the tide of goals Day was conceding for fun. Despite this – and Pop Robson and David Cross firing in goals themselves regularly – West Ham could only finish in 5th place; their 'goals for' tally being negated by their goals conceded.

Promotion wasn't going to be as easy as they'd imagined and the disappointment was evidenced by an exodus of players at season's end. Jennings, Taylor – [Alan **and** Tommy] - McGiven and, most lamentably, Pop Robson all departed. Most surprising exit though was that of 21 year old prospect Curbishley; who complained that he was always 'in the shadow of Trevor Brooking'. [*Otherwise known as stalking!*]

The following season would bring an amazing mixture of fortunes; for West Ham United **and** for Great Britain.

*

INTERLUDE
A WEST HAM FAN'S MEMORIES.   NO.3

Name: Paul McEvoy. **Age:** 49. **Profession:** Graphic Designer. [And drummer in the Punk/Mod group *'Friends of Luca Brasi'.*] **Born:** East Ham. [Now living in North Essex.] **Connection to West Ham:** Fan. [And designer of this book cover; the clever little descendant of the Irish race!]

Why do you support West Ham? [Early memories.]

"A number of reasons. They were a working-class team and I grew up in a working-class family and area. The

138

main reason though was that – on the corner of our road – was a little greengrocer's / sweet shop called 'Boyce's'. It was run by Bill Boyce, whose son was Ronnie Boyce and – occasionally – you'd go into the shop and Ronnie would be there, and that got all of us local kids excited; seeing a famous footballer on our doorstep.

I became a regular fixture in there; always going 'round, just to see if Ronnie Boyce was in there!

My dad used to go to Upton Park with his mate and me and my brother. We went to a few evening games at first and then it just kind of grew from there.

[Although we attended the Home games, my all-time favourite strip was the Away strip of that time; the sky-blue shirt with the two claret hoops across the chest.]

Once we were old enough to 'pay our own way', my brother and I used to go to the Saturday afternoon matches on our own. We went for quite a few years but then it all started to get a bit silly with all of the hooliganism. It all got a bit too 'heavy' for us and so we stopped going."

Who is your all-time favourite West Ham player and why?

"Bobby Moore, of course!

I liked Geoff Hurst too. I started going there when I was about 5 or 6, and so they were both still in the team. Then, later on, I liked Trevor Brooking, Billy Bonds and Clyde Best.

I used to really like Bobby Ferguson – the goalie – as well. I thought he was a great keeper and should've been in the England team".

Author: "He was Scottish; so that would've been difficult!"

"Ah, I didn't think about that, did I? Cut that bit out of the interview".

[**Author:** *(To himself):* 'He really doesn't know me very well, does he?']

Who was your least-favourite West Ham player of all-time and why?

"I can't actually think of anyone from the early years". [Laughs.] *"Though there's quite a few from the later years!*

I'm not that keen on Frank Lampard anymore, but that's mainly because of his 'turncoat' son. I think Lampard Junior's influenced how I feel about his dad now.

I think I've actually had more 'issues' with managers than players. Lou Macari made a complete 'balls-up' when he was there!"

What's your strongest single memory of supporting West Ham United?

[Pause.] *"I'm not really sure about that one...I remember when we played West Brom and the crowd wouldn't leave Jeff Astle alone. They kept chanting: 'Astle is a fairy', over-and-over again and you could see that he was really p****d off with it!"*

What was the best game you ever saw, or best experience of supporting West Ham?

*"It's got to be the evening game in 1971-2, when they played Coventry. It was p*****g down with rain that night and the players were sliding all over the place because the pitch was so wet, and yet the goals were flying in from everywhere".* [4-0 to West Ham.]

"Another game I vividly remember was beating Leicester City 6-2. Brilliant atmosphere that day at Upton Park".

[**Author:** I agree; one of the best Hammers performances I ever witnessed.]

What was the worst game you ever saw / worst experience?

"My worst experience was football-violence related. It was against Manchester United and darts started flying about in the crowd. People were throwing all manner of things at each other and it wasn't a nice feeling, being caught up in the middle of all that.

Football-wise, it was against Wrexham in 1978-9, after we'd been relegated. We needed to beat them in our last home game of the season, in order to stand a chance of being promoted, and we couldn't do it. It was a really boring game and we played poorly and, not long after that, I stopped going".

Any non-football pitch related anecdotes around supporting West Ham?

"You'd see a lot of Mods, at Upton Park, at one time. It started with just a few people in Parkas, and then there were more-and-more, and it got to the stage where there were hundreds of Mods standing on the terraces.
[I guess that was all started by Grant Fleming.]

Also, because we used to go to the 'Bridge House', in Canning Town, to listen to live music, you'd see a lot of the guys from the terraces there, listening to the 'Cockney Rejects' and other punk-type bands.

Football, music and fashion were inextricably linked at that time".

Ever had an affinity for another club and / or hated another club, and why?

"I've always liked Celtic, because of my Irish roots.
Manchester City, in the late 1960's / early '70's, when they had the likes of Francis Lee and Colin Bell playing for them; I used to enjoy watching".

141

[**Author:** Significantly; the Man City side managed by one of the key figures behind the 1950's 'Hammers revolution', Malcolm Allison.]

"Other clubs?...No. Certainly no other London club." [Laughs.] *"It's safe to say, actually, that I dislike most clubs that aren't West Ham!"*

*

Chapter Four: 'Champions!...[well; almost.]'

Oi! An East End music revolution.

The late 1970's had seen the most startling musical revolution since rock'n'roll had exploded from America in the 1950's. This time, it was centred around London and Punk Rock mirrored the football terraces of the period with its aggressive visual image and foul-mouthed ranting lyrics. The Establishment was suitably shocked as punk rockers preached anarchy and working-class revolution. If you were middle-class and middle-aged, this would have been your worst nightmare. [*This, or the baby-sitter introducing himself as 'Paul Gadd'.*]

The vibrant British music scene also incorporated the re-emergent Rockabilly's, 'new' Mods and second-generation skinheads and many of these music fans also followed football clubs. By 1980, there was a massive cross-over between football hooligans and punks, mods and skins and much of the violence seen at music gigs in this period was football related. The terrace wars were moving into the music venues and a perfect example of this 'blending' were the Glory Boys; a group of new-generation Mods who included many West Ham hooligans in their ranks.

'The Bridge House', in Canning Town, was one of the most energetic live music venues in London and –

because of its East End location – attracted many West Ham followers. Football hooligans, Glory Boys and punks all merged together at this venue and a new East London-based sound soon emerged.

The 'Oi!' movement was a purer, angrier working-class punk; post Sex Pistols, Clash and Siouxsie Sioux and more 'street'. These weren't middle-class youths pretending to be something they weren't and shouting 'anarchy'; these were young unpretentious working-class 'geezers'; ditching the Mohican and safety-pin look and re-adopting the skinhead style; who angrily shouted their lyrics of frustration and celebrated simple pleasures in song; such as football violence.

'The Cockney Rejects' were the most well-known Oi! Band. Managed by journalist Gary Bushell – [who'd coined the term 'Oi'] – they recorded West Ham's anthem *'I'm Forever Blowing Bubbles',* in 1980 and featured *'West Side Boys'* on the B-side; a song celebrating the I.C.F.

[The Rejects were actually pre-dated by another West Ham-supporting Oi! Band, 'Cock Sparrer', who featured pictures of West Ham hooligans on their record sleeves.]

It seems amazing then that, during this period of rebellious working-class musical anarchy, the Conservative Government should return to power. [?]

Margaret Thatcher had replaced Ted Heath as Tory Leader, following his dismal performance as Prime Minister; whilst Harold Wilson had shockingly resigned in 1976; handing the country's leadership to James Callaghan. [*Akin to giving the keys of your Jaguar to a monkey.*]

Callaghan was widely perceived to be a weak Leader and the economy nosedived. In 1978 Callaghan's

143

attempts to enforce a pay-freeze, in order to combat rising inflation, merely inflamed the unions and widespread strikes led to the infamous 'Winter of Discontent'; whereby nurses, refuse collectors and postal workers were amongst many who refused to work; resulting in foul-smelling, rubbish-strewn London streets and the very real possibility of rat infestation.

Ford car plant workers in Dagenham, Essex, meanwhile, simply ignored Callaghan's pay-freeze restrictions and loudly demanded a pay rise to match inflation; which was granted by their worried employers.

The Tories, sensing blood, called for a General Election and Margaret Thatcher made no secret of the fact that – should she come to power – she would restrict the influence of the unions, so that there would never be a repeat of the chaos of that winter.

Callaghan was duly deposed by Thatcher in May '79 and I developed my first intense dislike of a human being. [*Outside of someone wearing a Chelsea shirt.*]

*

Meanwhile, there were far more important things in life than politics and strike actions; namely, getting West Ham United out of the bloody Second Division; which would once again prove surprisingly difficult.

Pop Robson was replaced by the veteran Manchester United striker Stuart Pearson and John Lyall also splashed out £430,000 on Dundee United defender Ray Stewart; who would turn out to be one of the best acquisitions the Hammers ever made. These purchases, plus the rapidly-improving form of young centre-half Alvin Martin – [born in Liverpool but on West Ham's books since his teen years] – seemed to pay immediate

144

dividends, as the Hammers made a storming start to the 1979-80 season. However, an alarming and largely unexplainable slump in form saw West Ham finish in a hugely disappointing 7th place; even further away from promotion than they'd been the season before.

It beggars belief what went wrong in the League that season. A team which featured two of the most creative and skilful midfielders in the country - England international Trevor Brooking and the ever-improving Alan Devonshire – plus the combative captain Billy Bonds; superb shot-stopper Phil Parkes in goal; tenacious full-backs Stewart and Lampard; commanding centre-half Martin and reliable experienced strikers Pearce and Cross; somehow contrived to drop so many points against inferior opposition.

Nevertheless, every cloud…etc. Despite Lyall's inability to lift the Hammers back in to the First Division, there was much for the Upton Park fans to cheer about that season; namely, a much-desired return to Wembley Stadium, for the showpiece match of the season. It was another marvellous FA Cup run, culminating in a showdown with London rivals Arsenal. Somehow, a totally dominant West Brom failed to defeat the Hammers, at the Hawthorns, in the 3rd round. Stuart Pearson scored West Ham's goal in the 1-1 draw but it was the goalkeeping heroics of Phil Parkes which kept West Ham in the tie.

From *The Hammers'* [1997]:

"Parkes looks back on his performance in the 1-1 draw as the best of his career. He says: 'I made quite a lot of good saves that day – West Brom were all over us – but the one that really stands out in my mind was from a Gary Owen free-kick on the edge of the box. I read what he was going to do – bend it round the wall with his left foot – but as I've started to go, the ball takes a deflection and so I've suddenly got to readjust. The ball's going one way, I'm going another. I don't know how I did it – it was just an instinctive thing – but I managed to get a hand to the ball and tip it over. Gary Owen just came over to me and said; "I don't believe that".'

…In the second half, Parkes continued in the same vein. Thus, though West Brom did finally manage to get the ball past him, they ended up as demoralised as West Ham were jubilant. Indeed, it says much about the nature of Parkes' performance that, at the final whistle, West Brom's players all made a point of seeking him out to congratulate him. So too did West Brom's manager Ron Atkinson…who described it as 'the greatest goalkeeping performance I have ever seen'."

However, the reason Parkes was called into action so often – not only in that game but throughout the season – could be explained simply. As Parkes elaborated, regarding his Upton Park debut:

"My first game for West Ham was against Oldham. We won 3-0 but the strange thing about if for me was that I still had a lot to do.

You had the right-back turning up on the left wing; the left-back running down the right wing – that's not unusual, I know, but the two of them doing it at the same time is!

I said to someone afterwards; 'I've never played in a team with ten attacking players and no defenders before'."

West Ham won the replay 2-1, via goals from midfielders Brooking and Pike and then faced fellow Division Two side Orient; now skippered by ex-

Hammer Tommy Taylor and also featuring Mervyn Day and Billy Jennings. West Ham scraped through 3-2, thanks to two goals from Ray Stewart and an own goal and were equally unconvincing when defeating Swansea 2-0, due to two goals in the last five minutes, from young Paul Allen and David Cross.

It had been an immensely unimpressive cup run by this point but the 1-0 quarter-final victory over First Division Aston Villa alerted observers to the fact that West Ham might well go 'all the way'.

The Hammers completely dominated the game, before a vociferous 36,000 Upton Park crowd but were frustrated by Villa's stubborn defence, until the very last-minute, when a thumping Ray Stewart penalty deservedly took them into the semi-finals.

Ironically, Villa Park was the neutral venue for West Ham against Everton. This entertaining but bad-tempered encounter ended in a 1-1 draw – [Pearson scoring for the Hammers] – and the Elland Road replay was evenly poised at 0-0 when it into extra-time.

This match was an absolute classic; full of all the excitement and end-to-end action, fans – especially the neutrals – long for in cup ties.

A Devonshire wonder goal put West Ham in front but Everton unsportingly equalised and, as the game ticked towards its conclusion, both sets of fans grew increasingly nervy; neither wanting to lose a match of such importance, so late on. With two minutes remaining, it was the Hammers supporters who exploded into euphoria.

Left-back Frank Lampard, nearing the end of his lengthy playing career with West Ham – [an eventual 658 appearances] – turned up uninvited, in the penalty box and scored with an unlikely diving header from a

147

Brooking cross. [*It was as likely a sight as Cheryl Cole singing live…or in tune.*]

An ecstatic Lampard danced a 'middle-aged-white-man-at-a-wedding' jig around the corner flag and West Ham United prepared to be the underdog's yet again against their mighty North London neighbours – and defending FA Cup holders - Arsenal, in the Final.

Alan Devonshire later stated that the semi-final replay with Everton was; "the best game of football I ever played. It was as near to perfection as I ever got".

Again - in the Final - Devonshire would prove to be immensely important to West Ham; although the game itself would be an anti-climax after the heart-stopping excitement of the Everton semi-final.

[Plus, there was something weirdly wrong with West Ham playing in their now all-white away strip for the Final. The absence of claret-and-blue was a visual let-down; almost like we were watching Leeds play football. *Only without the violence and foul tactics of Hitler's protégé Don Revie.*]

Despite his failure to once again escape from the cloying clutches of the 2nd Division, John Lyall got everything right tactically against Arsenal. Known for having the meanest defence in the country; with central defenders David O'Leary and Willie Young practically impenetrable; Lyall elected to drop Pearson back into midfield and leave David Cross as the lone striker.

This was a thankless task for Cross, who admitted afterwards that he'd been unhappy at having to sacrifice his own chance for goal-scoring glory in the name of dogged teamwork, and yet he gamely ran himself ragged against Arsenal's stoic defence. The tactic successfully confused the Gunners. Instead of deploying the ball-player O'Leary into a more advanced position and leaving the less mobile Young to mark Cross, the Gunners stubbornly adhered to a rigid back four and thus allowed West Ham to dominate the midfield with sheer numbers.

The only goal of the game had 'destiny' written all over it. [*Actually, it had UMBRO written on it but that doesn't sound as good.*]

Back in 1975, a newspaper critic had written: "Trevor Brooking simply ignored the mud and gave a display which had to be seen to be believed. He floated like a butterfly and stung like a bee, inspiring West Ham to win a superb match against Queens Park Rangers, much more comprehensively than the 2-1 scoreline suggests".

Prior to the 1980 Cup Final, however, sarcastic Nottingham Forest manager Brian Clough commented: "Trevor Brooking floats like a butterfly...and **stings** like a butterfly! I have never had a high opinion of him as a player. I believe his lack of application – and that of other players like him – have meant relegation for West Ham in the past, and a failure to win promotion this season.

Brooking will only be able to have an influence on this Cup Final if Devonshire, or another of his more willing and enthusiastic team-mates, battles to win the ball at the front or back, so that Brooking can pick it up from midfield".

In reality, Trevor Brooking had resisted the temptation to leave his beloved West Ham and ply his silken skills where they really would have been better appreciated; the First Division. Thus, on his 500th game for the Hammers, it was fitting that Brooking's header brought the coveted FA Cup back to Upton Park after a five year absence, and stuffed Clough's damning words down his arrogant throat.

[Little were we to know that the following 34 years would be a barren trophy-less wasteland for the Hammers; although we would come agonisingly close to major success on several occasions!]

A Devonshire jinking run-and-cross down the left flank was miss-hit by Stuart Pearson but Brooking dived to divert his wayward effort into goal, via his stooping head.

17 year old Paul Allen – at the time, the youngest player ever to appear in an FA Cup Final – may have made it 2-0 but he was cynically brought down from behind by that carthorse Young, when clear through on goal. [This was before such a challenge – the stupidly-named 'professional foul' – resulted in an automatic red-card for the assailant.]

Nevertheless, it was an immensely satisfying victory, against the odds and West Ham badly needed to build upon the confidence gained in winning the FA Cup and finally find a way out of the quagmire-like Second Division, in the 1980-81 campaign.

Lyall decided to sign a young striker, to challenge the veterans Pearson and Cross and thus QPR's 20 year-old prospect Paul Goddard became the Hammers record signing, at £800,000. Goddard would prove to be a shrewd acquisition, although he would finish the season 10 goals 'lighter' than his strike partner David Cross.

West Ham finally achieved the promotion the bookies had predicted for them three years earlier, at a canter; comfortably winning the 2nd Division Championship, with games to spare. The season's highlights included 5-0 victories against Bristol City and Preston and 4-0 wins over Notts County and Chelsea; amongst many other high-scoring triumphs.

Club captain Billy Bonds considered this title-winning side to be the best team he ever played in; despite the fact that he'd previously played alongside legends such as Moore, Hurst and Peters.

Bonzo felt that the overall strength in depth of the 1980-1 team was the strongest, in **every** position, that he'd been a part of; with the likes of Parkes, Stewart, Devonshire, Allen, Martin, Brooking, Goddard and the under-rated Cross; whom Bonds regarded as one of the best strikers he ever played with.

Trevor Brooking agreed with Bonds, stating that not only was the '80-81 side one of the best teams he'd ever played in but it was also 'the most enjoyable season of his career'!

Although they surprisingly went out of the FA Cup at the first hurdle, to lowly Wrexham; West Ham again made it to Wembley that season; this time in the League Cup.

In the second round they disposed of Burnley – [*those imposters*] – 6-0, with goals from Goddard [2], Cross, Stewart, Pike and an own goal. Charlton and Barnsley were both beaten 2-1 – [Cross scoring 3 and Martin 1, of the 4 goals] – before they met arch-rivals Spurs in the quarter-final.

West Ham fans always take great delight in beating Tottenham and the packed Upton Park duly went into raptures when David Cross scored the winning goal. [*Surprisingly, regardless of who they're actually playing, West Ham supporters will always find time to chant anti-Tottenham and Millwall songs. It's a little thing, but it makes them happy!*]

The two-legged semi-final saw the Hammers triumph 4-3 on aggregate, over Coventry, with goals from Bonds, Goddard, Jimmy Neighbour and another own goal;

151

setting up a Wembley Final with the mighty Liverpool, who would go on to win the European Cup for the third time, later that season. [*Just greedy, if you ask me!*]

The Final was a tense affair and ended 0-0 after 90 minutes. It was only in extra-time that the game really exploded into life. Liverpool took the lead and West Ham responded by pouring forward; desperately searching for an equaliser. To the delight of their baying fans, the Hammers won a penalty with just seconds remaining and the ever-reliable Ray Stewart dispatched it with his customary aplomb.

The last kick of the game had salvaged a remarkable draw and the West Ham fans went berserk as the final whistle resonated. Their delight only lasted as long as the replay. Goddard gave West Ham an early lead but this time it was Liverpool who responded by stepping up a gear and they eventually ran out 2-1 victors.

The real drama and controversy in that 1980-81 season though, wasn't in the promotion victory, nor the League Cup run but occurred during the European Cup Winner's Cup campaign.

It commenced with a 3-1 defeat away to Spain's Castilla but it was the performance of their fans, rather than the players, which earned West Ham United all of the headlines the following day.

Members of the I.C.F. fought with Spanish fans and the police, both inside and outside of the ground and the repercussions were huge.

Trevor Brooking had been an outspoken critic of football hooliganism, in the late 1970's / early 80's; believing that it was the reason behind football 'no longer being a family game'.

Brooking had been about to take a corner, at Newcastle's St James's Park Stadium, in 1980, when a petrol bomb had been launched into the West Ham section of the crowd. Brooking thus became a rather 'un-politically correct' advocate of a return to corporal punishment and 'tougher discipline in schools', to eradicate this epidemic.

And yet, it was Billy Bonds who suffered for comments he'd – **allegedly** – made. A newspaper quoted the Hammers skipper as calling West Ham's fans 'scum'; something Bonds vociferously denied. However, mud sticks – [*as does chewing gum, poo, warm toffee apples and Velcro*] – and when Bonds led the players out at Upton Park for the next league game, he was stunned to hear his own fans booing him!

From *'Bonzo'*:

"I was totally unprepared for the reception I got from the terraces, when we ran out for the match. For a few moments it just didn't register that the crowd were booing me. Then they began chanting; 'We're not scum, Bonzo!'

I couldn't believe the reception they were giving me. I went over to one section of the ground and tried to tell them that I'd never said anyone was scum but they clearly didn't want to hear my side of it. Exchanges became increasingly hostile before team-mates pulled me away.

Play started with me seething; badly upset. I'd always had a very good relationship with our crowd. They had known me long enough and it really hurt that they seemed only too ready to believe something in newspapers, which anyone with an ounce of grey matter wouldn't have dreamed of saying.

Throughout the ninety minutes parts of the ground kept up almost non-stop barracking. Over the years I'd had plenty of that from opposition fans but never before from my own!

...By Monday morning I was even more angry. The 'hate mail' began to flood in. Some of it was unbelievably nasty – the worst of it anonymous. I tore them up but, understandably, my wife Lyn was very worried.

...A couple of days later, after further thought, I 'phoned the newspaper that had printed the 'you scum' report. I asked them if they realised what my family had been going through and what it could have done to my career...I asked them to print an apology. They finally did so, but just a couple of lines tucked away somewhere, with nothing like the prominence given to the cause of all my problems."

As punishment for the behaviour of the hooligans, UEFA forced West Ham to play the return leg against Castilla 'behind closed doors'. [*They'd rather have played 'The Most Beautiful Girl in the World' but Charlie Rich still owned the copyright on that one.*]

Thus, only the back-room staff and match officials witnessed a remarkable game of football, played to a deafening silence; West Ham winning 5-1, thanks to a Cross hat-trick and two more goals from Goddard and Pike.

In a reversal of their previous European exploits, West Ham scored an emphatic victory in the first leg against the Romanians Poli Timisoara and sailed through 4-1 on aggregate, with goals from Bonds, Goddard, Stewart and Cross.

However, the European expedition rudely ended in the next round, when they were soundly beaten by a very good Georgian side, Dynamo Tbilisi, 4-2 over the two legs.

Regarding the afore-mentioned football violence, Cass Pennant sheds some light on this particular period of the ICF's history.

From *'Congratulations:…'*:

"Attaching yourself to West Ham's East End following was a buzz like nothing else in those days, when football violence was sweeping the terraces. It was as dangerous as it was exciting. At one time our following had a bigger reputation than our team. The fighting prowess of the East End mob was growing on a nationwide scale.

Our reputation was built on the respect given us for coming out on top against the odds – usually away from home, where the opposition would have the numbers. Even if we were to come unstuck in a row, we had built a reputation that West Ham lads stood and stuck together, no matter what. It meant that to get a result against our little firm, you would seriously have to trade blows…

Throughout the Seventies we continued taking it to anybody; whoever wanted to know, just to show beyond doubt that we were the firm to reckon with in Britain. As the Seventies gave way to the Eighties, the football authorities and the police became determined to get to grips with the terrace warfare that had been going on for over a decade. To beat their desperate clampdown on hooliganism, we would have to step activities up to another level…

We had become too predictable. You'd come out of the opposition's station and head for the same boozer every time. Drunkenly, you'd attempt to take their end, at roughly the same time you'd entered it the season before. And after the match you'd meet them in the same street you'd had it with 'em last time. To be honest, we were making the Old Bill look wise!

We had to change from a mindless thug army to a thinking army; a new era was dawning. We abandoned the Dr Marten boots and smartened ourselves up; started wearing casual fashions. The Farah strides, Pringles or Gabichis we wore out on a Friday night, we now sported to matches on a Saturday. Anything to get as far away as possible from the authorities stereotyped image of what they thought they had to look out for...

Our exploits had become legendary; the I.C.F. was fashionable on the street in a big way. In its early issues 'The Face' magazine printed huge articles on 'the football casual' – and they weren't written as a put-down in any way. The emergence of the football casual was growing in strength around the nation's grounds and the I.C.F. gained in reputation from being one of the first 'casual firms'.

The Seventies 'scarf, boot-and-punch' aggro had been replaced by a quick in-and-out with a craft knife; all the time being careful not to get blood on your designer labels..."

Pennant and Bill Stokes recall that infamous petrol bomb incident:

"March 15th, 1980; Newcastle away. That was the day the fuse was lit – literally – between West Ham and the Geordies. The day a Geordie bastard threw a petrol bomb...Until this match it had never gone off between us and the Geordies on a scale worthy of a vendetta. In all fairness, they were one firm we'd always given some amount of respect to.

While they left themselves wide open to having the piss taken out of them with their donkey jacket clothing style, you couldn't deny the fact that they were a game

156

lot; as up for it as anyone. If fighting had been as high on their agenda as getting another tattoo and drinking they might have had a shout as to who the number one firm in the country was.

For teams with half-decent mobs it was a sad joke to be stuck in Division Two. The only two firms regularly doing the business there were Chelsea and Newcastle and we had terrorised Chelsea all season. We had quite a travelling support now, so it was time to have a proper go at the Geordies at theirs…

The skinhead had a Bowie-sized sheath knife. All I had was a plastic carrier bag in my hand, which I had been holding onto since I got off the train. I swung the carrier bag and the big Geordie buckled as it hit him – I think more out of fright than anything else, as they don't see too many black men up in those parts. I hit him again and he crashed on to the floor near the doorway, as the big Liebfraumilch bottle inside the carrier bag shattered against his head…

We started chanting **'I.C.F, I.C.F'** repeatedly. It was like we had stirred something in the crowd and from then it was all happening. Judging from the noise coming from the Geordies all around the ground, you would have thought we were playing a local derby. You could feel the passion and hate and it made the hairs on the back of your neck stand up. The whole ground shook with hostility…

We saw what looked like a box of matches that had been set alight, only bigger, spinning over us. At first I just thought it was lighted rags but, as it smashed just in front of me, flames flared up instantly from blacked, broken glass….It was a petrol bomb! At that point everyone had the same thought; 'kill the Geordie bastards.' And we **meant** it!

157

Once they had thrown the bomb that was it. We began punching and kicking Geordies; battering people…chasing them out into the streets, up hills and into the city centre."

Whilst the football 'Casuals' grew in popularity at Upton Park, another part of the East End 'culture' was dying.

*

Both sides of my family had worked in the Docks for generations and the Docks had been a major provider of employment for a large proportion of the East End of London for well over a century. However, the advent of containerisation and the use of larger ships to transport the various previously self-contained goods within the bulky new containers, meant London's aging Docks struggled to cope.

By 1978 the Port of London Authority was on the brink of financial collapse; the Docks having failed to be a profitable enterprise since the late Sixties. The Government looked at financial packages to enable the Docks to continue but it soon proved unfeasible and a decision was taken to commence closing London's Docks in 1980; resulting in thousands of men being made redundant.

[*My dad took a year off, courtesy of his generous redundancy pay and single-handedly managed to keep Scotland's whiskey distilleries in profit.*]

In 1981, the last ship was unloaded in East London and only Tilbury – outside of London – was still able to handle the 50,000 plus tonnes container ships.

The sad demise of the Docks meant that the area quickly became desolate; a huge grey expanse of concrete; abandoned warehouses and rusting cranes. Poor transport links to other parts of London and

158

extremely poor housing conditions were highlighted by the sudden absence of the previously over-powering presence of the multitude of ships along the Docks.

This ghostly wasteland led to the formation of the London Docklands Development Corporation and the consequent Canary Wharf Development; a mixture of huge new commercial buildings and an ultra-modern housing improvement scheme; which would come to dominate East London's skyline.

As part of this long-term project the marshland of Beckton, in Newham, was drained and an industrial park built; plus low-rent and low-cost housing for local people developed. Likewise, aging tower blocks were demolished in Silvertown and an 'urban village' built instead.

London City Airport was opened in 1987 and improved road links and Underground rail extensions ensured that this previously isolated part of East London was now accessible from other main areas. The whole face of the East End was changing and the young-and-wealthy now began to migrate from the swank of West and Central London and re-locate in the fashionable modernity of Canary Wharf and the surrounding areas. However, by the end of the decade, these stretches of expensive luxurious apartments overlooking the Thames, would only highlight the aging terraced housing and continuing deprivation in other parts of the East End.

*

In 1981-2 the Boleyn Ground's West Stand re-opened as an all-seated area and '3 points for a win' was introduced that season, in a bid to stimulate more attacking football and recapture the supporters; conspicuous by their increasing absence.

Their initial season back in the First Division was a successful one; the Hammers starting strongly and finishing in a respectable 9th position.

Lyall had added Scottish defensive-midfielder Neil Orr to the squad and purchased Belgian international striker Francois Van Der Elst – [back in the days when it was still reasonably rare to see top foreign players in Britain] - to bolster West Ham's roster of attacking players, but David Cross and Paul Goddard still ran out the Hammers top goal-scorers that season.

[Cross endearing himself even further to the fans when he scored all four goals in West Ham's stunning 4-0 victory away to Spurs!]

Unfortunately, at the end of the season, Cross announced that he wanted to leave and Lyall reluctantly sold our most reliable goal-getter to Manchester City.

Now, all attention turned to the World Cup and the remarkable finale to the Ron Greenwood story.

*

'Greenwood for England'…who'd've thought it?

In 1977, professional Yorkshireman Don Revie walked out on England, like the complete jerk we always knew he was. [*Though he speaks highly of me, apparently!*]

Revie's tenure had not been as successful as his ego had anticipated and England were left in limbo; looking highly unlikely to qualify for the 1978 World Cup Finals. The Football Association decided that a more mature approach was needed, to steady the rocking ship and – to many people's surprise – approached ex-West Ham United manager Ron Greenwood and asked him to take temporary control.

The 55 year old immediately recruited his former protégé Geoff Hurst, to assist him in coaching the players; recognising that his recent absence from the

160

game may mean that he struggled to 'talk the same language' as his young charges and thus needed an intermediary closer to their age.

Greenwood's first game in charge was a 0-0 draw against the less-than-fearsome Switzerland; followed by a lacklustre 2-0 victory against the even weaker Luxembourg, in a World Cup qualifier.

England now needed to defeat the much more powerful Italy in order to stand even a chance of qualifying and Trevor Brooking and Kevin Keegan stepped up and scored the goals which temporarily put England top of the qualifying group. Unfortunately, the beaten Italy had a 'game in hand' and their subsequent victory against Luxembourg saw the Italians qualify, in place of England. [*Who had, nevertheless, beaten Italy in World War 2 and so were – obviously – a far superior nation. Not that I'm a bad loser!*]

However, both the FA **and the players** liked the 'family atmosphere' Greenwood had engendered in training camps and the former Hammers supremo was offered the role on a permanent basis. [Reinforcing Bobby Moore's comment that the astute tactician Greenwood would thrive, if he were to have a group of international class players at his disposal.]

A fantastic run of 10 wins, 2 draws and just 1 defeat, in his next 13 matches, saw England enter the 1980 European Championship as one of the favourites. The 1-1 opening draw with Belgium was marred by extreme violence from England's travelling hooligans and, in the next game, we were disappointingly beaten by the host nation Italy 1-0. Although we then defeated Spain 2-1, it didn't matter; we had again come second-best to Hitler's favourite bitch Italy.

Attention immediately turned to qualification for the 1982 World Cup in Spain. England commenced their quest with a 4-0 victory against Norway at Wembley but this was followed by a 2-1 defeat to Romania and an unimpressive 2-1 win over Switzerland.

3 consecutive 'friendly' defeats were followed by a 0-0 World Cup qualifier draw at home to Romania and then a shocking 2-1 defeat to minnows Switzerland. The 'honeymoon' was over for Greenwood and the frustrated press and supporters began to turn against him.

Two goals from Brooking and another from Keegan gave England a much-needed 3-1 victory over Hungary but Greenwood had become demoralised. On the plane back home Ron told Geoff Hurst that he was retiring from football and asked Hurst to relay this news to the players.

Geoff reluctantly moved down the plane's aisle; informing England's finest of the manager's decision. However – evidencing the affection the players felt for Ron – Keegan and Brooking left their seats and huddled with the manager. By the time the plane had landed, Greenwood had been persuaded to change his mind.

Despite the obvious camaraderie in the England camp, they somehow contrived to then lose 2-1 away to Norway! This meant that they had to secure at least a draw against Hungary to qualify for the World Cup. England thankfully won 1-0 and headed, gratefully, to Spain.

[As do all Englishmen; just prior to being sick in the pool, following 12 hours of binge-drinking in their package-tour hotel and drunkenly sleeping with a fat bird from Doncaster named Brenda, who's proud that she's never shaved her legs...Or so I'm told...]

162

The 1982 World Cup was Ron Greenwood's glorious farewell to the game he loved. The format of the competition had been changed, in order to allow more nations to compete. There were now **two** group stages before the knockout rounds were reached. Impressive victories over France, Czechoslovakia and Kuwait, in the first group stage, were followed by solid 0-0 draws against Germany and Spain in the second group phase. England were unbeaten but, sadly, this wasn't enough for them to progress to the semi-finals. Regardless, the fans and the media were happy enough with the stirring performances they'd witnessed and England's pride on the world footballing stage had been restored, thanks to Greenwood.

Trevor Brooking had been one of England's most important players in the lead-up to the Finals and had developed a wonderful understanding with England's new talisman Keegan but, unfortunately, Trevor carried a groin injury into the tournament itself, which inhibited his performances and which necessitated an operation immediately afterwards.

Two other West Ham men were even unluckier. Centre-half Alvin Martin had made his England debut in 1981 but injury prevented him from going to the World Cup, when he may well have made the centre-back position his own.

Billy Bonds, meanwhile, could only rue his bad luck. Three times Ron Greenwood had called his former Hammers skipper into the squad and, on two occasions, after being told by Ron that he'd "definitely be playing", Bonds had to withdraw due to injury. On the third occasion; when widely tipped by the media to play against Italy – Bonds was a frustrated unused substitute.

As it is, Billy Bonds is generally regarded as the best player never to have played for his country.

*

Bombs, pit closures, race riots...welcome to England under that sweet little Thatcher lady!
[She was only a greengrocer's daughter...In the same way that Myra Hindley was 'only' a typist!]

Trevor Brooking's groin injury was severe enough to keep him side-lined for the entire 1982-3 season and yet somehow West Ham managed to finish in a lofty 8th place; despite the absence of their star player and creative genius.

Paul Allen was showing increasing maturity in midfield; whilst Alan Devonshire – now established on the England scene himself – continued to run defenders ragged with his mazy cross-field dribbles.

As Alvin Martin commanded the central defence, Billy Bonds moved back, into a sweeper role; mopping up any danger the imposing Martin may have missed.

Tommy Taylor had always been my favourite central defender but I have to admit, he had never instilled the confidence that Alvin managed; for Martin rarely gave the impression that he could be beaten. Yet, his early performances gave little indication of the 'rock' he would become.

From *'The Hammers'*:

"Instead of keeping it simple, I started to attempt more difficult things at the wrong times. At that time in my career I have to admit that I was maybe a bit arrogant and cocky and some of the senior players weren't slow to pass by an opportunity to put me in my place.

I would beat two or three people and then lose the ball in a really bad position. I was getting more and more frustrated with myself and the way I was playing. It

164

became a mental crisis for me and I was very fortunate I came through it. There were times when, at just 18 years old, I did go into the office to see Mr Greenwood and John Lyall and asked them if I could go back home to Liverpool but Mr Greenwood always replied with an emphatic 'no'."

Superb in the air, Martin was rarely beaten to a header and he developed into an immensely reliable defender; eschewing the ball tricks he'd attempted as a teenager and clearing his lines impassively.

Ray Stewart, meanwhile, had established himself in the Scotland side – *as had the grocer's cat* – and would finish the season third highest goal-scorer, behind Paul Goddard and Francois Van Der Elst – all three of them scoring in the Hammers biggest win that season; 5-0 against Birmingham.

17 year old striker Tony Cottee made his debut mid-way through that season and scored in the side's 3-0 victory against Spurs; impressing enough that Lyall sold Van Der Elst at the end of the season and gave home-grown Cottee his chance for an extended run in the team.

The fans had every reason to look towards the 1983-4 campaign with hope; especially with the return of Brooking to the side. However, injuries conspired to dent West Ham's hopes of European football and provoke Trevor Brooking's decision to retire.

Separately; Brooking made 635 appearances for the Hammers and Alan Devonshire 446. Together, they played a wonderful midfield duet for 8 seasons. Both men were laid-back personalities, who never reacted to the physical abuse they invariably received from less-skilled opponents. [Brooking admitted that the only time he ever swore was when he was annoyed at himself for not delivering the 'killer pass'.]

With 12 O-levels, 2 A-levels and a Diploma in 'Commerce, Economics, Statistics and Accounts', the well-spoken Trevor was never the most stereotypical of footballers and was jokingly referred to as 'Hadleigh' by his team-mates; after the 'proper English Gentleman', played by Gerald Harper, in the TV series of the 1970's.

A supreme passer of the ball, Brooking made creating goal chances look remarkably easy but he too credits Ron Greenwood for refining his skills and helping him to reach another level with his game.

From his autobiography, simply entitled *'Trevor Brooking'* [1981]*:*

"Ron Greenwood had a favourite expression; 'always make sure you've got pictures in your mind'. He meant that you should have an impression of where the other players are standing before the ball reaches you, so that you can react accordingly. If a defender is tight on you and someone nearby is free, then a first-time pass is the obvious choice.

Usually, when the ball is coming in my direction, I will glance behind me to see who is there. I can do this because I am fairly confident that I can still control the ball, although I have taken my eye off it. Some players cannot do this. They feel they need to give all their attention to the ball.

My control is so good because I spent so much time trapping balls bouncing off walls, drainpipes and ledges, when I was a boy. It is like learning to read or type. It is a skill that never leaves you."

The former fork-lift truck driver Devonshire would seem to have been an odd 'soul-mate' then for the well-educated, precise-speaking Brooking but the two men gelled like a perfect showbiz double-act and it was Devonshire's bad injury midway through the season which many people attributed as the main reason behind Brooking's shock retirement announcement. When it was stated that Alan would be out for approximately 18 months, the 35 year old Brooking quietly declared his intention to quit.

Devonshire wasn't the only long-term absentee that season; Paul Goddard missed most of the campaign through injury; Allen and Bonds both missed several months themselves and Alvin Martin suffered a car crash which forced him out of action, just after he'd re-established himself in the England side.

Despite West Ham United's worst-ever injury crisis, that season, the fact that they still managed to finish a respectable 9th place, spoke volumes for the fact that John Lyall was finally getting the formula for success consistently right; for, without the myriad injuries to key players, West Ham would definitely have qualified for Europe that season.

Young striker Tony Cottee – *usually politely referred to as 'diminutive'; in the same way that Snow White had seven diminutive friends* - continued to show his promise and was the Hammers top scorer; whilst the highlight of the season was the record-breaking 10-0 victory against 3rd Division Bury, in the Milk Cup. [Formerly the League Cup. It was the beginning of sponsorship exploding in football and West Ham sported AVCO TRUST across their shirts that year. The visual magic of the claret-and-blue was being spoiled by filthy lucre.]

A paltry crowd of just 10,000 people witnessed Cottee smash four goals, Brooking and Devonshire score two each and Martin and Stewart grab the others, in a veritable goal-fest.

After the final game of the season the supporters poured onto the pitch and that masterful, elegant midfield maestro Trevor Brooking was carried around Upton Park on the shoulders of his adoring fans.

*

37 year old Billy Bonds and 35 year old Frank Lampard decided to follow Brooking's lead and also announced their retirements; although – for Bonzo – saying 'farewell' would prove an extraordinarily difficult task.

John Lyall, too, almost left Upton Park at this point. His work – despite financial constraints and myriad injuries – had been much appreciated by Queens Park Rangers; who tried to entice him to Loftus Road, with promises of more money – both for himself, and to spend on players – but West Ham chairman Len Cearns persuaded Lyall to stay; a decision which all parties may have regretted if West Ham's 1984-5 season had gone any worse!

With Brooking, Bonds and Lampard retired and Alan Devonshire a long-term injury absentee, West Ham didn't need anything else to go wrong. Consequently, Phil Parkes suffered a knee injury, which required an operation and which would keep him out for the bulk of the season.

Tony Gale was purchased from Fulham, to replace Bonds in defence, alongside Alvin Martin, and he settled in well; plus, the diminutive [lol] Tony Cottee continued to bag goals for fun, and Paul Goddard returned from injury. However, despite the strikers enjoying a good season, a midfield minus Brooking **and** Devonshire looked worryingly lightweight; whilst the

168

defence was leaking like elderly women in a nursing home.

West Ham – who had looked so strong since their return to the First Division - were shockingly sucked into a relegation battle and a desperate Lyall convinced his former captain Bonds to return to battle. Thus, the 38 year old rolled up his sleeves – *metaphorically; long sleeves had departed top-level football ages ago; around the same time as success had departed at Spurs!* – and Bonzo's endless drive and boyish enthusiasm in the tackle helped West Ham ensure their safety; finishing 16th. Indeed, in the 5-1 victory over Stoke, which ensured West Ham's survival, Bonds scored twice and was voted 'man of the match'!

Nevertheless, John Lyall needed to provide some talented cover in the yawning gaps created by retirements and injuries, if West Ham were to avoid their old routine of regular relegation battles. It didn't augur well, then, when Lyall decided to sell popular midfielder Paul Allen to Spurs, for just £400,000. This was hardly the actions of an ambitious club, who wanted to make their fans happy. But then…the Conservative Government could hardly have been accused of 'wanting to make the British people happy', either, around this period.

*

In April 1982 Argentina invaded the Falkland Islands. Even though 90% of the British public responded; 'The who?' Margaret Thatcher convinced everybody that Britain owned the islands – *presumably in the same way we'd once 'owned' India and half of Africa, etc* – and that we needed to 'take them back'. Troops were sent halfway across the world and – 74 days later – the Argentinians surrendered and Alf Ramsey smiled.

This 'Iron Lady' persona Thatcher assumed won her much admiration at home and abroad and conveniently distracted from the fact that she'd just raised VAT and taxes, right in the middle of a recession.

By 1984, though, most people were beginning to doubt that the Conservatives were very nice people. Principal amongst these doubters were the miners and the IRA; both of whom attempted to bring down the Tory Government in their own unique ways.

The Provisional IRA bombed the hotel which the Tories were using for their annual conference but Thatcher and her Cabinet emerged unscathed. [*Although her wardrobe and nice antique dining set were dented; thus reducing their value on eBay.*]

Also, in '84, the Conservatives announced that they wanted to close 20 pits; meaning the loss of around 20,000 mining-related jobs. The mines had been heavily subsidised for some time and were no longer profitable. However, the Unions obviously resisted this decision, as their primary concern was the welfare of the workers and thus Arthur Scargill led the National Union of Mine-workers out on strike.

I remembered how it was a decade earlier, when the miners had striked and our house was lit by candles. Unfortunately for Scargill, Margaret Thatcher remembered those days too and so had been secretly stock-piling coal for just such an eventuality. [*Although her neighbours complained, as it was blocking the sunlight!*]

Violent clashes between the Yorkshire miners and the police became a daily scenario on our TV news-screens, as neither the Government nor the unions would give ground.

In March 1985, the miners finally accepted defeat and forlornly returned to work. The one-year strike had been wholly unsuccessful and had resulted in the pointless deaths of six picketing miners but Thatcher had achieved her stated intention when she came to power; to break the influence of the Trade Unions.

Although this may have been interpreted as a success for middle-class 'polite' society, it was a worrying moment for the working classes; who often depended upon the unions to secure reasonable pay and working conditions for them, and the majority of the East End had supported the striking miners cause.

Meanwhile, there were other, more worrying, things for the Conservatives – and Britain – to be concerned about. Racial tensions had been steadily rising since the late 1970's and the rise of the racist National Front; followed by the British Movement, was a vivid sign of white unease.

At Upton Park there had been a noticeable increase in the presence of skinhead National Front members and a black friend of mine told me that he'd switched his allegiance, from West Ham to Arsenal, because he was sick of hearing the word 'n****r', hurled around the Boleyn Ground.

The black Cass Pennant, himself, was concerned at this rise of racism in the East End and decided to test the waters. He entered the section of the ground where the NF skins were most conspicuous and blatantly walked amongst them and then stood at the front of that section of supporters; daring them to react. Not even the NF skinheads wanted to try their luck though with one of the I.C.F.'s most prominent figures and Cass remained untouched by the suddenly very quiet racists; who

171

remembered that they'd left the gas on at home and had to leave.

In Brixton, South London, in 1981 this racial tension detonated into actual violence and the Brixton Riot – which exploded on the streets for days – highlighted the barely-concealed hatred which young black men felt towards the perceived racist white police and authorities.

280 police officers were injured, along with 45 members of the public. 82 rioters were arrested; 150 buildings damaged and over 100 cars – mainly police vehicles – were burned.

The TV coverage of the riots inspired similar violent scenes in Liverpool, Birmingham, Manchester and Nottingham. Racial tension was erupting around Britain and Lord Scarman's report on the disturbances found that the disproportionate use of 'stop-and-search' on young black men had destroyed the already fragile relationship between the black communities and the white establishment.

Of course, Margaret Thatcher dismissed these findings; claiming that the rioters were 'simply criminals'. This head-in-the-sand attitude towards the rampant increase in racial tension led to the 1985 Brixton riots and the far worse Broadwater Farm, Tottenham, North London riot; which resulted in bloody violence and running battles between petrol-bomb throwing youths and the police.

This was bad enough but then gunfire was heard and five people were hit – two police officers and three members of the watching media – and fire-fighters were assaulted when attempting to extinguish the various shop and car fires.

Sickeningly, PC Keith Blakelock was surrounded by a group of men with machetes; who savagely chopped him to death; unsuccessfully attempting to decapitate him in the process. Thatcher's Britain was falling apart in an orgy of uncontrollable brutality and it was perhaps significant that the first airing of *'EastEnders'*, in February 1985 – a soap-opera set in the fictitious East London Borough of Walford – featured a death, and set the tone for what many consider to be one of the most depressing TV programmes ever made, but which the producers argued 'reflected real life in the East End of London'.

*

Apart from the insidious racism, football was also suffering from this 'violence epidemic'.

In 1982 an Arsenal fan had been killed in a clash with the I.C.F. at Finsbury Park tube station. The press had a 'field day' with this and regurgitated old stories of the *'Congratulations: You have just met the I.C.F.'* calling-cards being deposited on victims battered and unconscious bodies.

The police Criminal Intelligence Unit stepped up its infiltration of known hooligan firms, via undercover officers entering the grounds and mingling with the fans; seeking to identify the ringleaders of the various gangs.

Documentary film-maker Ian Stuttard decided to get inside several of these firms himself and try to discover what it was that gave them so much pleasure from violence. His resultant *'Hooligans'* TV programme gave a shocking insight.

Stuttard recalls:

"I arranged to meet Cass Pennant and after a long discussion, during which I made clear my intention to approach the subject without prejudice, he agreed to help me. He stressed that he could introduce me and guide me but that the measure of my success would depend upon the relationships I made. My access would be based on trust and I would be excluded from certain activities. So began a period of six months in the company of the I.C.F.

In getting to know these people I was to discover that much of their world was very different from its depiction in the press. Among the unemployed thugs were office managers, builders, soldiers, publicans, a solicitor's clerk and an assistant bank manager.

In the early weeks I also sought links with Millwall hooligans, who enjoyed equally fearsome reputations. Millwall thugs were the implacable enemies of the I.C.F. The two groups were dissimilar though; the West Ham people being thinkers and planners, while Millwall were less subtle. They appeared to have fewer strategists and tacticians…

All-out thuggery was not the I.C.F.'s way. For an away game they laid plans, which would vary according to circumstances. The challenge for them was to evade arrest by the police and to find the best way to combat the opposition. Should they surprise them by ambush or formally arrange to meet and fight? Should they employ deception? Should they divide their forces and strike in several places at once? There had to be structure, which informed the way the I.C.F. operated and there had to be leaders to whom people could turn for guidance during these encounters.

…As the I.C.F. regrouped at the back of the terrace, behind the goal at the back of the packed Southampton end, Cass said to me; 'Are you ready?'

174

I said 'yes', thinking that they were going to move off again, to another part of the ground. I was wrong. Mayhem broke out! Using shock and surprise, Cass, big Natley and the others, though vastly outnumbered, tore into the Southampton people surrounding us. The element of surprise was such that a number of the Southampton supporters just froze.

The ferocity of the attack had left several Southampton supporters injured and we were surrounded by enraged supporters. I had no time to use my camera and I was concerned that the second the opposition realised that there were just twelve of us we'd be slaughtered...

I wanted to show that this activity was **not** mindless; that there was a structure to it and that there was a reason why some young men wanted to pit themselves against each other. There are so many different aspects to it; the expressions of rivalry; the notion that their simple differences – such as being from a different place, having different accents or simply representing different teams – were enough to inspire young Englishmen to fight. They desired to be the best and just as their football teams aspired to be champions, so they aspired to be the 'top boys'. The tradition of having men who will fight – especially against men who represent other areas - was established in Victorian times, before football gave it such an appropriate setting."

There was even humour to be found amongst the violence. In February 1984 West Ham were drawn away to Birmingham in the FA Cup and played dismally that day. At 3-0 down the travelling I.C.F. decided to do something about it and attempted to invade the pitch, in order to get the match abandoned;

succeeding only in causing several lengthy delays before the match – and defeat – resumed.

At that time ' *'The Britannia*' pub, in Plaistow, was the I.C.F.'s favourite meeting-place and just happened to be owned by Hammers left-back Frank Lampard. The day after the Birmingham fiasco, the *Britannia's* pub side were losing 2-0 to another local pub team. None other than Lampard himself sauntered over to the touchline and asked a watching fan what the score was. When told they were behind 2-0, Frank replied dead-pan; "Right; if they make it 3-0, we run on to the pitch and get it abandoned!"

However, football violence was about to reach another horrific level; one which would ultimately bring its downfall.

In the 1985 European Cup Final, at Heysel Stadium, Belgium, thirty-nine Italian fans were killed when Liverpool hooligans charged the Juventus end of the stadium and caused widespread panic. In their attempt to escape the marauding Liverpool supporters, the Juventus fans pushed frantically for the exits and, in their blind panic, a huge stadium wall gave way under the pressure of the fleeing fans; collapsing upon them and killing the aforementioned.

The football world was stunned and English teams were subsequently banned from competing in Europe for five years.

West Ham's I.C.F. then made the situation worse – in conjunction with Manchester United's 'Red Army' hooligans – and caused the ban to be extended by another year.

Both teams were playing in pre-season 'friendlies' in Holland and, on the cross-Channel ferry returning to England, Manchester's hordes realised that there were a handful of West Ham on board. Cue *'Assault On Precinct 13'*, as approximately 150 Man Utd fans tried to invade an upstairs bar being 'defended' by just 14 West Ham fans.

This bloody pitched battle effectively wrecked the ferry; every object that wasn't nailed down being used as a weapon.

When the beleaguered ferry finally docked, fourteen fans were arrested and three West Ham supporters received six-year sentences for their part in the riot. There had been four stabbings and many injuries and it was a minor miracle that no-one was killed that day.

Margaret Thatcher wrung her hands – *I'd like to have wrung her neck!* - and pledged an end to this 'mindless violence' and she pretty much succeeded.

ID cards were introduced, in order to make the hooligans instantly identifiable and thus easy to ban from stadiums but this was unpopular with both supporters and the clubs and didn't last. [Although Luton Town took the drastic step of banning all away supporters from their ground. *Thus leaving three men, a dog and twenty-seven pigeons to root for the home side.*]

In 1987, Operation Own Goal saw the police capitalise on the undercover infiltration, which had been taking place for years, and the leaders of Chelsea's Head-hunters and West Ham's I.C.F. were arrested in dawn raids on their homes. Heavy sentences were handed down, as a deterrent to others and the 'heyday' of football hooliganism was over.

Cass Pennant would use his time inside to write his autobiography, which was finally published in 2002 and subsequently turned into a movie, *'Cass'*, in 2008.

Fellow I.C.F. 'legend' Carlton Leach also wrote a book, which was turned into a hit movie *'Rise of the Footsoldier'*; chronicling his journey from football hooligan to doorman to friend of major drug dealers 'The Essex Boys'.

Leach remembers: "I revelled in the fear we brought to towns and cities all over the country, the way they shut the pubs and shops when they knew the ICF was in town; the way a path would clear through 10,000 fans as the 300-strong West Ham mob swaggered through the streets, standing our ground in the face of bombardments from snooker balls, bricks and chair legs; defying the police as they charged you with horses and batons, dragging you off and giving you a good hiding. I loved it! You've got to be able to take a good hiding, as well as dish it out. I've had my nose broken and been kicked in the face by Arsenal and Chelsea fans, stabbed in the back by Millwall fans, but all I wanted to do was get back in there next week and get my revenge. It was ten years of sheer madness.

But the spies from the football intelligence units were everywhere and things had to change. Self-preservation played a big part in me quitting the terraces. It was only a matter of time before I got nicked for something serious. I got a tip-off from a copper I knew. Scotland Yard was launching a f***ing great anti-hooligan operation. He said: 'Do yourself a favour Carlton; knock it on the head or you're going to get nicked for something heavy'. He was talking about charges for conspiracy to incite violence, with a probable five-year stretch. The geezer did me a big favour. I thought: 'What the f**k am I doing?' I knew it was time to back off...

My passion for West Ham as a football team never totally waned. My whole mood for a week could be determined by the West Ham result. I still go to the odd West Ham game, but that urge to run amok and scare the s**t out of people has long gone. I've got different priorities now".

Other I.C.F. based movies would follow, such as *'Green Street'* and *'Stand Your Ground'*, as the notorious I.C.F.'s fame continued to expand, even as the original 'top boys' faded into middle-age.

*

In the late '70's and throughout the 1980's there were **other** East London men fighting too; some legally, others…not so.

The East End had a proud tradition of boxing and for decades the Noble Art had provided a financial escape from the grim poverty, for many young working-class males; men whose names would become heroic upon the lips of numerous East End kids: Sammy McCarthy, Jack 'Kid' Berg, Terry Spinks, Billy Walker and, towering above them all, the legendary former World Welterweight Champion, Ted 'Kid' Lewis. [To this list of names would soon be added that of Britain's first World Heavyweight Champion in over a century; West Ham-born Lennox Lewis.]

Bethnal Green's atmospheric York Hall played host to countless classic encounters; whilst Canning Town's 'Royal Oak' gym was a magnet to young boxers seeking to fulfil their raw potential, and based there was West Ham-born Terry Lawless; **the** premier boxing trainer of that period; tutoring a selection of men to British, European and World titles; including the diminutive Maltese flyweight Charlie Magri, whose family had settled in Stepney.

Canning Town-born middleweight Mark Kaylor, meanwhile, took to entering the ring in claret-and-blue shorts – *lest we forget that this book is, in fact, mainly supposed to be about West Ham United!*

[Largely pointless reminiscence...When I was 15, my dad and uncle took me to an amateur boxing evening. It was a dinner-jacket and bow-tie affair and so I was stuffed into a rented suit, in order to make me look 18, as that was the criteria for the evening.

*For **me** to look 18, that is; not my dad and uncle and all of their pals. No amount of liposuction and Botox could have achieved that. 18 stone was the closest they could have managed!*

Anyway...as we left the venue we were 'treated' to the sight of former World welterweight champion John H. Stracey urinating drunkenly in the street. I was transfixed; not by the sight of his willy [!] but by the fact that a famous sportsman was so publicly rat-assed.

*As we climbed into my uncles less-than-impressive car – [I never understood how he could be a car-dealer and yet always drive around in bland cars himself] – Stracey shouted: "Oi. With all your f*****g money, you should be driving a Roller!"*

*This obviously touched a raw nerve, because my uncle replied; "And no wonder you're not welterweight champion anymore, you piss-head"; at which point we drove away **very** quickly.*

The only reason I mentioned all of this was the fact that Stracey came from Bethnal Green and, thus, drunkenly qualifies for this book by birth-right!]

Another man who would emerge as one of the country's top trainers, via a very circuitous route, was Canning Town's Jimmy Tibbs but his story was closer to that of East End gangland than of Marquis of Queensbury.

Post-Kray Twins, various other 'hard men' had attempted to control parts of the East End; notably, the Dixon brothers, George and Alan. [George Dixon had actually survived an attempt upon his life by Ronnie Kray.]

However, the police attention upon the vendetta between the Stepney-based Nicholls family and the Canning Town Tibbses, was not because they were all feared gangsters, vying for power and supremacy, but because of the sheer bloody savagery of their 'war'.

Albert Nicholls, a man in his twenties, had badly beaten Georgie Tibbs, an elderly man, in his sixties, in a pub fight. Consequently, Albert was 'visited' by Georgie's son George and brothers Johnny and Jimmy Tibbs; resulting in Nicholls suffering severe shotgun wounds.

At their trial, though, the Tibbs' were sensationally acquitted; with the Judge coming out with the classic understatement: "Living in the part of London where you live, there is a great deal too much violence."

Two years later, in 1970, an attempt was made on Robert Tibbs's life by an alleged friend of the Nicholls and thus began an incredible series of reprisals and counter-reprisals, involving guns, knives and axes, as the two families and their allies sought ever-more brutal methods of revenge.

Eventually, Jimmy Tibbs was arrested and accused of attempted murder and was fortunate to escape death himself, when a car-bomb intended for his demise, exploded when he was with his young son.

Tibbs received a sentence of 10 years, in 1972 and six other members of his family and friends were also sentenced to various terms, as the vendetta finally reached its conclusion via the Law courts.

When Jimmy Tibbs emerged from prison he resolved to alter the course of his violent life and the Born-again Christian - and former promising young boxer - took up a position with Terry Lawless, as an assistant trainer. By the late 1980's Tibbs had become a highly-respected and motivational trainer in his own right and would go on to work with some of Britain's top fighters; notably the 'Dark Destroyer, Ilford's knockout artist Nigel Benn.

East London also produced two of the most infamous bare-knuckle / unlicensed fighters of this period; the massive physical presence that was debt-collector and nightclub doorman par excellence Lenny 'the Guv'nor' McLean, from Hoxton and his nemesis Roy 'Pretty Boy' Shaw; the former armed robber turned Essex and East London 'hard man' supreme and bare-knuckle legend.

Probably the strongest East London-based organised crime 'firm' of that violent period were the 'Canning Town Cartel'; consisting of a loose alliance of several different crime families and various independent gangland 'enforcers'. The cartel specialised in drugs, kidnapping, extreme violence and murder.

One of the first youth street-gangs, meanwhile, to carry a moniker were the 'Croydon Road Gang', from Canning Town. They were not an 'organised crime' firm but, rather, a group of racists, responsible for countless assaults upon young Asians and culminating in the deaths of three Tamil men.

Largely in response to these kinds of racist attacks, young Asian men too began forming into recognised street gangs and, by the end of the decade, there were Tamil, Sri Lankan, Bengali and Pakistani youth gangs, only too happy to meet violence with violence.

Older Asian organised crime gangs also began to proliferate; predominantly around the East Ham area, and drug-trade-related murders sadly began to increase in the East End.

*

There were other areas of tragedy and concern in football, in the 1980's, unconnected to hooliganism. In April 1985 a fire at Bradford's old wooden stadium raged through the terraces, causing the tragic death of 56 supporters.

[The investigating Safety of Sports Grounds Act compelled all clubs to replace any remaining wooden structures or terracing, with modern concrete and metal stadia.]

Then, in 1989, 96 people died at Hillsborough Stadium, in an FA Cup semi-final between Liverpool and Nottingham Forest. Police failed to properly control the flow of Liverpool fans at the entrances and far too many surged into a single 'caged-in' section of the ground; causing those already there to be crushed to an agonising death against the crowd barriers.

The Taylor Report into the tragedies concluded that standing terraces should be phased out and replaced with the much easier to control all-seater stadia. Also, the metal fences which most grounds had erected, as a response to football hooliganism – to deter fans from running onto the pitches - were removed, in light of the fact that the supporters were unable to spill onto the pitch at Hillsborough and thus avoid the crush.

Meanwhile, throughout all of the various dramas, tragedies, riots and scenes of unrest, Thatcher's popularity began to wane. As the decade wore down, even her own MP's no longer agreed with many of her policies and, when she received a Leadership challenge from Michael Heseltine, the following decade, she resigned rather than fight what would be an obviously losing battle.

As comedian Kenny Everett commented: *"When England was a kingdom, we had a king. When we were an empire, we had an emperor. Now we're a country, we have...Margaret Thatcher."* [A joke which contributed towards his being fired from his radio station!]

*

The Fantastic 'Boys of '86.'

The Government introduced a ban on the sale of alcohol within grounds, in an effort to reduce the likelihood of booze-induced crowd violence and – in a bid to re-entice younger supporters and their parents, who had been deterred from attending football matches, by the ever-present threat of hooligan violence – West Ham United introduced a family seating area, with ticket-price concessions, in the East Stand; as well as installing closed-circuit TV cameras, in an effort to discourage the 'rowdier' fans.

Even so, it would be late in the season before attendances finally began to approach capacity; by which time the East End faithful had realised that 'something special' was occurring at Upton Park.

The West Ham side of the mid-to-late 1960's, which won the FA and European Cup Winner's Cups and which included the likes of Moore, Hurst, Peters, Byrne and Sissons, is generally considered to be the greatest-ever Hammers team.

After that, the promotion-gaining and FA Cup winning team of the early 1980's; which included Brooking, Bonds, Devonshire, etc, is thought to be one of their strongest sides ever.

And yet, a team which actually won nothing is probably the most 'complete' unit of players West Ham United ever possessed; the footballers who so gallantly contested the First Division Championship in 1985-6 and who came closer than any other Hammers squad to tasting the ultimate in success.

Despite his best-laid plans to retire, Billy Bonds had been enticed back by John Lyall, to help the Hammer's in their fight against relegation, the previous season and so it was sadly ironic that he should miss their most successful League season ever, due to a serious toe injury!

Paul Allen had moved on to Spurs, at the end of the previous campaign and Hammers fans were anxiously awaiting news of who would be replacing him. The name Frank McAvennie produced a resounding '...**who?**'

Lyall purchased the St Mirren player for £340,000; supposedly as an attacking midfielder in the Allen mode but the former ginger-turned-dyed-blonde McAvennie became a former-midfielder-turned-instant-strike partner to Tony Cottee, when Paul Goddard was injured and ruled out for most of the season.

However, McAvennie struggled to settle initially. From 'The Boys of '86', [2001]:

"I had been warned that the people of London could be cold at times but I didn't expect that to bother me because it normally takes me only two seconds to settle in anywhere. I just thought that, because no-one was talking to me, they didn't like me. I did feel lonely at that point.

The problem stemmed from the fact that the players didn't understand a word I was saying! Then Tony Gale explained to me that every time I shouted for the ball,

185

the lads thought I wanted to fight them! It was my Scottish accent.

I don't know what John said to the players but soon after my chat with him about feeling homesick, the boys had a big night out and that did the trick. We started off drinking in the '*Ship*' in Gidea Park, moved on to the '*Slaters Arms*' in Romford and ended up at '*Stringfellows*' in the West End. I remember thinking to myself that night that my new team-mates were all poofters, because it was the first time I'd ever seen blokes dancing together."

Alvin Martin was made captain in Bond's absence and responded to the responsibility admirably. States Martin, modestly: "I took over from Bonzo – **the** ultimate player! He was a role model and although I tried to live up to him, it was an impossible job."

Alan Devonshire made a welcome return from long-term injury, whilst Alan Dickens established himself that season, in midfield and drew comparisons with a young Trevor Brooking; a judgement he was never going to be able to live up to. Like Alan Sealey and Alan Taylor before him – [*there's a pattern emerging here!*] – Dickens would enjoy a wonderful season and then slowly fizzle out.

[*Dickens had an unsuccessful spell at Chelsea and ended up retiring, aged just 30 and becoming a black cab driver; which was ironic, as he could barely find his way around a football field towards the end of his career.*]

The man who would – effectively – become Allen's replacement on the right side of midfield / right wing was the little-known Mark Ward; purchased for £250,000 from 2nd Division Oldham. Ward would rival McAvennie as the 'bargain of the season' that year;

becoming 'provider' for many of the Hammers goals, via his electric runs-and-crosses from the right flank.

Ward and Cottee would both have their separate concerns, though, pre-season. Ward remembers:

"I was mesmerised by the likes of Alan Devonshire. It was all one and two-touch football and I wondered whether I would be good enough to be in this team. The pace and the quality I witnessed in that first training session was unbelievable and that was the first time I'd ever doubted myself as a player. I'm glad there was just the one training session before my first game, otherwise the self-doubts may have increased, but all the lads made me feel very welcome. They were such a great bunch; quality players and quality people as well."

Tony Cottee: "I was concerned about what the coming season would hold. We had some good players at the club and Alan Devonshire was just coming back after being out so long with a bad knee injury but I just didn't know how good Frank and Wardie were going to be. I was really worried about relegation!"

Cottee needn't have been so anxious. McAvennie scored twice in the 3-1 victory against QPR and made himself an instant favourite with the home fans. The team that delighted Upton Park that day would be the basis of the side which would shockingly challenge 'the big boys' for the title.

Parkes returned in goal; at right-back was the ever-dependable Ray Stewart, left-back Steve Walford; central defenders were captain Alvin Martin and the quickly-developing Tony Gale; right-wing, the new signing and unknown quantity Mark Ward; left-wing, the returning, hero-worshipped Devonshire; central midfield Neil Orr and Alan Dickens and new strike duo,

187

the consistently high-scoring Cottee and the second unknown quantity McAvennie.

After a mixed start to the season, a 2-2 draw against championship favourites Liverpool – [two more goals from McAvennie] – seemed to suggest that there were potential good times ahead with this new-look Hammers side.

But it was a players meeting, called by captain Martin, which finally brought the players together as a tight-knit unit. At their Chadwell Heath training ground, Alvin opened a 'frank' discussion on why the team weren't performing to their fullest potential; by criticising Tony Cottee's workrate.

Cottee had been a goal-scoring revelation ever since he'd burst into the team aged 17. However, he was also lazy; choosing to hang around the penalty area and wait for the ball to be delivered to him, rather than dropping back and helping his team-mates to retrieve the lost balls and pressure the opposition in possession. In complete contrast, his new strike partner McAvennie ran himself ragged in pursuit of the ball.

Eventually, **everyone** knew how they were perceived by their team-mates and all agreed – amicably – to work upon their supposed 'weaknesses'.

Cottee remembers; from *The Boys of '86'*:

"At the time I was 20 years old and I was pretty arrogant, which isn't a bad thing because it helps you to become a good player. I felt I was a goalscorer. I didn't think I had to contribute anything else. It was a case of the others around me playing to my strengths, giving me opportunities and letting me score goals. It was arrogant but that's how I saw it then."

Despite the Board's valiant efforts to stimulate interest from the 'family fans'; on 14th September 1985, the players walked out to Upton Park's lowest league attendance in many years; a paltry 12,000. It appeared that the years of frustration and on-going relegation battles had finally taken their toll on the loyal EastEnders and – regardless of the on-going hooliganism issue – the fans had voted with their feet.

It was a terrible shame, as a rampant Hammers destroyed Leicester 3-0, with goals from McAvennie, Cottee and the rejuvenated Alan Devonshire. However, Devonshire himself quickly realised that he was no longer quite the force he used to be.

From *'Boys of '86'*:

"As soon as I had the chance, early in the game, I used to like to run their right-back on the outside, just to test how quick he was. But I wasn't able to do that anymore, so I'd tend to come inside, onto his weaker left foot and make the play from there. Looking back, I know I was only playing 80% of my true potential after the injury. The '85-6 season should have been the peak of my career but it wasn't as good as it would have been if I hadn't done my knee. The team played well and I had a good season but I do regret the fact that it could have been even better for **me** personally."

Devonshire then praises McAvennie:

"Frank was the best striker I ever played with! I think he had everything. He was good in the air, could hold it up, would 'dig' a centre-half if he needed to, and he could finish…

He was just magnificent that season. Players know who are the good players, as much as the fans do, and I could tell that Frank was a top-class player by the way he handled himself on the pitch. And he was a team player too. I like to think that I was the same, in that I would work my b******s off for the team when I

189

didn't have the ball. The accolades I received from my team-mates over the years mean more to me than anything else."

McAvennie returns the compliment to the player who created so many chances and goals for him that season.

"Devonshire used to have a simple philosophy on the game. 'The ball's round', he would say; 'so let's get it down on the grass and play it'.

Dev's right up there among the best players I've ever played with, along with Kenny Dalglish. They played in different positions but they're both top quality. Dev was unbelievable – a breath of fresh air to me – but he's the worst finisher I've ever seen. He'd go past six players, beat the keeper and then knock it wide of the post. I'd look at him and he'd shrug and say; 'I was f****d!' He's a great fella."

There were further signs that this was going to be a very good season when West Ham stuffed Brian Clough's highly-rated Nottingham Forest 4-2, in October. But a better indication of the growing confidence of the Hammers could be found in the personal wager Cottee and McAvennie had developed at this point; whereby the front two bet that they'd score 'more spectacular goals' than their partner.

From *Boys of '86'*:

"Cottee seemed to have one hand on the winnings when he burst through in the 57th minute and blasted a volley past Aston Villa keeper Nigel Spink from 25 yards.

Cottee says; "When I scored with that shot, Frank ran up to me, laughing and said; 'you little s**t!' He knew it would be hard to top that'.

There were 10 minutes of a one-sided match remaining when McAvennie capitalised on a mistake. Knowing it would take something special to beat Cottee's long-

190

range strike, the canny Scot ran with the ball and took it as close to Spink as he dared before executing the most audacious chip from just inside the penalty area.

'When Tony scored a cracker from 25 yards, I thought, I'm never gonna top that. Then I was clean through on goal with Spink, who's about 6 ft 4 in, in front of me. I just kept running towards him and he must have been wondering what the hell I was up to by not shooting but I dug the ball out of the ground like I was using a seven iron and it went up so high before dropping into the net. It was arrogant stuff and it was also good fun."

In December, two goals from McAvennie were enough to defeat defending champions Everton, at Upton Park and the belief throughout the team gathered momentum; as did the attendances, which began slowly rising as the fans realised that **this** West Ham side were something special.

By this time McAvennie had been called up into the Scotland squad and Cottee to the England side and their partnership was being talked about excitedly in the media. Remarkably, West Ham were in third place, behind Liverpool and Manchester United, and Upton Park was finally buzzing again.

Just before Christmas, West Ham made it 18 consecutive matches without defeat; equalling the club record but then suffered a disappointing Boxing Day defeat to Spurs.

They then suffered another set-back when they were soundly beaten 4-1 by Liverpool at Anfield but managed to rebound with a marvellous 2-1 victory over top-of-the-table Manchester United. [They would also knock holders Man U out of the FA Cup that season; winning even more impressively, 2-0 at Old Trafford.]

191

A 4-0 thrashing of Chelsea, at Stamford Bridge, - [2 goals from Cottee, the others from Devonshire and McAvennie] – moved the Chelsea skipper Colin Pate to remark: "If West Ham play like that for the rest of the season, they'll win the Championship. They were brilliant – the best team to come here for a very long time".

Several of the West Ham players cited that match as one of the highlights of their season. From *'Boys of '86':*

"Devonshire still maintains that the Hammers have probably never played better than they did at Chelsea that afternoon. He says; 'We were both on the fringe of the title race and it was a big game. Even though the pitch was a mudbath, some of the football we played that day was breath-taking. It all fell into place that day and there is no better feeling than when things come together like that'.

Cottee also singles out the emphatic win at the Bridge as the pinnacle of West Ham's season, saying; 'If ever one game stood out above all the rest, this is it. We absolutely pulverised them. This was the result that made people sit up and take notice of West Ham. Not only that, but the players started to believe that perhaps we could go on and challenge for the title.'

John Lyall, a man not given to exaggeration, couldn't conceal his pleasure after such a thrilling spectacle. 'That was as well as we've played all season. We won in spectacular fashion and everything went right. It was a very special performance. You get days like that; days when everything you try comes off. If I'm not happy now, I never will be!'"

This was followed by a 2-1 victory over Spurs but, just as everyone was talking about the possibility of a

192

Hammers title win, Nottingham Forest defeated them 2-1 and Cottee admitted afterwards:

"It was towards the end of the season and I definitely felt drained. It had become harder for Frank and I to keep scoring the amount of goals we were getting earlier in the season. Teams had done their homework and, particularly at Upton Park, were tending to man-mark us both. We had found it hard to beat Sheffield Wednesday at home and even harder against Southampton."

Showing just how crazy football can be, Chelsea – just weeks after suffering a 4-0 home drubbing against the Hammers – came to Upton Park and won 2-1. The match was a sell-out; most of the fans coming to see a hoped-for repeat of the Stamford Bridge performance.

[I particularly remember this match, as I feared that I was going to be on the receiving end of a 'kicking' from my own fans!

I'd gone to Upton Park with my mates Danny and Gary – both Chelsea supporters – and, as is Danny's preference in life, had stopped off at more than several pubs on the way to the ground.

After eventually shoe-horning Daniel out of the latest alcohol emporium, we arrived at the Boleyn to discover the gates shut and the tickets all gone. I was less-than-pleased but we decided to retire to a small boozer around the corner, where – in these pre-Sky TV days – the match could be heard on the radio behind the bar.

*Chelsea scored and the pub went silent. I prayed to God / Allah / Rastafari / Bobby Moore and Bruce Lee, that Danny and Gary wouldn't celebrate. **Good boys;** they didn't.*

West Ham equalised and the pub went berserk – minus Danny and Gary – and all was well with the world.

Then, Chelsea scored again and – amidst the violent silence of the pub – Gary let out an almost imperceptible 'yes!' and punched the air.

I saw the man, as if in slow-motion – watching us from across the bar – begin to stride purposefully towards us and my adrenalin started pumping as I realised that I couldn't abandon my mates, and so I'd have to suffer the painful ignominy of getting pasted by the I.C.F.

The guy asked; "Are you two Chelsea fans?"

Anyone with a grain of common-sense would, of course, have laughed and said 'no'. Consequently, Gary said 'yes' and I closed my eyes and waited for the pain and the beer-glasses to start smashing.

"Thank f**k for that", stated the now-obviously-non-I.C.F.-member. "Can I stand with you?"

And so I finished the evening with three Chelsea fans and a renewed hatred of everything connected with Stamford Bridge.]

As my old mate Jimmy Greaves often remarked to me, just before collapsing in a drunken heap – *him or I? Only his libel lawyers will be able to tell you;* - "football's a funny old game", because West Ham followed this set-back with an **amazing 8-1 thrashing of Newcastle!** It was their biggest league win since the 8-0 drubbing of fellow North-Easterners Sunderland, back in 1968. [Alvin Martin managed a hat-trick; the other scorers being the returning Goddard, McAvennie, Stewart, Orr and an own goal.]

And the wins just kept on coming but West Ham were always playing catch-up to the Merseyside top two, Liverpool and Everton, who – unfortunately – **also** kept on winning. [Man Utd having fallen off the pace as the season neared its conclusion.]

With two matches remaining there was still a possibility of West Ham United defying all the odds and winning the First Division title for the first time in their history. Despite defeating West Brom 3-2, though, Liverpool too won that day and with their victory came the League Championship.

Ray Stewart and Frank McAvennie broke down in tears when they discovered that their efforts against West Brom had been in vain but John Lyall consoled:

"Don't cry. Instead, be proud of what's been achieved. Don't be too disappointed. Think of what progress this side has made to get up among the big boys and give them a shock or two. And think, too, of what we can achieve with these players over the next two or three years. The future looks marvellous."

[*In fact, what Lyall achieved was relegation and the sack!*]

The Daily Mail's Patrick Collins stated: "West Ham have proved that attractive football can also be effective football. They have grown into the most appealing side to watch in England."

[*They had **always** been that, you silly little sausage…but 'thanks'.*]

A draw in their final game of the season would have been enough to secure second place but a mentally and physically demoralised Hammers tamely surrendered 3-1 to Everton and finished in 3rd position; **still** their highest-ever placing.

[There was no European adventure, due to the awful events of Heysel.]

Defender Tony Gale later remarked upon that season: "I will never forget those days, as long as I live. That was a dream team – wonderful to play in and wonderful to watch…it's far and away the best side I ever played in.

West Ham will be lucky if they ever get one as good again."

The unheralded McAvennie had established himself as a top-class striker; amassing 28 goals that season and Cottee was snapping at his heels with 26. Winger Mark Ward was suddenly 'hot property' and Alvin Martin headed off to the World Cup with England. How then, could this group of players – who had challenged so magnificently for the title – fail so dismally over the following seasons?

[It wouldn't be unique. Leeds United and Blackburn Rovers would both win the League in subsequent seasons and then dramatically drop down the divisions; proving that complacency is the biggest enemy to continued success.]

*

A large part of the blame for the failure to build upon this season's success must lie with John Lyall; for it was total naivety to believe that the squad didn't need strengthening. As evidenced in later campaigns – particularly by the likes of Manchester United and Chelsea – strength in depth was all-important and yet Lyall felt that his young stars would continue maturing into a championship-winning unit **but** he failed to take into account both injuries and fluctuations in form, which all players go through.

It was certainly stupidity of the highest order to sell fit-again Paul Goddard, in the belief that he was no longer needed; for McAvennie could only manage a paltry 11 goals in the 1986-7 season, as his playboy persona surfaced and fame went straight to his formerly-ginger head. [*Along with cocaine to his little Scottish nostrils.*]

The Hammers started the season well enough and Tony Cottee managed to maintain his own outstanding form

196

and improved his total to 28 goals that season. However, with McAvennie suddenly misfiring and Alan Dickens's form deserting him, West Ham slumped dramatically and Lyall suddenly realised that he needed to 'splash some cash' and reinforce his stuttering midfield; spending £700,000 on Arsenal's Stewart Robson – [*a complete waste of bloody money*] – and also recruiting the veteran former Gunners hero Liam Brady.

Even with these acquisitions and the emergence from the youth ranks of talented youngsters Paul Ince, Steve Potts and Kevin Keen, it still required yet another S.O.S. call to the old warhorse Billy Bonds to save West Ham from a ludicrous relegation battle and the fans responded to the 41 year old's magnificent performances by voting him '*Hammer of the Year*', yet again.

It has to be worrying when you need a middle-aged man to dig you out of a hole – [*unless you're a Chilean miner!*] – and Lyall was obviously pinning his hopes for the 1987-8 season on the promising young Academy members Ince, Potts and Keen hitting top gear, for he made no new purchases; despite the previous season's struggle.

Once again, a bad injury caused Alan Devonshire to miss the entire season, whilst Tony Gale and Phil Parkes also missed a sizeable portion of the campaign, due to injuries.

Lyall had decided to 'cut his losses', regarding the out-of-form McAvennie and sold Frank to Celtic for £750,000. This was all well-and-good but Lyall didn't replace him; instead choosing to play Tony Cottee as the lone striker. [?]

197

This tactic was never going to work, as the pocket-sized Cottee wasn't a Geoff Hurst or David Cross-type big, strong target man, who could hold up play and wait for support. Cottee was a Greaves / Pop Robson-style penalty box predator and Lyall **finally** accepted this, with the season almost over; purchasing Leroy Rosenior from Fulham, who promptly scored 5 goals in the Hammers remaining few games – including two in the 4-1 victory over Chelsea, which condemned the Blues to relegation. *Bless him!* – and which helped West Ham escape the drop again.

It was too little, too late though, for a disillusioned Tony Cottee, who realised that the team which had come so close to the title just two years previously, had deteriorated almost overnight into relegation candidates. It's bad when a die-hard West Ham fan such as Cottee announces that he wants to leave, and Everton paid a British record fee of £2.5 million for the young England striker.

After 795 appearances, meanwhile, Billy Bonds decided to **definitely** 'call it a day'. Bonds' game had been built around his unceasing enthusiasm, endless running and hard tackling and he trained as hard in his forties as he had at 20 years of age but it was his wife who commented to him that he was 'beginning to look gaunt'.

In his efforts to continue competing with much younger men Billy was pushing himself ever harder in training but it was actually having an adverse, weakening effect on his body. Realising this, Bonzo decided to retire before his standards started to slip and he began to be exposed by less-talented foes. In appreciation for his years of sterling service to the Hammers, John Lyall made Billy the youth team coach; believing that

Bonzo's visible fervour would inspire the Academy's youngsters.

Lyall bought instant Bonds-alike Julian Dicks, from Birmingham but stubbornly persisted in treating West Ham's finances as if they were his own and was rewarded with this continuing near-sightedness with an almost incomprehensible relegation and the sack, at the end of the 1988-9 season.

Leroy Rosenior was West Ham's top scorer but **he** only managed 11 goals and there lies the story of the Hammers' season and Lyall's blinkered attitude in not investing in some new talent.

Devonshire returned – **again** – and young midfield general Paul Ince was hitting top form but it takes more than a couple of class players to make a successful team and West Ham – after contesting the First Division Championship several seasons before – were soon embroiled in their third consecutive relegation dog-fight.

Desperation set in when Lyall re-purchased Frank McAvennie [!] towards the end of the season for £1.25 million but it was a futile gesture. Frank couldn't manage a single goal – *although he did manage to locate 37 different nightclubs* – and the defence continued to leak goals by the bucket-load; the injured Parkes's replacement Allen McNight being universally hated by the fans and getting his revenge on the boo-boys by pretending that he was a professional goalkeeper. [*Oh, how we laughed.*]

With two games remaining, the Hammers needed to win them both, in order to stay up. I attended the game at Nottingham Forest's City Ground and was **hugely vocal** in my delight at West Ham's 2-1 victory. [*'Hugely vocal' enough that a nice policeman on a very*

199

*nice horse escorted me all the way to the train station; despite my protestations that I actually 'lived in Nottingham'! I **did**, at that time but it's not something I would recommend. Full of Midlanders!]*

Despite this brief ray of sunlight, West Ham were then stuffed 5-1 at Anfield. *[I **definitely** wouldn't recommend living in Liverpool! It's full of Scousers, and they even gave us Jimmy Tarbuck and Cilla Black; with a straight face. I know they're famed for their 'humour' but that's just plain nasty! (Although, to be fair, we did give them Plaistow-born Reg Varney!)*

*The only consolation being that Arsenal dramatically 'robbed' Liverpool of the title by winning 2-0 at Anfield; courtesy of that incredible last-minute goal from Michael Thomas, which broke Scouse hearts. LOL. **There's** a guy I need to buy a drink for!]*

A dreadful West Ham side – *and I admit that, as a fan!* – were duly relegated and, after 34 years of service to the club, John Lyall was brusquely sacked.

[He was offered the manager's position at Ipswich Town and managed to gain them promotion from the 2nd Division in 1992. After which, he retired to his farm in Surrey and – upon his sheepdog's death – re-purchased Frank McAvennie for 50p.]

It was also nearing the end for Alan Devonshire, whose best days were behind him due to the awful series of bad injuries he'd endured over the years, which had robbed him of most of his pace. No longer able to set off on his mazy, jinking runs, he became more of a passer / crosser of the ball, in the Brooking mould.

From 'The Hammers':

"It is easy to see why the West Ham fans found it so easy to relate to him. Even at the height of his career,

Devonshire thought nothing of 'going to work' from his West London home on the London Underground.

'I knew what it was like to get up at seven in the morning and work until five, for not a lot of money', recalls the ex-forklift truck driver, 'so I loved every minute of being a full-time professional footballer. I can't believe that some players don't work their socks off all the time because, at the end of the day, you're only working two or three hours a day and you should be able to give 100% to that.'

Devonshire reflects on the effect of his injuries, at the end:

'Previously, whatever situation I was in, I knew I could get out of it, just by stepping up a gear. Now, I couldn't do that. I was able to kid people to some extent – some opposing players would still be wary of me taking them on and I could beat them by dropping my shoulder, to pretend that I was going to take the ball past them on the outside and then just come inside. But, generally, I had to play a lot differently and although people felt I was doing well, I knew – deep down – that I wasn't the same player. It hurt, to be honest with you.'"

It was the end of another era and the next decade would bring shocks, intrigue, drama but, unfortunately, no real success. The glory days were gone; it was time instead for back-biting, foreign 'talent' and the enigma that is Harry Redknapp.

*

INTERLUDE
A WEST HAM FAN'S MEMORIES.   NO.4
Name: Alan Burgess. **Age:** 64. **Profession:** Bus Driver. **Born:** Barkingside. [Now living in Leyton, East London.] **Connection to West Ham:** Fan. [Home and Away Season Ticket holder.]

Why do you support West Ham?

"I didn't actually start supporting them until quite late. My dad liked non-league football and used to take me with him to watch matches. It was only when I was about 13 that my next-door neighbour took me to Upton Park. That was it!"

Who is your all-time favourite West Ham player and why?

"My second choice would be Billy Bonds; best player never to have played for England. But my all-time favourite would have to be Trevor Brooking. The things he could do with a ball – especially when you consider how muddy and uneven the pitches used to be in those days – was unbelievable.

If he was playing now...well; you couldn't afford to buy him!

I've seen Bobby Moore, Geoff Hurst; all those players, since I started supporting West Ham in the 1960's, but I still think Brooking was the best player I've ever seen. He'd've fitted right in to that World Cup winning side of '66."

Who is your least-favourite West Ham player of all-time and why?

*"I **would** say David Kelly –"* [**Author:** striker from the late 1980's and **so** poor as to not previously rate a mention in this book!] – *"but, to be fair, he was bought to replace Tony Cottee, and Cottee was always going to be a hard act to follow. Kelly was never going to score the amount of goals Cottee did and so...I'd say Bobby Zamora.*

*I can't understand why people rate him. I thought he was a terrible player! If anyone looks at his goal-scoring record – especially if you look at **who** he scored* his goals against – he didn't score many against the 'bigger' clubs.

I really think he'd've been a better midfielder. I don't rate him as a striker at all."

[**Author: I do**, but...hey. It's all about opinions, I guess, and you've had enough of mine stuffed down your throat, by this point in the book.]

What's your strongest single memory of supporting West Ham United?

"I've got a few really good memories. One is from a game we played against Cambridge United, just before Christmas 1979. We were expected to beat them easily but, at half-time, we were losing 1-0.

There was a really poor crowd there that night; whether it was because it was Christmas, or because it was freezing cold, but there were only about 8-or-9,000 of us there".

[**Author's note:** I know I said I wouldn't be boring about statistics **but**, there were 11,721 supporters at Upton Park that night. Memory can be a funny thing; as evidenced when friends owe you money, or in the movie *'Total Recall'*.]

"At half-time the DJ / Stadium Announcer, put on...I think it was 'Tubular Bells" – [**Author:** See what I mean about memory? It's a wonder he remembers his bus route.] – *"and the whole crowd started 'dum-de-da-de-da-de-da' to it.*

Then, a guy – bearing in mind it's freezing cold and snowing – did a 'streak' on the pitch. The crowd were all laughing and singing and then they began dancing to the tune as well.

When it finished, the DJ put it straight back on again and the crowd all carried on singing-and-dancing; having a great time.

When the players came back out for the second half the DJ had to stop the music but the entire crowd just continued singing-and-dancing. The players looked up at us as if we were all mad!

We ended up winning 3-1 and that was one of my favourite-ever nights at Upton Park, because of the atmosphere.

Funnily enough, though, the DJ tried it again at our next home match against Watford, and even though we had a much bigger crowd that day, nothing happened!

*Another of my favourite memories regarding 'atmosphere', is of when we played Den Haag, in the Cup Winner's Cup. We'd lost the first leg away 4-2 but then beat them at Upton Park 3-1, to win on away goals. That was a **really** fantastic atmosphere there that night."*

What was the best game you ever saw or, best experience of supporting West Ham?

"The best game I ever saw was when we beat Tottenham 4-0, in 1981.

We'd just been promoted and our first Away game was against Spurs, on a Tuesday night. I couldn't get a ticket but I went there anyway, with my missus, and decided to go in the Tottenham end, with all of the Spurs supporters.

*David Cross scored all four goals and I managed to bite my lip and say nothing, for the first three goals but, when the fourth one went in, I shouted: **'YES!'***

My wife – who was my girlfriend at that time – made me go home at that point, in case we both got into trouble, and so I missed the end of the match".

What was the worst game you ever saw / worst experience?

"My worst memory is of when we went to Brighton, in the late 1970's. On the way back to the car there was this big, fat – he must've been about 25-stone – Brighton fan and he was surrounded by West Ham fans. He was too fat to try and run away from them and so he just stood there as they abused him. One of them caught him with a punch and knocked him down and this other guy kicked him in the head.

Well, he was 'out cold' and it was obvious that he was unconscious, but they all just carried on kicking him. It was horrible to watch and I wanted to go over and help him but I'd've got a kicking myself, and so I just walked off.

Yea...that's my worst memory".

Any non-football pitch related anecdotes around supporting West Ham?

"My eldest boy was studying for his exams; trying to get into Uni, and my youngest boy was annoying him. 'Get him out of the house, dad', he said. 'He's driving me mad', and so I drove him over to West Ham's training ground, but they weren't training that day.

Because we didn't really have anything else to do, we went over to Tottenham's training ground instead; just to get him some autographs. So, we turned up and there he is, amongst all these Spurs supporters; wearing his West Ham shirt, and they wouldn't let us in.

They said it was a 'closed training session' that day and told us that we'd just have to wait outside if we wanted to meet any of the players, when they'd finished training.

*Anyway, we're standing there – amongst all these staring Tottenham supporters – when this car pulls up alongside us and a bloke shouts: 'Oi! What are **you** doing here? You support West Ham!'*

I turned around and there was Pat Holland." [Former West Ham midfielder; then working as a Coach at Tottenham Hotspur.]

"I explained to him that we'd gone to see West Ham but they weren't training that day and so we'd popped over to Spurs, but they wouldn't let us in.

*'Stay there; **I'll** get you in', he said, and a few minutes later this bloke came out and says: 'Mr Burgess? Come with me'.*

Well, the faces of all these Tottenham supporters who can't get in to watch their own team train, and yet see these guys in West Ham shirts walking straight through, was a picture!

Pat Holland says to me: 'Wait here. Help yourself to a coffee' and, with that, he's taken my boy off for about half-an-hour, to meet all of the Spurs players".

[**Author**: At least, that's what Jimmy Saville told him later!]

"So, after that, we went out onto the pitch with Pat Holland and watched the Spurs players train. Players like Klinsmann, Ginola, Fox. My boy was so excited. I remember they were practising corners.

When they'd finished Pat Holland came back over and said: 'Right. I've booked you two a meal here tonight. The reserves are playing; so you can stay and watch'. So, we had the meal and then left! I didn't want to watch Spurs Reserves!" [Laughs.] *"Love Pat Holland; hate Tottenham!"*

Ever had an affinity for another club and / or hated another club, and why?

"When I was younger, because my dad didn't like professional football, we used to follow our local amateur team Barking. We followed them all over the

country; until I started to support West Ham, but I still look for their result, every Saturday.

The reason I hate Spurs may surprise you. It's not just your typical anti-Spurs thing that West Ham fans have.

I told you that my next-door neighbour took me to see West Ham play and that's how I started supporting them. Well, my neighbour on the other side was a Spurs fan. Now, to be fair, the Tottenham side of 1960-61, that won the Double, was a really good side and for the next couple of years they remained a good side, and so this neighbour used to really 'wind me up' about supporting West Ham.

Anyway, that winter – when I was about 13 – we'd had some really bad snow. I was going out to get the Sunday papers and when I reached my front gate, the neighbour was there, clearing the snow from the pavement.

He said: 'West Ham are rubbish, you know?'

'They're better than Tottenham', I replied.

***'What?'** he shouted. 'They're rubbish!' and, with that, he knocked me to the floor and started shoving snow down my back; pinning me down and trying to make me say: 'West Ham are rubbish'.*

*'No, I won't', I kept saying, but I just couldn't get back up. He held me down in the freezing cold snow and kept angrily repeating: **'Say West Ham are rubbish'.***

*'I'll **never** say that!' I replied and, eventually, he let me up.*

*All the way to the paper shop I was shaking and repeating to myself: 'I hate Tottenham...I **hate** Tottenham!'*

Even years later; when I used to go back to visit my mum; if I saw him standing outside, I'd say to him: 'I hate Tottenham. Always have, always will'.

*It sounds silly, at my age, I know but that experience made me feel the hatred of Spurs; because of what **he** done to me.*

It's even got to the stage now where, if West Ham ever went bust and couldn't play in the League anymore, I'd go to Tottenham every week; sit in the Away supporters end, and cheer for whoever the visiting team are!

*One bloke laughed at me, when we lost in the FA Cup Final to Liverpool, but I said: 'That don't bother me. At least we stopped Spurs getting into Europe. **That** was more important to me!"*

[**Notice from the Publisher:** Any readers who may have been emotionally affected by Alan's sad story and feel that they may need to contact someone for help and advice…should **snap the f**k out of it and get a life!**]

*

Chapter Five: 'H' is for far worse than Heroin.

'This is the end of a beautiful friendship...'

With the sacking of John Lyall, following the heartbreak of relegation to the 2nd Division, West Ham United's Board broke with tradition and surprisingly installed someone with no previous connection to the club whatsoever, as their new manager.

Ex-Celtic and Manchester United midfielder Lou Macari was appropriated from his position as Swindon Town manager and enticed to Upton Park but the fans were less than appreciative of this move; as Macari had never been the most popular of visiting players, in his prime.

Macari clashed immediately with several members of the squad, as he attempted to introduce discipline to the 'family atmosphere' of Upton Park and tried to impose a stricter regime of diet and fitness. [Particularly unpopular with left-back Julian Dicks; whose method of 'warming up' was to sit in the dressing room and consume a supermarket trolley's worth of Coca-Cola. Dicks later admitted that he'd had 'no respect for Macari', or his plans for 'change'.

Macari's method of motivating his players to lose weight had included blatantly calling Dicks; 'a fat b*****d'.

Julian kindly responded by kicking the crap out of his manager, in a 5-a-side game.]

Midfield prospect Paul Ince, meanwhile, enraged the fans – and assured himself of the position '*Most Hated Former Player*', for years to come – when he was photographed wearing a Manchester United shirt, in a *Daily Express* newspaper article and musing about 'how nice it would be to play for a club like Man U.'

Ooh, here's a surprise! Manchester United – immensely flattered, no doubt by this 'totally unexpected' comment from this nice young East End chappie [!] – tabled an offer of £800,000 for Ince, which the Board resentfully accepted.

Bad enough that one of our best players didn't want to stick around and try to help get us promoted back to the First Division; worse, was that he'd 'play' the club in that way and show a total disrespect to West Ham United and its supporters. [*Though he wouldn't be the last to do so!*]

Frank McAvennie broke his leg in the first game of the season – *though it was hard to tell, judging by his recent form* – and the loss of the striker **and** Ince forced Macari into the transfer market.

QPR midfielder Martin Allen and Nottingham Forest defender Colin Foster were duly purchased and Macari exchanged want-away winger Mark Ward for

Manchester City pair; midfielder Ian Bishop and striker Trevor Morley.

[Mark Ward was one of the saddest stories to come out of the 'Boys of '86' squad. Mark would later claim that John Lyall's departure had really upset him, prompting his transfer request. Ward would go on to enjoy considerable success at his boyhood club Everton before retiring. However, post-football, Mark quickly fell into financial difficulties and was shockingly jailed for 8 years for possession of £700,000 worth of cocaine, with intent to supply. *Presumably, to supply Frank McAvennie.*]

Lou Macari also found a replacement for the aging Phil Parkes, in Czechoslovakia's Ludek [Ludo] Miklosko, who would become a huge favourite with the Upton Park fans, *as well as a winning score in Scrabble.*

Indeed, Morley and Bishop would prove to be an astute capture as well and the 'new' team certainly looked stronger than the one which had been relegated.

Looks can be deceiving! As Macari continued to fail to 'win friends and influence people', West Ham toiled away in mid-table obscurity and were humiliatingly dumped out of the FA Cup by 4th Division Torquay United.

Surprisingly – considering their total lack of a relationship – Macari made Julian Dicks his captain, when Alvin Martin was ruled out for the remainder of the season, with a foot injury; Macari obviously seeing leadership qualities in his left-back, despite the fact that Julian couldn't tolerate his manager, and the attack-minded Dicks even finished the season as top scorer.

Then came the news that Macari was being charged by the FA for allegedly making illegal bets on games, when manager of Swindon, and a further allegation that he had made 'irregular payments' to his players.

Macari immediately resigned; stating that he needed to concentrate all of his attention on 'clearing his name'. West Ham fans breathed a collective sigh of relief *and Julian slipped back into his elasticated-waist trousers and warmed up half—a-dozen Pukka pies and a KFC bucket.*

Ronnie Boyce became caretaker manager for a short period but he was quickly superseded by the man who **should** have been given the job before Macari; the legend that is Billy Bonds!

Bonds's presence at the helm had an immediate effect and a run of late victories – which included 5-0 and 4-0 wins over Sunderland and Wolves respectively – saw the Hammers rapidly climb the table but, it was too late and by the time they reached 7th position, the season was over and they'd just missed out on the play-offs.

Nevertheless, there was a positive vibe again around Upton Park and most fans – including myself – welcomed the elevation of Bonds to manager and firmly believed that he would lead us to promotion the following season and then on to even greater success. [*Maybe the World Cup? Or, at least, the Grand National;* **anything** *was possible with Bonzo! After all, we would've been lucky to have made the Donkey Derby under Macari.*]

*

A Billy Bonds-inspired West Ham United managed an incredible 21-game unbeaten run, at the start of the 1990-91 season; which included a marvellous 7-1 victory over Hull and the sun shone once more on Upton Park. [*When it could squeeze through the tower-blocks.*]

211

They also reached the semi-finals of the FA Cup that year.

After destroying lowly Aldershot 6-1 and Luton Town 5-0, West Ham scraped past Crewe 1-0 and then defeated First Division Everton 2-1, before a crazy semi-final against Nottingham Forest.

With the game evenly poised, Tony Gale was controversially sent off, for the most innocuous-looking challenge you're ever likely to see. [*Not counting Audley Harrison's embarrassing 'performance' against David Haye. He'd been looking for the Ladies Room and found himself inside a boxing ring.*]

Still, 10-man West Ham attacked, trying to rectify this perceived 'wrong' and hitting the woodwork twice before the Forest players – who were either related to the referee or having an affair with him; *or **both**, if the match had taken place in Louisiana!* – scored.

Once the first goal went in West Ham never had a hope; eventually losing 4-0 but their supporters roared them on until the end; seeing the injustice of the Gale sending-off and the dogged pursuit of victory by the weakened Hammers, as worthy of their approbation.

Julian Dicks was sidelined for the remainder of the season, with a bad knee injury and the in-form Ian Bishop – who was proving himself to be a flair player in midfield; the kind always popular with West Ham fans – was given the captaincy.

Trevor Morley would finish as top scorer that season but may have scored far more than his 17 goals had he not mysteriously been absent for a period after a 'domestic incident', involving his wife and a knife, led to an unspecified injury. [*Though, fortunately, not John Wayne Bobitt-like. Every time I think of that it puts me off sausages.*]

212

Although form became more erratic towards the end of the season, West Ham still clinched promotion, with a second place finish and Bonzo had achieved that which we always knew he would; returning us to our rightful place in the First Division.

[*'And Like My Dreams'...etc, etc. You get the picture by now.*]

The 1991-2 season couldn't have gone any worse. [*Short of a nuclear strike; which, as Bernard O'Mahoney commented to me once: "is the only thing which will improve parts of the East End". I laughed...even though he comes from Birmingham; home of the worst accent known to man.*]

The club's Directors announced 'the Bond Scheme'; their idea to help finance improvements to the Boleyn Ground, demanded by the Lord Justice Taylor Report, following the Hillsborough debacle. £500-£975 would give fans 'the **right** to purchase a season ticket'. This money would be used towards the estimated £15 million pounds worth of remodelling required to turn the stadium into a modern all-seater arena. The Board then added insult to...well, insult, by suggesting that; if the loyal East Enders didn't part with their hard-earned cash, then the stadium wouldn't be fit to meet the new standards and so they wouldn't be able to watch **any** football at Upton Park. [???!!!] What kind of monkey-brained idea was this? Well, some would call it 'emotional blackmail'!

The fans predictably responded with outrage and the season would be blighted by angry vocal protestations and even pitch invasions. [*It would have taken an Alien Invasion, to knock some sense into West Ham's Boardroom!*]

213

Morale was low at Upton Park; as the players and staff reacted to the atmosphere of resentment engendered by the supporters, and they were soon embroiled in a now-familiar relegation battle. Instead of consolidating their position back in the top flight, the Hammers were plunged into a Bond Scheme-inspired depression and, eventually, even manager Billy Bonds admitted; "I thought it was a diabolical liberty".

Returning captain Julian Dicks was even more forthright, stating: "**I** wouldn't pay £975 to watch a load of crap!" [Dicks – and the rest of the players – were politely asked 'not to air their private views in public'.]

In all honesty, the club captain was right; West Ham largely **were** 'a load of crap' that season. *The famous commentator gaffe: "Julian Dicks is everywhere. It's as if West Ham have eleven Dicks on the pitch"; was never more appropriate.*

Alvin Martin had returned to fitness but, surprisingly, his former team-mate Bonds told him that he thought he was 'finished, as a first-team player'. [*With friends like that...*] Determined to prove him wrong, Martin re-discovered his form and regained his place in the team.

[Alvin was badly injured once more in 1993 and spent another 10 months out of action but surprised everyone **again** by returning to the centre-half berth he had made his own for nearly 20 years; finally leaving Upton Park in 1996, after 22 years of sterling service. *I had a sterling service once but some b*****d stole it.*]

Highlights that season were few. A 1-0 victory at Highbury, against defending champions Arsenal and a 1-0 win over the Manchester United 'All-Stars', which effectively handed the title to their arch-rivals Leeds.

[A result which delighted the Upton Park faithful, as they witnessed the hated Paul Ince miss out on a League

Championship winner's medal but which enraged Man Utd manager Alex Ferguson, who declared that West Ham's effort that day was "obscene" and that, if they had performed like that consistently, 'they wouldn't have been relegated, but just seemed to save such performances for the likes of Manchester United'. (*Red Grapes were very sour, that season! Although, in truth, he had a point.*)]

On a sentimental note; for many fans the real highlight of the season was Frank McAvennie – who had been largely out-of-favour under Bond's reign – scoring a hat-trick against Nottingham Forest, in his final game for West Ham.

[Unlike his down-to-earth former strike partner Tony Cottee though, who made a successful career for himself after retirement, Frank was more akin to another ex-team-mate Mark Ward, in the way that his life spiralled downhill upon retiring from football.

Years later, he told *The Daily Mail:*

"I was depressed. I was on everything I could lay my hands on. Alcohol, drugs, you name it. I was waking up in places I'd never been before in my life, with people I didn't even know.

It was a horrible time. I had nothing to get up for in the morning. As a player, you would get up every morning and have some structure to your day. It was the dressing-room banter I missed most. I always felt safest on a football pitch. It was my sanctuary from life. Then, suddenly, it stopped.

I knew that I was doing too many substances, drinking too much alcohol, taking too many painkillers, but I didn't want to talk to anybody about it. I didn't want any help!

I would go out at night and drink and take drugs; do this for a couple of days, get depressed all over again; go out and get drunk again. I was stuck on a wheel".

It wouldn't be until Frank reached his fifties that he finally managed to kick his various habits and 'straighten himself out'.]

*

What was most upsetting about our instant relegation was that West Ham United missed out on the inaugural Premiership campaign.

A major restructuring of English football was taking place. Sky satellite TV was pumping millions of pounds into the game, in order for the right to show live action throughout the season. The 'highlight packages' were now joined by something better; as fans were given the unique opportunity to watch their team in action, 'as-it-happened', on a weekly basis.

Sponsorship increased and, slowly, so did attendances and British football was suddenly booming again. The reformation of the leagues reflected the need to modernise and re-brand English soccer and thus The Premiership was created, to replace the First Division. [Confusingly, the 2nd Division was re-named The Championship and the 3rd Division became League One; as the powers-that-be decided that this made the lower leagues sound more compelling.]

Thus, West Ham United prepared for life in 'The Championship', as the '91-2 season spluttered to a climax. Despite new Managing Director Peter Storrie announcing that the club was 'dropping the Bond Scheme', the damage had been done and a set of players, clearly intimidated by their own fans loudly-vocalised anger throughout the season, trudged away from a demoralised Upton Park.

As Billy Bonds admitted: "We were asking players to perform in an atmosphere that was very hostile. In 25 years at the club, I've never seen anything like it!"

*

Whether because of the stress of the previous season or because he was struggling to 'connect' with several of the players – [notably, his captain Dicks,] - Bonds decided to bring in his old friend Harry Redknapp, as his Assistant Manager. This would lead to one of the most controversial periods in the club's history.

After leaving West Ham United's playing staff back in 1972, Redknapp had moved to lower-division Bournemouth, but his career was ended by a knee injury in '76. Harry relocated to America and coached in the booming U.S. soccer scene; returning to Britain only to join his old mate Bobby Moore, as his assistant at lowly Oxford. [One of Bobby's abortive attempts at lower-league management.]

From there Harry returned to Bournemouth as first-team coach and then manager, and oversaw their promotion to the Second Division in 1986-7.

When John Lyall was sacked at the end of the 1988-9 season, Bobby Moore recommended Harry to the West Ham Board; recognising the blossoming coaching talents of his former playing colleague. However, the Board – in their infinite wisdom – went for Macari instead and now, three years later, Billy Bonds made a 'phone call to Redknapp, asking Harry to join him at Upton Park. It would be 'like the old days'. [*Black-and-white TV; petrol rationing; my nan's knitted tank-tops...*]

Redknapp had actually been slightly in awe of Bobby Moore, when they had first played together in the 'sixties – most people were – but Harry was a 'laugh-a-

217

minute' socialiser and one of the after-match regulars at *The Black Lion* pub, in Plaistow and quickly became close friends with Bobby.

Like Mooro, Harry – or 'H', as he was popularly known – enjoyed a pint or twelve, but Billy Bonds was unlike his contemporaries in that he shunned partying with his team-mates and always returned straight home to his wife and family after the game. Thus, Billy and Harry seemed – on the surface – an odd friendship; the introvert Bonds and the extrovert Redknapp, and yet Billy had chosen Harry to be the 'Best Man' at his wedding and turned to him again now when he needed help at West Ham.

When Redknapp returned to Upton Park, he admitted to being 'shocked' at how low the morale was and at the generally depressing atmosphere; not eased by the dour Bonds; who needed the 'chirpy Cockney' persona of his friend Redknapp to 'lighten the mood'.

From *'Always Managing'*:

"There was a lot of anger about. This was a relegated team, and the fans weren't happy with the players at all. Ian Bishop was a superb player, but they hated Bishop, and they hated Morley, the main striker and goal-scorer. The fans were spiteful towards the players and the players were scared to make a mistake. There was no confidence about the team at all.

It wasn't just the team that were copping it. Some fans would give Billy Bonds abuse like I've never heard. Billy was the manager who had got them relegated and so, regardless of his fine standing and fantastic service to the club as a player, he was a f***ing w****r as far as some fans were concerned and deserved all the abuse he got. I was so disgusted, but Bill just shrugged his shoulders…

218

At times like that I think back to the days of going to *The Blind Beggar* with Bobby Moore, and how much the game has changed. Yes, we came across the odd nutter who wanted to show off to his mates by having a pop at a footballer, but mostly there was a great atmosphere between the players and the fans. The locals loved West Ham United, and we were local boys who played for West Ham.

We'd go to *The Black Lion* in Plaistow after the game, and there'd still be a lot of fans in there who'd been to the match. There was never a problem, even if we'd got beat. You couldn't do that now. Lose a match and people take it personally. And Billy and those players had got West Ham relegated. So that season was hard for us, with the fans."

The Poplar-born 'H', whose dad had been a Docker, was as down-to-earth as you could get and had a very positive attitude to life but even Harry was taken aback by the poor attitude of some of the players; notably centre-half Colin Foster, who allegedly didn't turn up for training one day because 'his wife needed the car to go shopping'!?

[Redknapp would soon make Foster one of his first 'transfers out'.]

Gone, it seemed, were the days of players routinely travelling to the ground via several buses, or even – in the recent case of Alan Devonshire – across London on the Underground. Redknapp was left speechless at some of the things he witnessed, but not so was captain Julian Dicks, who continued to clash verbally – and **almost** physically – with Bonds.

Dicks was very similar to Bonzo in the way he played with total commitment to the cause and with an aggression absent in most of his team-mates. However,

219

this 'aggression' was often uncontrolled and Dicks verged on being 'a dirty player'; something which Billy could never have been accused of.

I must admit that I was never a great fan of Julian and felt that his lack of discipline, at times, affected the team negatively. Bonds also worried about Dicks's inability to 'reign himself in', when his team-mates needed his motivational presence and not his unhinged behaviour.

From *'The Hammers'*, Dicks recalls:

"There was one incident at Coventry. I elbowed Flynn, I think, or whatever his name was. I came in at half-time and Bonds has had a right pop at me. The kid had been on my back and I'd given him a little elbow to dislodge him and get him off me but he'd gone down like a sack of s**t.

We've come in at half-time and Bill's come at me, ranting and raving. He said; 'I should take you off'. So I've taken my shirt off; thrown it at him and said; 'Take me off then!'

He wanted to fight me. He said; 'I'll see you in the gym on Monday'.

I said; 'See me **now,** if you want to have a row!"

[*Bonds admitted years later: "I'd love to have chinned him, a few times."*]

Although many supporters idolised Dicks, West Ham United were promoted from the Championship that 1992-3 season **despite** Julian Dicks's actions. His indiscipline resulted in three sending offs and suspensions totalling a remarkable thirteen games; more than any other player in the Hammers history.

A dismayed Bonds stripped Dicks of the captaincy and gave it to the unheralded defender Steve Potts; who would repay him with some masterful displays in defence that season and earn the admiration of the fans too, being named '*Hammer of the Year*', at the end of the campaign; eventually amassing 445 appearances in his lengthy West Ham career.

Best wins that season were 5-1 over Bristol City, 4-0 against both Bristol Rovers and Brentford and a whopping 6-0 victory over Sunderland; the mobile, skilful striker Trevor Morley again being the Hammers top scorer.

It seemed that the Bonds / Redknapp partnership was the 'dream pairing'. However, the joy of instantaneous promotion was diluted that season by tragedy.

*

Death of a legend.

On February 24th 1993, the world was shocked by the news that Bobby Moore had died, aged just 51, from bowel cancer.

Journalist and friend Jeff Powell remembers:

"When the news broke, it released a tidal wave of admiration, a flood of tributes, an ocean of nostalgia and a river of tears.

All were of such overwhelming magnitude that our society found itself challenged to accept the real significance of this footballer of humble birth and simple origin but princely integrity and regal aspirations; challenged to realise his importance to a succession of generations; challenged to assess his influence over the English way of life, both now and in the future.

It came swelling up, as he would have wished, not from the privileged socialites who had sought briefly to bask in his reflected glory but then turned their backs on him; not from the self-important football institutions which

221

had failed him in later life, but from the vast body of 'ordinary' people.

Suddenly, as if feeling guilty at having failed sufficiently to acknowledge its debt to this heroic defender of forgotten virtues and collapsing standards, England recognised the loss of something pure, something honest, something good, something intangible but something impossible to replace."

The Guardian's Hugh McIllvanney - one of Britain's most highly-respected journalists – eloquently reflected: "The tributes paid to Bobby Moore are astounding. Sir Alf Ramsey called him 'my captain, my leader, my right-hand man. He was the spirit and the heartbeat of the England team. A cool, calculating footballer I could trust with my life. He was **the** supreme professional, the best I ever worked with. Without him England would never have won the World Cup'.

Pele said he was 'a friend, an honourable gentleman, and the greatest defender he had ever played against'. Franz Beckenbauer went even further, calling him 'the best defender in the history of the game'...

By being not only the captain but the unmistakable leader of the England team who, in 1966, brought the World Cup home to the island that liked to consider itself the birthplace of football, the incomparable central defender made himself an abiding presence in countless lives. The timing of that achievement helped to give it a lasting resonance, for the decade was a genuinely distinguished period for football in England, with Moore, George Best and Bobby Charlton at the apex of a broadly-based pyramid of exceptional talent.

Viewed from the vantage point of the present grey era in the game, that was a golden age, and the blond, upright, regally composed figure who orchestrated the

222

defeat of West Germany at Wembley, was naturally freeze-framed in the mind's eye as its golden symbol. That he should become the first of the glory boys of that distant summer to die was sure to make the jolt all the more sickening, when he was claimed by cancer of the liver and colon at age 51...

His nerve under siege was awe-inspiring. It was never simply a matter of not being frightened; whether confronted by physical risk or mountainous responsibility. The impression was of a nature so comfortable with challenge that it needed crisis to show its true strength. Of the supreme sports performers I have seen in action, perhaps only boxer Muhammad Ali was a more conspicuous example of grace under pressure...

When connoisseurs of Moore's game are listing his assets, they are obliged to start with his almost supernatural aptitude for divining the intentions of opponents; his capacity to identify a threat before even its perpetrators were fully aware of what they were doing. 'There should be a law against him', Jock Stein, a giant among managers, once told me with mock bitterness. 'He knows what's happening out there 20 minutes before anybody else'...

As he patrolled his extensive area of influence, straight-backed, handsome, head-up and eyes sweeping the field like a radar scanner, he was everybody's ideal of the thinking footballer. But if attackers decided that they were outgunned tactically, it was inadvisable for them to seek a more physical duel. Moore was six feet tall, with a playing weight of slightly under thirteen stone, and in his prime was as fit and as hard as a prizefighter...

Operating through most of his senior years as free man in defence, charged with scenting trouble and smothering it at birth, his comparative frailty in the air was seldom damaging. [The frequency with which he positioned himself perfectly to collect the ball on his chest was freakish.]

His tackling was precisely timed and uncompromising and his brilliantly early and economical distribution constantly transferred pressure from his own to the opponents' goal area...

His most influential attributes as a player were firmly related to the confident rationalism that underpinned all his attitudes. 'OK, if speed is only a matter of taking yourself physically from A to B, then I'm not fast. But isn't it important to know earlier than the next man that it's necessary to go from A to B? Isn't speed of thought as vital as how fast you can move your legs? Of course pace is a good thing to have, but I like to think that I compensate for my slowness by seeing situations quickly, by anticipating and reacting before others realise what is happening'.

As understatements go, that one should have been auctioned as a collector's item. Somehow though, the drive, leadership and perceptiveness that made him such a potent force on the field did not translate into a worthwhile career in football coaching or management, and his business ventures were equally disappointing. Undoubtedly greater effort should have been made to give him a more prominent role in English football than the radio commentating he had done for years and which, with typical courage and lack of fuss, he insisted on continuing to do within a week of his death."

Fellow *Guardian* journalist David Lacey added:

"Moore had a presence which turned heads when he entered a room. He never forgot the first piece of advice he had received upon joining West Ham United as a 17 year-old, in the summer of 1958. 'Stand big', Malcolm Allison told him, and throughout the 1960's and early '70's no-one in the English game stood bigger.

Fame was Bobby's natural companion. He first captained England against Czechoslovakia in May 1963, less than a month after his 22nd birthday. The following year he led West Ham to victory in the FA Cup Final and in 1965 he was holding aloft another trophy at Wembley, the European Cup-Winners Cup.

The picture of Bobby etched most deeply in the nation's consciousness though is the moment he received the Jules Rimet trophy from the Queen, after England beat West Germany 4-2 in the 1966 World Cup Final. Wembley is in uproar, Bobby Charlton is crying, Nobby Stiles is all gap-toothed glee, Alf Ramsey has quietly disappeared into his own thoughts. Moore is the calmest person in the stadium as he leads the England players up to the Royal Box. Completely in control of his emotions, he carefully wipes the sweat from his palms before the presentation is made and the handshaking of royalty begins.

That air of inner calm, of a man completely at ease with himself and his achievements, never deserted Moore. It served him admirably, but – eventually – his apparent detachment was to mystify even those closest to him."

In 2005, James Corbett wrote a poignant article for *The Observer,* reflecting upon Moore's sad final years:

"One afternoon 28 years ago, a remarkable meeting took place over lunch, between one of the country's most famous pop stars and the finest English footballer of his generation. Elton John had recently taken over

Watford football club and needed a new manager. Bobby Moore was in the final week of his playing career and, like so many players at that stage of their lives, was looking for a break into management. It seemed a perfect match and a deal was agreed in principle. The two men shook hands and John promised to call Moore to finalise the details. Moore thought it was 'a done deal'.

For three weeks Bobby waited by the 'phone. The call never came. One day Moore read in the morning paper that the job had been given to Graham Taylor, a young and successful manager with Lincoln City, but a man who had been a very ordinary player in the lower divisions.

By 1993, 16 years later, Taylor was England manager, while Moore was a commentator for London's Capital Radio. England were playing a mid-week World Cup qualifier against San Marino and Moore was there in the commentary box. But that night was different. Bobby Moore was a bigger story again than Graham Taylor or what happened on the football pitch. The previous day, the world had learnt that he had cancer. The press cameras were all trained on Bobby; the collar of his jacket turned up to hide his gaunt and pallid face. A week later he was dead, and football grounds across the country were hushed in memory…

Nobody asked what had happened to Bobby Moore until it was too late. Between his last game in 1977 and his death in 1993, he was almost the forgotten man, shunned by the football authorities, ignored by club chairmen, seemingly unwelcome even at West Ham, the club to which he had given his best years.

Only posthumously it seemed, did people recognise his grace, not just as a player, but as a man. Why was this?

226

What went wrong with Bobby Moore's life? Why did he end up as no more than a local radio pundit?

Moore's first wife Tina still expresses disbelief that no club came in with a coaching or managerial offer. 'How could anyone who had Bobby's knowledge and expertise be overlooked in that way?' she asked. 'Kids would have looked up to him and learnt things just by being in his presence'…

Tina Moore recalled that her husband found the struggle to build a post-playing career increasingly hard to take. 'I could see that Bobby was being torn apart', she says. 'Self-doubt started to creep in. Mentally, it was a dreadful time for him'.

She will not say whether Moore's sense of rejection and depression had anything to do with the break-up of their marriage. Tina and Bobby were football's golden couple in the 1960's and '70's; the Posh and Becks of their day, though with less glamour and far less scandal. But, in 1979, Moore met a 29 year-old air stewardess named Stephanie, and by 1984 he had separated from Tina and moved in with Stephanie…

In 1991 Bobby was diagnosed with bowel cancer, and it was terminal.

'It was very late in the day to diagnose it', recalls Stephanie, 'so we knew he wasn't going to survive; although we didn't know how long he had to live.

He decided not to make it public because we didn't want to have journalists crawling all over us. We only had another two years, as it turned out, and we wanted to lead our lives as privately and as normally as possible in that time'.

He and Stephanie married in December 1991 and travelled widely during his final months. 'Bobby was never a complainer, and he never criticised the cards that had been dealt him', Stephanie recalls. 'Even when he was diagnosed with terminal cancer, he was never angry about it – it just wasn't in his nature'.

The news remained a secret, even to close friends and colleagues. 'I had a cancer scare myself that year', radio co-commentator Jonathan Pearce said. 'Bobby helped me through it, speaking to me about it every day, reassuring my wife that I'd be okay. Not once did he ever let on to us about his own illness, even though he knew it was terminal'…

Following the England - San Marino game, Moore was determined to cover the West Ham match against Newcastle on the Saturday. 'I think he must have known it would be the last time he would get to watch West Ham', said Pearce. 'But Stephanie called me on the Friday, saying that she didn't want him to go; that it was too much for him, after all the press attention during the week.

I 'phoned Bobby and told him that I didn't think it was a good idea that he came'. What he said will stay with me forever: 'I must admit, I'm very disappointed'. I'd never intended disappointing Bobby Moore. And that's the last time I ever spoke to him'.

Moore died at his home on 24th February 1993, a week after his stricken appearance at Wembley. He was aged just 51, and the nation had barely even known about his illness. Only when he was gone, it seemed, did people appreciate what they had lost.

English football was then in a dismal state – [the national team would fail to even qualify for the 1994 World Cup] – and Moore recalled a lost era of pride and achievement.

Upton Park was turned into a temporary shrine and West Ham United belatedly invited Stephanie, and

228

Moore's daughter from his first marriage, Roberta, to attend a match as their guests. The following year Moore's close friend Harry Redknapp was appointed manager."

Harry Redknapp himself recalled Moore's final days in his autobiography *''Arry'*:

"Bobby died after a long illness, but for so long no-one apart from his family knew that he was ailing. He never told a soul. Even when his illness was getting too much for him he never felt sorry for himself…

He spent a few days in Bournemouth with me, towards the end of his life and we went to watch the horses. Not once did Bobby complain that things were getting too much for him. He'd go for his treatment to a clinic in Scotland and not say a word to anyone. I remember when I went to see him after he'd had his operation. I could have cried.

Bobby was always a big lad; big legs, powerful build, but suddenly his trousers were hanging off him because he'd lost so much weight. It slaughtered me to see him like that. He'd say to me that he was 'doing okay' but he knew all along he wasn't. He knew what was coming but faced it with incredible bravery. That was how he was – unflappable. You couldn't help but love him."

Similarly to with Redknapp; Bobby quietly arranged to meet with most of his closest friends and associates, in those final days and 'say his dignified goodbyes'.

Within hours of his 'passing', the Boleyn Ground's gates were covered with scarves, flowers, shirts and all manner of fan memorabilia, as East London commenced its extended mourning of its much-loved son.

There was a minute's silence before all of the following weekend's games; by which time the stadium was completely swamped with floral tributes.

Before West Ham's next home game, a week later, a selection of fans carried more flowers onto the pitch but it was the sight of Geoff Hurst, Martin Peters and Ron Greenwood, walking towards the centre circle with a huge wreath in the shape of the number six, which brought most fans to tears that day; including myself.

Ian Bishop had been the latest inheritor of Moore's old shirt number but, out of respect for the legend, Bishop declined to wear it that day and wore the number 12 shirt instead.

The number 6 shirt had always been associated with its most famous wearer but, after Moore's death, it assumed even greater significance and, eventually, West Ham United decided to 'retire' the shirt from use; so that no other player would ever again wear the number forever linked with England's greatest-ever defender and captain.

[The Board also announced that the South Stand would be renamed the Bobby Moore Stand, as a lasting tribute to Bobby; as well as a bronze bust of the captain installed in the club's foyer.

Later still, a statue of 'the Holy Trinity' was erected at the corner of Green Street and Barking Road and, when the 'new' Wembley Stadium was complete, a statue of the World Cup-winning Moore stood proudly at the entrance.]

Fittingly, West Ham defeated Wolves 3-1 that day and Upton Park bade farewell to **the** supreme player ever to lace on boots for West Ham United.

Harry Redknapp though, remained bitter towards West Ham United, for what he considered to be their hypocrisy.

From *'Always Managing'*:

"When I go to Upton Park these days there are two gigantic portraits in the corners at each end. One is of Sir Trevor Brooking, the other of Bobby Moore. Think about that. *Sir* Trevor Brooking; plain old Bobby Moore. No disrespect to Trevor, he was a great footballer and a fine ambassador for the game, but it doesn't seem right. How was Trevor knighted and Bobby ignored? How was the greatest footballer – and one of the greatest sportsmen – this country ever produced, reduced to living his final years as a commentator for Capital Radio; rejected by his club, his country, and those who should have placed him at the heart of the game? The hypocrisy that followed his tragically premature death in 1993 sickened me.

Bob's got it all now. The old South Bank stand named after him at Upton Park, statues outside the ground and at Wembley Stadium. They even use his name to sell West Ham merchandise. *'Moore than a football club'* is their slogan. When he was alive they didn't want to know him. I saw him get slung out of there for not having a ticket!

Bobby Moore. *The Bobby Moore*. Thrown out of a half-empty stand at West Ham because he didn't have a ticket. Now he's dead you can't move for pictures of him around the place. It disgusts me. I don't think he ever went back after that".

Redknapp wondered at the lack of a position for Moore at the club following his retirement from football, and speculates that the likes of John Lyall were too intimidated by the legend:

231

"John was a young manager, and he didn't want a huge presence like Bobby around overshadowing him. It would have been the easiest thing in the world to get him back. If John had said to him, 'Come over to the training ground Bob. Just drop in, let the kids see you're about. Watch their training; maybe put on a training session for them'. I'm sure Bob would have done that and the kids would have loved it. But John didn't want him anywhere near the place. I think he felt he might be undermined. Maybe John thought that Bobby would be too big, that the players would start looking to him for advice. He probably thought that Bobby would be a threat to him. That didn't make any sense to me. Bobby wasn't like that. He didn't have a bad bone in his body…

You'd have thought that someone, somewhere, would have snapped Bobby up and given him a chance. They only had to have seen him play to know the way he read and understood the game. He was Sir Alf Ramsey's captain. Surely **that** should have meant something?

To this day I don't know why he couldn't get a break. I still believe that, with the right support, he could have been the greatest manager in West Ham United's history. But we'll never know…

When I was assistant manager at Upton Park I spoke about it with the directors, but there were apparently never any positions for him at West Ham. And then he died. That same week Terry Brown, the chairman, started talking about naming a stand after him. I'll admit, I went spare.

'When he was alive, you wouldn't even give him a ticket. Now you want to name a f***ing stand after him! He should have been sat beside you at every game'."

*

The 1993-4 Premiership campaign highlighted the importance of having huge financial backing behind-the-scenes, as the top clubs in Britain began to inexorably pull away from the chasing pack.

Manchester United, Chelsea, Liverpool and Arsenal had the deepest pockets and this allowed them the cream of the world's best players and – during this period – foreign footballers began to dominate the English game, as Sky TV poured money into the Premiership's coffers and attendances continued to increase, as football hooliganism waned and soccer became 'fashionable' again; especially with the likes of the pop-star handsome David Beckham beginning to ply his trade on the nation's screens.

[Sky certainly knew how to promote and 'sell' the game to the average fan and their extended 'expert' previews and post-match analyses took the sport – on television – to another level; as well as packing out public houses, with their live presentations.]

Crowd capacity at Upton Park was temporarily reduced, as the modernisation of the stadium picked up apace, and West Ham enjoyed an unspectacular but solid first season in the Premiership; finishing mid-table. [Trevor Morley, **once again**, the Hammers top scorer.]

The biggest 'event' of their campaign had been the shock transfer of Julian Dicks. Billy Bonds decided that Dicks was just too much of a loose cannon; whereas Liverpool's manager and ex-midfield general Graeme Souness liked what he saw whenever he watched Julian battling his opponents. He reminded Souness of himself, in younger days – *what; talented but a nasty b*****d, you mean?* – and swapped him with Bonds for defender David Burrows and midfielder Mike

233

Marsh, plus £250,000. *And a boxed-set of Star Trek videos, a Sinatra CD and a Spiderman comic.*

The passage of time has mellowed Julian's memories of this abrasive period, and particularly his inflexible relationship with Bonds.

Dicks later recalled, with more than a little respect: "I joined West Ham when I was very young, and all I knew about the team was John Lyall and Billy Bonds, but I quickly grew to love the place. Being voted *Hammer of the Year* four times was a bonus. Overall the highlight was playing for West Ham at Upton Park, in front of such great fans...

I played with some real legends. Alan Devonshire was so graceful for a footballer, but I'd have to go for Billy Bonds as 'the best player' I ever played with. He had such passion on the pitch...

When Billy took over as manager we were too much the same; peas out of the same pod. We fought, because if I thought I was right I'd argue about it all day long and Billy was the same. When we argued neither of us would give in, and that's because we were both winners!"

All was not well, though, behind the scenes at Upton Park. The Board had been closely monitoring the management partnership between Bonds and Redknapp and believed that Harry was actually the one 'pulling most of the strings'. Thus, when his former club Bournemouth tried to entice Redknapp back with a better financial package and more 'power' than he was receiving at Upton Park, the Hammers Board acted quickly to ensure that Harry didn't leave.

Bonds and Redknapp were summoned to meet with Chairman Terence Brown and Managing Director Peter Storrie; whereupon it was announced – to Billy's utter

234

dismay – that they 'wanted Harry to be the manager' and for Billy to 'take a more back-seat role'.

It was a stab in the heart for one of West Ham's most beloved icons and a perceived stab in the back, when he realised that his 'best friend' Redknapp had accepted the role!

The two men have never spoken since but their recollections of that event differ vastly.

Redknapp claimed that he initially turned down the management offer and that he only – finally – agreed to take it once it had become clear that an upset Bonds had decided to leave anyway. Harry also claimed that Billy had even told him to 'take the job'.

From *''Arry'*:

"With that I was almost bundled into a press conference announcing me as the new manager. Yet it wasn't something that I'd wanted to happen. I allowed myself to be pushed into it too quickly and that was a mistake. I was deeply troubled, so deeply that I stayed the entire week in Bournemouth. The next morning I picked up a paper and read a story that I'd knifed Bill in the back. But that's not my game; not my nature. I would never do anything like that. I am not ambitious enough to jeopardise a friendship for the sake of a job, and certainly not to Bill, of all people…

In the early days after his departure I rang him for a chat on a few occasions but looking back it must have been very hard for him. I don't know if Bill bears me any ill-will. It bothers me more than anything to think that he might. Of all the people in football I've met, he'd be right up there at the top. I would never have done anything to harm him. I'd rather not have the job than anyone think that."

Bonds's reaction was rather different, when explaining why he stopped speaking to Redknapp; a succinct: "I've got no time for the man! He keeps calling me a 'friend', but I don't see **him** as one."

Former team-mate of both men and keen observer of 'all things West Ham', Trevor Brooking quietly commented: "The situation could have been handled much better."

With the benefit of further hindsight, Redknapp again reflected upon that period, and the bitter ending of his friendship with Bonds, in the 2013 version of his autobiography *'Always Managing'*:

"Billy Bonds was the most fantastic player. What would West Ham United give to have him now? He could play central midfield, centre-back, full-back; he was fearless in the tackle and he could run all day.

He was one of my closest friends in football. But was Billy in love with being a manager? I don't think so.

I loved Bill to bits, he was a fantastic fella. But in the modern world of Premier League football he was increasingly a man out of time.

In an era when man-management was more important than ever before, with foreign internationals coming into the English game and wages soaring, Bill wasn't really a 'people person'. He loved the game but didn't care much for footballers or their problems. He would get the hump with the ones who weren't as talented as him, or who didn't work hard in training, or who didn't have the same attitude. I think he looked at the players sometimes and they just all got on his nerves…

I think Bill's love of the game began and ended with pulling on his claret and blue shirt as a player. He loved playing football but when that final whistle blew, he'd be halfway through the Blackwall Tunnel and home before some of the lads were even out of the shower.

Training was the same. There would still be people ambling off the pitch as Bill's tail-lights were disappearing out of the car park. He was a home-loving man; he loved his wife and family, and he didn't want to hang around the football club all day. He wasn't a great one for talking to other managers or footballers."

Bonds himself admitted: "You can forgive players for not passing a ball properly; although that's bad enough, but when they're not putting the effort in, or they don't give a s**t...I found that very difficult to take. In all honesty, it was the most difficult part of the job".

Regarding the fateful meeting with Chairman Terrence Brown and managing director Peter Storrie, Redknapp recalls:

"Brown asked me: 'Why don't **you** be our manager? Bill can be the director of football, with a ten-year contract'.

This wasn't what I had expected and I felt very uncomfortable being offered Bill's job with him sat there next to me.

'Bill's the manager', I said. But Terry Brown had shown his hand.

'It's obvious you want Harry instead of me', Bill interrupted. 'You think he's a better manager than me and you want to replace me'.

There was an awkward pause. 'Right', Bill continued. 'What does 'director of football' mean then?'

Brown began outlining the job. Go to training when he liked, turn up on match days and be the club's ambassador. Complete job security and no pressure. I was beginning to wish they'd offered it to me.

Bill said he needed time to consider and we all parted company. We had dinner together that night and there wasn't a squeak of difference between us. I don't know what the final straw was for Billy. On Monday he called me and said, 'I'm packing up'. I couldn't talk him around. I even offered to stay on as his number two, if he still wanted the manager's job, but he was set on resigning. He went in to see Terry Brown and he quit.

Immediately, Terry called me and asked if I would be the manager. I said I needed time to think it over, but the club was eager to put on a united public face, and the biggest mistake I made, in hindsight, was agreeing to a press conference. I should never have agreed. I wasn't ready to be manager...

What I didn't expect was to lose Bill's friendship over the decision to take the job. All these years later that still hurts, and I would swap having Billy as a mate again, for all my seven years as manager at Upton Park.

Let me get this straight: **I** didn't push Billy Bonds out of West Ham United. In fact, for two weeks after I took the job we continued to speak. Yet, each conversation grew more stilted and, in the end, I could tell things weren't right between us. I knew what was happening. People were mixing it for us. There is always someone who can't wait to tell you a story – that's how it is in football – and Billy probably heard too many stories about me and things I was supposed to have said about him. The difference between us was, he believed them!"

*

London's having a blast!

The Docklands Redevelopment was finally completed by 1994 and the shiny new Canary Wharf, Surrey Quays Shopping Centre – [not a part of the East End but sufficiently close to be included in this book;

238

especially as its development was allied to the rest of the Docklands Regeneration project] – and Excel Exhibition Centre, thrust their imposing selves into the consciousness of East-Enders – old and new – as the young and affluent joined the 'native' population of East London.

Historically, 90% of East End housing had been rented, but this modernisation drastically altered those figures, as home ownership – particularly via 'affordable housing' and shared-ownership offers – proliferated.

The Canary Wharf offered ultra-modern office and retail space and soon became the headquarters of many multi-national banks, media organisations and high-earning professionals; providing around 90,000 new jobs.

New Health and Leisure Centres accompanied these offices and housing schemes; along with Community and Watersports centres. Also, training and further education initiatives were aimed at ensuring that the 'native' EastEnders enjoyed the revamped community just as much as the new 'high-fliers' who migrated there.

Soon, East London was home to a thriving art community, as it suddenly became fashionable and 'trendy' to live or work in the East End. [The Spitalfields and Hoxton areas, particularly, became the focus for artists and media professionals to congregate.]

With the concurrent completion of the short-haul flights London City Airport and the Docklands Light Railway, the shape and skyline of East London was forever altered. Which is not to say that the IRA weren't continuing to **try** and alter it further!

Margaret Thatcher – *or Satan, as she's known to her friends* – had finally relinquished her stranglehold on power, at the start of the decade; largely because of the widespread riots and resultant violence between protesters and the police, due to the hugely unpopular Poll Tax.

Her successor, the personality-free John Major, was – ironically – discussing Britain's involvement in the Gulf War, when those nice chaps in the Provisional IRA decided to allow him a glimpse of what life must be like for the soldiers, by launching a mortar bomb at Downing Street.

Further attacks followed and £350 million of damage was caused to buildings in the financial district; resulting in hugely increased security around the City of London, and the new architectural landmark 30, St.Mary Axe; better known simply as 'the Gherkin' tower, replacing the damaged buildings.

A 17 month 'ceasefire' agreement was broken in 1996, when the IRA turned their attention to the sparkling newness of East London's Docklands; this time causing £100 million of damage and – fortunately – only two deaths.

[It would be the end of the decade before the Northern Ireland 'Peace Process' brought an end to this terror.]

Meanwhile, as the Docklands Development reached its conclusion, Stratford – in East London – also began its own modernisation, in a concerted effort to continue attracting consumers to its huge shopping centre and its thriving pub, restaurant, theatre and nightclub 'evening allure'.

A new train and bus station were built, to both improve transport links to Stratford and to reflect its new 'modern' image. [Before long, Stratford – and its surrounding environs – would undergo far greater change, as East London became the focus of the world.]

It would be funny if it wasn't so awful…Harry's transfers.

Upon assuming the manager's mantle Harry Redknapp recruited his friend, former team-mate and brother-in-law – *all the same person; not the ultimate example of nepotism* – Frank Lampard, to become his Assistant Manager, and wasted no time in dipping into the transfer market.

In 1994-5 the Prodigal Son returned to Upton Park, when Tony Cottee made a welcome reappearance in claret-and-blue. Although he'd been Everton's top goalscorer for six out of the seven seasons he'd been with them, they had never really idolised him in the way that Hammers fans had. [*That's because A) they're silly, B) they're Scousers and, C) they're silly Scousers!*]

Cottee would immediately re-establish his warm relationship with the Hammers supporters, by finishing the season as West Ham's top scorer. It was as if he'd never been away.

Two other buys looked good that season; attacking midfielders John Moncur, from Swindon and Don Hutchison, from Liverpool but the very average Burrows was quickly off-loaded to Everton.

The 'big surprise' – but welcomed by most of the 'Upton Park faithful'; even more than Cottee's return – was Redknapp's re-purchase of the shaven-headed cult figure Julian Dicks. [*At least, I **think** 'cult' is the right word. Might be a spelling mistake.*]

Dick's brief tenure at Anfield had not been successful at all but it had been a sobering experience for Julian. Used to being hero-worshipped by the Hammers fans, Dicks cut an unhappy figure at Liverpool. He didn't fit in; the Liverpool hierarchy not liking rebels at all and when Graeme Souness was 'removed' as manager, Dicks knew that his days too were numbered.

Fortunately for him – with Billy Bonds gone - Redknapp wanted him back and Julian was gratefully reunited with his adoring fans. Harry recognised that Dicks was more than just an aggressive tackler and that he brought another element to the Hammers, with his accurate passing and powerful long-range shooting and he had great faith that the Liverpool debacle had 'humbled' Julian and had 'calmed' his erratic temperament down.

Redknapp remembers his earlier dealings with the hot-headed Dicks:

"When I first got to West Ham the club seemed to be built around Julian Dicks. He was a cult figure and, no doubt, an outstanding player but the influence he wielded was unhealthy.

Dicksy didn't like running, so pre-season training was a nightmare. 'What's all this s**t?' he would say. 'I'm not doing that crap'. And then his little acolytes would join forces with him and it was mayhem.

Dicksy's talent wasn't in doubt, but if I say he was a pest I am guilty of an outrageous understatement. He was, and I stress **was**, the most disruptive professional footballer I've ever come across. An absolute nightmare.

The fans idolised him to an extent that was, in many ways, unacceptable. In one game at Derby he got sent off after just 15 minutes for two yellow-card offences; two absolutely horrendous tackles. Yet, for the next 75 minutes the visiting West Ham fans chanted his name. That was completely out of order, because as far as I was concerned he'd let the team down; leaving his ten colleagues to work their socks off for an unlikely victory. Yet **they** didn't get a mention from the fans…

For someone with such immense talent, he was an appalling trainer. Every day he'd have a blazing row with Bill over something petty and Dicksy would just walk off the training pitch. The feeling among the other players about Dicks was mixed. He had his little group of mates who loved him but, if truth be known, there was an equally large group glad to see the back of him, once we off-loaded him to Liverpool…

He couldn't touch his toes if you gave him ten grand! During training he'd be strolling around at the back, as everyone else was exercising, muttering to himself; 'What a load of b******s'. But then, once the ball came out, he was like a man possessed. If a ball was there, he'd play for his life! With a ball, no-one at the club had the quality Dicks had. He could put it anywhere he wanted…

He could pull those kinds of stunts at West Ham, where he was 'a big fish in a small pond' but Liverpool sorted him out. All of a sudden Dicksy wasn't the big 'I am', when he returned to Upton Park. How could he be, when he'd been such a failure at Liverpool?"

However, despite the Board's own faith in Harry Redknapp, the season was actually less successful than the previous Bonds-led one.

Striker Trevor Morley – who had been West Ham's main source of goals for the previous few seasons - had missed most of the campaign through injury and thus the projected Morley-Cottee strike partnership never transpired, as Morley eventually departed from West Ham, without returning to the first team.

Another striker, Joey Beauchamp, turned into one of the weirdest stories ever to come out of Upton Park. [*At*

243

least, until Marco Boogers decided to rival him for 'mentalness'.]

Beauchamp was a young prospect, whom Bonds had bought for a million pounds from Oxford United. Beauchamp turned up at Upton Park; announced he was 'homesick' [!!!] and that he 'didn't want to play for them'. [*Oh, boo hoo! I suppose Green Street didn't sell Zebra-flavoured Farley's Rusks, either, you fool?*]

When you consider how many African, South American and Australian players there are today in the Premiership; let alone the multitude of European footballers in Britain, it amazes any sane human being that someone could feel 'too far from home', when they've just travelled down the bloody motorway! Unsurprisingly, an irritated Redknapp showed Beauchamp the exit door. [*Lucky, I guess, that it wasn't 'too far away'!*]

West Ham could beat Arsenal at Highbury and Chelsea at Stamford Bridge but yet they continued their infuriating age-old pattern of dropping points against other teams they were expected to beat. Thus, with two games remaining, the Hammers had to win one of them to guarantee our Premiership safety. Who were they against? Oh, only those s**t teams, Liverpool and Manchester United!

Much to Julian Dicks's delight, West Ham stuffed Liverpool 3-0 and were thus 'safe', but this was not good news for Blackburn Rovers, who needed defending champions Man Utd to 'not win' their final game of the campaign, in order that they themselves could win the title.

Popular defender Tony Gale had been sold to Blackburn and promptly won the title-winners medal he'd come so close to getting with the Hammers in 1985-6, thanks to

244

his former team-mates **again** pulling out all the stops against Alex Ferguson's men.

We might not have needed the points anymore but that was of little importance to the Upton Park fans. They'd come to make sure that the hated Paul Ince didn't get his disloyal little mittens on another medal and in that, they were entirely successful.

Ince had angrily responded to the Hammers fans chants of 'Judas' by calling them 'morons'. However, many years later – after Ince had established himself as one of Europe's premier midfielders, via playing for the likes of Inter Milan and Liverpool; as well as captaining England - he admitted in an interview that he had been 'naive' in agreeing to be photographed, smilingly posing in a Man Utd shirt. He also claimed that, like Dicks, he'd had 'no respect for Lou Macari' and that **that** had been the principal reason behind his wanting to leave West Ham. *I had no respect for Macari but you didn't see **me** leaving Upton Park...Not until the grounds-man found me hiding in his shed, anyway.*

[I personally had mixed feelings here. As much as I too booed the 'villain' Ince, as if he were the Child-Catcher from *'Chitty Chitty Bang Bang'*, I resented the fact that Jack Walker's millions had effectively 'bought' the Premiership title for Blackburn, by simply opening his expansive wallet and amassing some of the best individuals money could buy. (*A la Chelsea, several seasons later.*)

The only consolation was that Blackburn's time at the top was a brief one and they soon returned to being an unsuccessful, boring team to watch. Unlike Chelsea, unfortunately, as Russian Billionaire owner Roman Abramovich has even deeper pockets than Walker and can afford to **keep** buying them bloody success; along with every decent West Ham player his managers take a liking to!]

A deliriously happy Upton Park watched West Ham fight tooth-and-nail to deprive the talent-laden Manchester United side the title, and Ludek Miklosko performed miracles that day, to defy Man U's bombardment of the West Ham goal.

The final 15 minutes was a red tidal wave crashing against the unmoving Hammers goalkeeper. Even Ferguson was moved to admit that; "Miklosko was fantastic".

The 1-1 draw was enough to gift Blackburn the title and a delighted Tony Gale led the Rovers players in a heartfelt rendition of *'I'm Forever Blowing Bubbles'*, as Blackburn celebrated this unlikely result.

*

The one thing which Harry Redknapp is best remembered for, in his stint as Hammers manager, is the - generally - woeful transfer dealings he began to engage in, in earnest, in the 1995-6 season. For every diamond Harry managed to unearth, there were half-a-dozen cubic zirconia 'foreign talents'.

Midfielders Allen and Hutchison were sold and, in their place, came a veritable feast of misfits. Winger Stan Lazaridis, from Australia and defender Slaven Bilic, from Croatia were actually useful additions, but couldn't-hit-a-cows-ass-with-a-banjo forward Ian 'is-that-your-real-face-or-are-you-still-celebrating-Halloween' Dowie became an object of derision to the Hammers fans. Worse, though – for at least Dowie **tried** to score – were the £2.5 million record signing, Romanian international striker Ilie Dumitrescu and aspiring mentalist Marco Boogers, from Holland.

Boogers was – supposedly – an undiscovered sensation; purchased for a million pounds and hailed as 'an exciting talent'. Well, we never found out if that was true because, after being sent off in only his second game for a ridiculous challenge on Manchester United's Gary Neville, which would've been more suited to the UFC, Boogers returned to Holland and simply didn't come back; claiming to be suffering from stress! *He should've tried being a West Ham **fan,** instead of a player. Then he'd've known what stress was all about...not that he actually tried to be a West Ham player. And at least Dowie **was trying!***

Dumitrescu, meanwhile, whilst undoubtedly talented, hardly appeared on the pitch; Redknapp claiming that the Romanian 'didn't like the physical nature of English football'. *At least Dowie didn't mind the physical...etc.*

Steve Potts – American born but who had represented England at Youth team level – had proven to be the consummate professional and an able captain, since assuming the armband from 'naughty' Dicks. However, Redknapp decided that Julian deserved to have another chance at the captaincy and so, of course, Dicks made a complete arse of himself yet again.

In the match against Chelsea, he was accused of deliberately stamping upon John Spencer's head and, in the very next game, was sent off against Arsenal, for an awful foul on Ian Wright.

It was surely only a matter of time before he ran on to the pitch, swinging some pool balls inside a sock and screaming; **"Who's the f*****g daddy, now?"**

[Hard-man actor Ray Winstone is a Hammers fan, funnily enough. Bless him.]

MP David Mellor refrained from calling Julian 'Scum' – *see what I did there?* – but publicly stated that Dicks was "an animal" and the FA took a dim view of Julian's unhinged actions; banning him for an extra three matches for 'bringing the game into disrepute'.

It was hard to see when it was all going to end with Julian; although he ended up second-top scorer that season, behind Tony Cottee.

Therein lay West Ham's biggest problem that campaign. Although they managed to finish in a much-improved 10th position, goals had been hard to come by and when it was announced that Tony Cottee was 'moving on' again, at the start of the 1996-7 season, it became obvious that Harry needed to sign a top-class striker to complement Dowie's obvious skills. Lol.

Dumitrescu was off-loaded and Harry continued his close-your-eyes-and-stick-a-pin-in-a-map-of-Europe method of choosing players by signing – and then almost immediately selling – another Romanian international misfit, Florin Raducioiu and Portuguese eccentric Paulo Futre – just to prove that Harry was a European Equal Opportunities bad judge – who made a massive four appearances before disappearing.

[To further highlight the craziness of this period, Redknapp later related how Futre was aghast to discover that he wouldn't be wearing the number 10 shirt he'd always worn at previous clubs. He remarkably – after initially throwing his dummy out of the pram and refusing to play, unless he be given the number 10 – offered current incumbent John Moncur £100,000 to 'buy the shirt from him'. *He could've bought one from the Hammers gift shop for £30! Mind you, it would've said 'Moncur' on the back.*

Sanity, eventually, prevailed and Moncur allowed him to take the shirt, in exchange for a fortnight's holiday in Futre's villa in Portugal. *If 'sanity' had **really** prevailed,*

248

*Moncur would've taken the money; as he would have got the shirt back within weeks anyway **and** been a hundred grand richer, thanks to that shmuck Futre buggering off.*]

Fellow Portuguese playmaker Hugo Porfirio proved to be a slightly better buy; managing 15 appearances and contributing 4 goals but, once again, goals were few-and-far-between that season and the fans – used to seeing the free-scoring West Ham sides of previous decades – began to voice their unease; no longer enjoying the spectacle of the stuttering football at Upton Park.

When the Hammers went out of the FA Cup, in the 3rd round, to lowly Wrexham, angry supporters invaded the pitch and protested. It appeared that Redknapp was making both ridiculously random transfers **and** team selections and many of the foreign signings seemed apathetic about wearing the famous claret-and-blue.

[Although Harry defended his transfer dealings by insisting that West Ham United simply didn't have the finances to buy 'the very best players' and so he had to take chances with ex-internationals who were past their best, or temperamental unknown quantities that had been recommended to him.]

As a disorganised West Ham side plummeted towards relegation Harry **finally** made some shrewd acquisitions and the three players he purchased, as the season wound down, basically saved the Hammers from demotion.

Midfield toiler and combative battler Steve Lomas, was bought from Manchester City for £1.6 million but it was the strike pairing of the nippy Paul Kitson – £2.5 million from Newcastle – and young powerhouse John Hartson – £3.25 million from Arsenal – that inspired a remarkable revival.

It all began with an incredible 4-3 victory against Spurs, in a real barnstormer of a match and survival was guaranteed when Kitson's hat-trick and Hartson's brace, helped West Ham thrash Sheffield Wednesday 5-1.

Remarkably, Kitson would tie with Dicks for the position of 'top scorer' that season; even though he'd only played in the last 14 matches; again highlighting the woeful strike rate, prior to Kitson and Hartson's arrival. [*Although Dowie's 2 Coca-Cola Cup goals proved invaluable.*]

Aside from the late arrivals, other plus points that season were the emergence from 'The Academy' of starlets Rio Ferdinand, in defence and Frank Lampard, Jnr in midfield; although many fans expressed reservations about Lampard; wondering whether dad's position in the Hammers hierarchy had influenced his inclusion. [The doubters would remain, right up until Lampard's eventual bitter departure.]

A negative was the loss of Slaven Bilic, at the end of the season. Bilic had proven to be a calm, cultured, steadying presence in defence, when others were 'losing their head' around him, but then he announced that he wanted to move to 'a bigger club'.

At this point Everton were hardly a 'bigger club'; having fallen away from 'the big boys' in the division – *unless you were comparing them with Dagenham & Redbridge* – but, nevertheless, they offered £4.5 million and, considering that Harry had only spent £1.5 million on Bilic, it was a nice profit for the Hammers.

*

In total contrast to the chaos of the ill-fated foreign transfers and resultant disjointed football and fan unrest of the '96-7 season, 1997-8 would prove to be –

completely unexpectedly – West Ham United's best Premiership season thus far.

It appeared as if Redknapp had suddenly found the winning formula at last and memories of '85-6 were provoked with some of the Hammers' stirring performances that campaign.

Harry purchased the Israeli playmaker Eyal Berkovic but then decided not to raid-and-pillage any other far-flung foreign locations and stuck to spending the remainder of the 'Bilic money' on Blackburn's solid defender Ian Pearce and Queens Park Rangers duo; defender Andy Impey and talented winger Trevor Sinclair.

Julian Dicks was ruled out for the entire season, after undergoing major surgery on his damaged left knee and, in the injured Dick's absence, Harry made the tenacious Steve Lomas his new captain.

There were two main stories that season; both centring around duos.

The emergence of Rio Ferdinand and Frank Lampard Junior, from the youth team, the previous season, continued apace, as both young men established themselves firmly in the first team.

Ferdinand looked particularly impressive, in the centre of the Hammers defence and the tall, gangling prospect was immediately compared to the young Bobby Moore. Many men had worn the number 6 shirt, since the departure of the legend but none had ever managed to live up to Mooro's over-powering reputation. Now, numerous observers believed that just such a man had been found; who **may** prove to become an enduring legend himself.

Comfortable on the ball; cool under pressure; quick and athletic, Rio appeared to have it all and this fact was not

251

lost on watching England manager Glenn Hoddle, who decided to include the youngster in his pre-World Cup squad. [Rio would go on to become – at 19 – the youngest-ever winner of the *'Hammer of the Year'* award that season.]

Unfortunately, Ferdinand's meteoric rise was temporarily halted when a drink-driving conviction caused a disappointed Hoddle to immediately omit him from the England set-up.

The situation wasn't helped by an overly-honest John Hartson commenting: "Rio's bad luck was to get caught. If we are honest, we must admit, we've all done it." [???!!!.]

[This omission, whilst understandable in 'wanting to set a good example', was slightly hypocritical in that Hoddle **had** included self-confessed alcoholic Tony Adams – *whose 'Addicted' is one of the better footballer autobiographies* – 'substance-using' gambling addict Paul Merson, and supremely talented but completely idiotic domestic abuser and regular drunkard Paul Gascoigne, in his squad. All that was missing was George Best as coach driver; Jimmy Greaves as caterer and Brian Clough as physio and England would have had the ultimate Stag Party from Hell! *But hey, I shouldn't criticise. 'People who live in glass houses...get very hot between July and September'!*

Even more hypocritical though, when you consider that Hoddle himself was later 'removed' from the England set-up by the FA, after the 'born-again' Christian claimed that some people had disabilities because it was God's way of punishing them for bad things they'd done in a previous life.

Wow! Whatever happened to the days of poor old Alfred Ramsey; whose only 'crime' was to pretend that he didn't come from Dagenham? Even Don 'abandon-ship' Revie seemed preferable to a man who held those sorts of retarded opinions being in charge of the national team!]

Fellow prospect Frank Lampard meanwhile, although also evidencing precocious talent, wasn't as warmly received by the cynical Hammers fans; who wondered whether he'd done enough to warrant an extended run in the side, or whether it was merely because he was Harry Redknapp's nephew that he'd achieved this.

The chunky teenager was given very little respect by some supporters and was regularly regaled with *'Who ate all the pies?'* chants, and the ever-popular Noel Coward ditty: *'One man couldn't carry,*
Couldn't carry Lampard.
One man and his forklift truck,
Couldn't carry Lampard.
Big Fat Frank, Big Fat Frank,
Big Fat Frankie Lampard'.

It was never going to be easy for the talented midfielder to convince a sceptical section of the support that he was anything other than an ex-players son and the manager's nepotism.

The main story that '97-8 campaign though, was the magical striking of John Hartson.

[*Actually, the **main** story was the incredible re-emergence of the Labour Party; although under the leadership of Tony Blair they were unrecognisable as the Labour Party 'of old' and even went under the moniker 'New Labour'.*

What this meant – effectively – was that Blair and Co had opted to target the middle-classes; recognising that

253

the John Major Government were widely perceived as 'weak', and thus altering Labour's historical targeting of the working-class vote, and widening the Party's appeal.

With the thumping tune of D-REAMS' 'Things Can Only Get Better', backing his campaign, Blair swept to victory in 1997's General Election; promising Britain 'a brighter future'...'And Like My Dreams...come on, you know the words by now...']

Hartson and Kitson had hinted at their strike-partnership potential when they'd jointly saved the Hammers from relegation, the previous season but Kitson was unfortunately injured, early in this campaign.

John, though, opened the new season explosively. Hartson was on fire. [*Oh no, it's alright; it's just his ginger hair!*] The physically imposing striker terrorised defenders with his bustling, all-action displays and smashed in goals for fun. If only Kitson had been around to help maintain John's focus and ease the pressure on the striker, West Ham would have qualified for Europe. However, Hartson's 'fire' dimmed and the hunger for goals abruptly left him.

By his own admission, a self-satisfied Hartson felt that he'd 'done his bit' for the side [!] and, after slamming in 20 goals in the first half of the season, he would add only a paltry 4 over the second half.

In fact, there was a danger that the striker was being possessed by the spirit of Julian Dicks, when he was sent off twice for blatantly violent offences, and the 9-game suspension he served for these transgressions effectively killed West Ham's hopes of a UEFA Cup berth.

For fans who had hoped that Hartson-Kitson were going to be the new Cottee-McAvennie, they were disappointed. Kitson would never rival the consistent strike rate of Cottee, but Hartson **did** prove to be surprisingly akin to McAvennie in that, after a storming start to his Hammers career, he would peter out with a whimper.

West Ham eventually finished in 8th place, after looking a certainty to qualify for Europe for most of the season and there can be little doubt that – had Hartson not imploded and Kitson not been injured – the Hammers would have tasted European football for the first time in years.

[Best wins were the 4-1 demolition of Crystal Palace and 6-0 thrashing of Barnsley but, perhaps, the most exciting games were the dramatic FA and Coca-Cola Cup quarter-final defeats to eventual Double-winners Arsenal, in which the Hammers went out on penalties.]

*

"Tell me quick…Ain't That A Kick, In The Head?"

Season 1998-9 carries special significance for me; not merely because it would turn out to be West Ham United's best-ever season in the Premiership but because it saw the introduction of one of the greatest players ever to wear the claret-and-blue and one of my personal all-time favourite footballers. [But more of him later.]

Dr.Martens became the new sponsors of West Ham United and there's never been a more appropriate benefactor than the purveyors of some of the finest boots ever to adorn the I.C.F.'s little tootsies.

One guy who would've really suited having '*Dr.Marten's*' emblazoned across his chest was the skinhead stomper himself Julian Dicks but he was

255

forced to retire from the game after an abortive attempt at a comeback, following his knee surgery.

The out-of-favour Ian Bishop returned to his former club Manchester City and Redknapp purchased a motley selection of characters to 'bolster' the squad.

Goalkeeper Shaka Hislop was recruited from Newcastle and would prove to be a solid procurement. Arsenal's goalscoring legend Ian Wright and Liverpool's 'hard man' defender Neil Ruddock, had both been great professionals in their prime. Problem was; that prime was definitely in the past tense by the time they arrived at Upton Park; although Wright had a reasonably good season and his ultra-competitiveness resulted in his being the Hammers top scorer.

The biggest 'busts' though, were the Chilean World Cup star Javier Margas – who hardly even appeared for the Hammers; claiming to be 'homesick' for Oxford. *Oh, sorry, I meant South America. It's so easy to confuse the two, as that chump Beauchamp thought that they were equi-distant from Upton Park* – and record £4.5 million signing, Cameroon international Marc-Vivien Foe; as Harry continued his less-than-impressive delves into the global market.

It was, actually, a pretty weird season altogether and, in hindsight, hard to understand how we managed to finally qualify for Europe, as West Ham's form was madly inconsistent throughout.

High-scoring 5-1 and 4-0 wins against Derby and Middlesbrough respectively, were outweighed by some awful defeats; notably, 4-0 and 5-1 losses to Leeds; 4-0 defeats to Arsenal and Sheffield Wednesday; a 6-0 hammering by Everton and a 4-1 loss to eventual Champions Manchester United.

However, the most ridiculous and plain **annoying** 'performance' of the season had to be when West Ham somehow contrived to lose 4-3, at home to Wimbledon, after leading 3-0!

It was fortunate that the Hammers managed to secure enough wins in their other fixtures, to negate these poor performances and manage a lofty 5th place position, when the season had climaxed.

But the real drama that campaign occurred off the pitch and behind-the-scenes, as Upton Park became a virtual den of iniquity. [*Ooh, I like that phrase!*]

The first home game of the season had 'welcomed' Manchester United to Upton Park and the hostile reception David Beckham received that day from the Hammers fans exceeded even the vitriol they usually reserved for Paul Ince.

Beckham had been roundly condemned in the media, as being the man largely responsible for England's World Cup exit against the hated Argentines, following his ridiculous sending-off. Beckham suddenly found himself 'public enemy no.1' and the foul-mouthed abuse he received at the Boleyn Ground gave little indication that he would soon 'redeem himself' and become one of England's most loved and influential players, as well as a pop-culture icon and fashion pin-up.

[The story of the noose-wearing effigy of Beckham, hanging outside the Boleyn Ground though, was unfounded and was later believed to have been a newspaper stunt; the dummy not even in East London. *He was in Oxford!*]

But this was minor news compared to the 'big story' that season; the infamous training ground 'incident'.

In the previous campaign fans had been shocked to see John Moncur and Eyal Berkovic 'square-up' to each other, in the defeat against Chelsea; seemingly ready to exchange blows.

Moncur had given Berkovic a tongue-lashing – *though not the same type as in 'Fifty Shades of Grey'* – and Eyal had angrily responded by slapping him around the face. [*Alright; maybe it **was** a bit like 'Fifty Shades'!*]

Although Moncur tried to laugh it off, Berkovic claimed that Moncur was 'jealous of him'. [?] There were rumours that Eyal was less-than-popular with the other players and that, one day; someone was going to 'iron him out' [*See what I did again?*]

An over-weight and sadly out-of-form John Hartson performed the two most accurate kicks of his season at the Hammers' Chadwell Heath training ground. The first was against Berkovic's legs and sent him crashing to the floor. The second was a stunning volley to Eyal's head that almost decapitated him!

Sky Sports were filming the training session, as part of their 'build-up footage' for West Ham's forthcoming live game with Southampton and the clip of Hartson's 'assault' on his team-mate became manna from Heaven for the salivating media.

Redknapp admitted, in his 1998 autobiography:

"The story was nothing without the pictures. It was the video footage, and its sheer savagery, that took the breath away. It was a horrific thing to see, and the more I saw it the more it sickened me."

There was a predictable media furore and an apparently repentant Hartson publicly apologised to Berkovic; who kindly accepted the Welshman's apology and then went to the papers and claimed that West Ham had initially tried to 'cover up the incident' and that Hartson enjoyed 'special privileges' at the club, because of his goalscoring exploits the previous season; adding that Hartson; 'should've been thrown out of the club', for the assault.

[It did appear somewhat strange that Redknapp claimed that it was 'a horrific thing to see' and that the attack had 'sickened him,' and yet then try and blithely dismiss the occurrence by claiming that incidents like that happened, in training, at every club.]

This all left Harry in a bit of a predicament, as many observers felt that he'd handled the situation badly and allowed it to fester.

Redknapp fined Hartson the maximum amount he was allowed to, but he was now equally angry with Berkovic, for the allegations he had made in the newspapers.

Speculation abounded that either John or Eyal would have to be sold, in order to put an end to the on-going controversy and the pressure increased when the FA announced that they would be 'investigating the incident' themselves. However, attention was temporarily deflected by a new drama; namely, a public bust-up between Redknapp and Managing Director Peter Storrie.

Prior to the game against Derby, Harry was instructed 'not to play Andy Impey'. [*The fans had been instructing him this, for months but, hey!*]

The Board had agreed to sell Impey to Leicester for £1.5 million but Redknapp wasn't happy in their 'meddling' with his team affairs and publicly said so.

From ' *'Arry':*

"I criticised the West Ham Board and said that the decision to sell Impey had been made by people who knew nothing about football. Remember that at that

259

stage we were in the top six of the Premiership and pushing for a place in the top four.

'I'm not a mug and I don't need a job that badly that I'll let people walk all over me', I blasted. 'If someone walks in and says they're selling Rio Ferdinand without telling me, then I'll resign. They probably thought it's all right to sell Andy because the fans don't like him too much and no-one will really care. I've been undermined in front of my players and everyone else. The day I stop choosing who I buy and who I sell is the day I'm not managing a football club any more. Will I resign over this? Other people can resign first – **I'm** more important than they are'."

Peter Storrie took exception to these comments and stated: "We had to get a certain amount of money in to balance the books and now they **are** balanced. Harry always knew we had to do this, from the start of the season.

But what he said about the decision being made by people 'who know nothing about football' is insulting and I have taken it personally. Harry should remember that **no-one** is more important than West Ham."

Eventually, the dual 'dramas' resulted in two people departing before the season's conclusion; John Hartson and Peter Storrie. [Berkovic would follow at season's end.]

Remarkably, 'little' Wimbledon came in with a massive £7.5 million pound offer for Hartson, which Redknapp gleefully accepted.

In one of those strange quirks which football often throws up, John made his home debut for Wimbledon against West Ham [!] and was taunted throughout by the travelling Hammers fans. Chants of *'Hartson, Hartson's going bald; Hartson's going bald'*, visibly

260

angered the going-bald Hartson, who snapped afterwards that he 'thought he deserved more respect from the West Ham fans' for all that he'd done for them. [*That* **was** *respect, compared to the reception Paul Ince – and, later – Frank Lampard would engender!*]

Ian Wright, who had caused a mixed reaction amongst the supporters; some liking his arrogance, whilst others considered him 'too mouthy' – *did you ever watch his 'Friday Night's All Wright' TV chat show? God, you'd've wanted to throttle the fool that came up with* **that** *'great idea'* – also moved on, and Redknapp needed to replenish his waning strikeforce.

Thus, he invested some of the Hartson money on Derby County's Paolo Wanchope and Sheffield Wednesday's Paolo Di Canio: Upton Park sucked in its breath.

*

INTERLUDE
<u>A WEST HAM FAN'S MEMORIES.   NO.5</u>

Name: Dave Garner. **Age:** 50. **Profession:** UNITE Union Shop Steward. **Born:** Rainham, Essex. [Now living in Leyton, East London.] **Connection to West Ham:** Lifelong fan, and Season Ticket holder.

Why do you support West Ham?

"I didn't have a choice! My dad and my grand-dad were both big West Ham fans and they dragged me along - literally – to my first game, when I was 6. I wasn't interested in football before that.

They took me to a reserve match first; as the crowds were small and they didn't have to worry about me in a big crowd. Soon though, they took me to my first 'proper' game and I was just hooked, as soon as I saw the claret-and-blue."

Who is your all-time favourite West Ham player and why?

*"Am I really only allowed to choose one? I've got **three** all-time favourites but, if I **had** to pick just one...it would be Trevor Brooking.*

*The things he could do on the pitch; the way he carried himself **off** the pitch; everything he did just exuded class.*

It still amazes me, when I watch videos of him. It doesn't even look like he's running! He glided. And the way he just stroked the ball on to players heads...

If I could choose a second player, it would be Julian Dicks. I loved everything about Julian – including the violence – and his total commitment.

Third, would be Paolo Di Canio, for the sheer excitement he brought on to the pitch."

Who was your least favourite West Ham player and why?

*"David Kelly! I'm not saying that he was the **worst** player we've ever had but – despite the fact that he came to West Ham with a big reputation – to me, he was just a 'journeyman'.*

*He didn't score enough goals; he didn't **do** enough, and he spent too much time on his arse!"*

What's your strongest single memory of supporting West Ham United?

*"My strongest memory is **also** my favourite game".*

[**Author:** Don't you just hate it when they pre-empt your next question? Although it saves on typing time and the amount of money I spend on alcohol when interviewing these people. Bless him!]

"You may find it hard to believe, but it's the 4-0 FA Cup semi-final defeat to Nottingham Forest!

That's purely because, from 2-0 down, all the way through to the end, we sang without a break: 'Billy Bonds's Claret-and-Blue Army'. The entire section of West Ham fans were bouncing up-and-down on the terraces, until the final whistle.

I heard that Bobby Charlton – who was one of the TV commentators – said that he'd 'never heard anything like it'.

That game showed – to me – what West Ham is all about. We had a player sent off unjustly; then we threw absolutely everything we had at them. Even when we were 2-0, 3-0 and then 4-0 down, the fans were singing. Even the Forest fans applauded us at the end!"

What's the worst game you ever saw / worst experience?

"Worst game I ever saw was the 6-0 defeat in the League Cup, against Oldham.

*It was p*****g down with rain; gale force winds; West Ham were in the uncovered end of the old Boundary Ground; I was freezing cold; soaking wet, and we lost 6-0 to a rubbish team and then had to travel home; and so I'll never forget that game. It was the worst experience of my entire life as a West Ham fan!"*

Any non-football pitch related anecdotes around supporting West Ham?

*"My **worst** non-football pitch related memory is of having my nose broken at Chelsea. I can't remember the actual year but I was only a young kid. I'd just started going to games with my mates, instead of with my dad, and we'd gone to Stamford Bridge but couldn't get in to the West Ham supporters end; all of the Away tickets were gone. So, we had to go into the Chelsea end of the stadium.*

There were about eight or nine of us, stood at the back of The Shed. These were the pre-I.C.F. days – or, at least, in the very early days of the I.C.F. – and you just didn't go into the opponent's end. We knew we had to keep quiet and not give ourselves away as West Ham fans, or we'd be in trouble.

Tommy Taylor kicked Peter Bonetti in the head and he had to go off injured. These were the days before goalkeeper substitutes. I can't remember who took over in goal but, from 1-0 down, we went 3-1 up and – when the third goal went in – I went mad.

Well; we got pulled out of The Shed by the St John's Ambulance men! We were basically kicked all the way from the back of The Shed to the front. I don't remember seeing the sky once. All I saw, with my head down, was the boots of the Chelsea boys kicking the s**t out of me!"

[**Author:** That match took place in 1972, and thus the 10 year old Dave's nose was broken by those brave Chelsea hooligans. The same men who would subsequently melt at the very presence of Bill Gardner and Co.

But, that's what happens when you marry your cousin. Your offspring discover an affinity for wearing blue football strips and appearing on Jeremy Kyle, with their obese mother-in-law, in her best velour tracksuit.]

Ever had an affinity for another club and / or hated another club, and why?

"One year, my mate and I decided that we'd follow a non-League club, as well as West Ham. Crawley Town were doing well that season and so we started to go and see them.

The first game we saw was against Luton and the atmosphere was terrific. Even though the crowds were very small, they were really enthusiastic and Crawley ended up winning promotion to the League.

So, we carried on watching them in League 2 and they promptly went straight up to League One".

[Laughs.] *"I've now got my Crawley Town scarf and consider myself a 'proper' Crawley fan but, if they ever drew West Ham in the FA Cup, I'd want West Ham to stuff them!*

Ever hated another club?...Millwall and Spurs!

The era I grew up in, you automatically hated Millwall and Spurs, if you were a West Ham fan, but we hardly ever played Millwall; we were always in different leagues, and so Tottenham were our 'natural' rivals.

[I think because they were so smug when they were a decent side, and wanted to rub everybody's noses in it. Thing is; they haven't been a decent side for years; and yet they still smugly act as if they are.]

The reason that I, personally, hate Millwall is because – as a Trade Union official – I'm aware of Unions, strikes and working class protest history, and the Millwall Dockers refused to join the East London and other Dockers in the General Strike of 1926, and subsequent strikes in which East London Dockers tried to make a stand.

None of the country's other Dockers liked Millwall; well, certainly, no-one in the East End liked them!

West Ham are working class, but Millwall can't call themselves that; they don't deserve to.

I loathe them – and their football team – for that very reason! Football's tribal – defending your territory, and all that – and West Ham-Millwall – along with most intense rivalries – is a modern-day tribal rivalry".

*

Chapter Six: *La Donna e Mobile. [Sung to the tune of Paolo Di Canio]*

'That Italian geezer's no pushover!'
[Alternate subtitle: *'Some People Think I'm Bonkers, But I Just Think I'm <u>Me!</u>'*]

You may well have noticed, as you perused this elegant tome, that I have enthused over several players; most notably, the incomparable Bobby Moore; the marvellous Geoff Hurst and the inspirational Billy Bonds, amongst others. Now, I would like to add another maestro to this list of West Ham United legends; the paradox that is Paolo Di Canio.

Paolo was raised in a rough environment in his native Italy and soon became passionate about football, as a child. By the time he was in his teens, however, it wasn't just by displaying his emergent skills on a football pitch that he exhibited his fervour; for the young Di Canio became 'caught up' in his team Lazio's football hooligan firm.

From his autobiography, simply – but oh, so elegantly – titled *'Paolo Di Canio'* [2000]:

"The thing to remember is that when you're in a mob, everything changes. All of a sudden, there is a mental transformation; you are no longer the same person. I've seen the calmest, most mild-mannered guys turn into absolute thugs. There's always a flashpoint, a moment when the strength and power of the mob overcomes you and you lose your sense of right and wrong. Or, rather, you develop a different sense of 'right and wrong'.

It's not something I really enjoy talking about now. After all, I'm 32 years old and I am a father, with two daughters. I should be an example to them. But I cannot turn my back on my youth, because that has contributed to making me what I am today…

There is so much talk these days of hooliganism, of fans getting stabbed. That is another matter. Punch-ups and fistfights have been a part of football support for some time. My father used to tell me stories about Rome derbies which ended in fisticuffs between the fans. There **is** such a thing as a 'healthy punch-up'. It's when it grows out of control; when it starts involving fifty, sixty people running at each other with knives or bottles, injuring innocent bystanders, **that's** when it becomes a problem.

That's the difficult part to understand; there's a fine line and, in some areas, it's pretty much invisible. But while violence is wrong in principle, physical confrontation can be beneficial.

Punch-ups are a fact of life. I'm not urging people to beat each other up, I am just saying that they happen and they can actually teach you a thing or two about yourself. Again, perhaps it's a function of where I grew up, but I got my ass kicked many times by people who were bigger, stronger or just meaner than I was…It was about surviving though, and it's a philosophy I have taken with me on to the pitch. Football doesn't have to be a battle but, if you treat it as one and you're a warrior, you will come out on top. On the pitch, you need that edge, that hunger which allows you to get to the ball first."

This aggressive side of Di Canio surfaced several times over the years, in dressing-room confrontations with his managers.

In Italy, Paolo swapped blows and obscenities with future England manager Fabio Capello and; after Di Canio angrily punched the much-larger Ron Atkinson in a dressing-room row, the manager – showing there were definitely 'no hard feelings' - made him captain of Sheffield Wednesday!

There was no doubting Paolo's supreme skill with a football but, there was also no doubt that his passionate temperament could get the better of him, and he was seen as a bit of a 'loose cannon' emotionally.

Thus, Di Canio had changed clubs many times in his career before he arrived at Upton Park; representing Lazio, Juventus, Napoli and AC Milan, in Italy, before moving on to Celtic.

Di Canio enjoyed his time in Scotland but was disappointed at the lack of competition in Scottish football – Celtic and Rangers being the only two teams of note – and so he jumped at the chance of a move to the English Premiership and Sheffield Wednesday.

Things were going well for Paolo until the fateful day he assaulted Martin Keown's elbow with his nose!

In the midst of a tussle with the Arsenal defender, Keown deliberately elbowed Di Canio in the face. Paolo reacted angrily and retaliated but was then dismayed when referee Paul Alcock – *or so he claimed, to the ladies* – only red-carded Di Canio.

Paolo pushed Alcock, in his frustration, and Alcock theatrically tumbled to the floor like Bambi on ice.

[Keown was confusingly red-carded, subsequently, on the advice of the linesman but then had the red card rescinded by the FA, upon appeal.]

An 'assault' upon a referee was virtually unheard of and, when Paolo appeared before an FA Disciplinary Committee, he was banned for 11 matches.

Sheffield Wednesday decided to 'wash their hands of him' – *ooh, like Pontius Pilate, you mean?* – and Harry Redknapp stepped forward and offered them a meagre

£1,750,000 for the Italian's services; knowing that they were keen to sell a player, whom they had come to view as a liability.

From *'Paolo Di Canio'*:

"I knew I would have to give a press conference when I signed. It would be the very first time I spoke in public to the British press, since the Alcock incident and I feared it could get confrontational. But Redknapp was excellent. He managed to tone everything down. When they asked me about Wednesday I simply said: 'I'm lucky to move to a better club than Sheffield Wednesday'.

Which was the truth! There was no comparison between the two clubs, on or off the pitch. One of the main differences was the atmosphere in the dressing-room.

Sheffield Wednesday was a small-minded provincial club and I could tell that some players were jealous of me. I think that they had some kind of inferiority complex and they reacted by turning on me.

They are people who didn't understand that they had a chance to play alongside a guy whose talent and experience was so much greater than theirs. I could have taught them so much…

At West Ham I found a perfect environment. There are plenty of talented players here, but even the most skilful understand that you're never too old to learn something. I think they understand that perhaps, in terms of experience and vision, I can give them a little bit extra. Rather than resenting my presence, they try to learn from me and I, in turn, learn from them.

When I first walked into the West Ham dressing room, everybody was laughing, joking. It was the polar opposite of Sheffield Wednesday. At first I thought to myself; 'My God, this is a lunatic asylum!' Then I

269

understood. This was the way it **should** be. Sheffield Wednesday was the **real** lunatic asylum.

I fell in love with that camaraderie right away. Each player was made to feel important; which is the way it should be in any team. I settled in quicker than I had anywhere else in my career."

As you can tell, Paolo's not exactly shy about sharing his self-confidence and belief in his skills with the reader! For once, though, a sportsman's egotism was well-deserved. Paolo Di Canio was a revelation at West Ham United and the fans immediately embraced this rare footballing treasure. Indeed, Redknapp would later describe him as his greatest signing.

As he walked out onto the Upton Park pitch, Paolo was greeted by the massed supporters with the simple chant, to the tune of the opera 'classic' La Donna e Mobile; *'Paolo Di Canio, Paolo Di Canio…'* He had finally found his spiritual home, in the East End of London.

*

Exodus!

Previously, finishing in 5th place would have been enough to guarantee European football but UEFA, in their infinite wisdom, decided to move the goalposts that season – [*Dowie still couldn't score!*] – and West Ham were forced to enter a qualifying tournament – the Inter-Toto Cup – in order to access the UEFA Cup proper.

Thus, the Hammers 1999-2000 season started early, as they dispatched Jokerit, of Finland, 2-1, Heerenveen of Holland 2-0, and the French side Metz 3-2, in order to reach the UEFA Cup first round.

In that first round they were paired with the Croatian side Osijek and destroyed them 6-1, over the two legs, with goals from Wanchope, Di Canio, Lampard, Kitson,

Foe and Ruddock; leading hopeful fans to believe that we were ready to conquer Europe's best. Consequently, we were dumped out in the second round, 2-0 on aggregate, by the Romanians Steaua Bucharest. All that was left to hope for was another good Premiership season and, perhaps, a decent domestic cup run. But, things are rarely that simple when you're a Hammers fan!

Reaching the quarter-final of the Worthington Cup – [the constantly re-named 'League Cup', of old] – West Ham triumphed over Aston Villa in a thrilling game, which epitomised everything gripping about cup matches. Unfortunately, the aftermath epitomised everything frustrating and demoralising for the average fan.

It emerged that the Hammers had fielded an ineligible player; someone who had been loaned out to another club, earlier in the season and who had represented that team in a previous round, before returning to West Ham.

The media leapt upon the debacle and West Ham became a source of ridicule. Who was to blame? Redknapp; for not realising that the player had already performed in the competition? The club secretary; for not checking the player's status? Or, as **I** prefer; to blame the player himself, - *and thus that's why I'm not even allowing the fool's name to appear in this book –* for not admitting to everyone that he'd already played in the Cup?

The League forced West Ham to replay the match and, of course, we lost and Villa duly advanced to the semi-final. As a result of this bitter disappointment, the club's secretary resigned and Redknapp offloaded the **chump** of a player.

[It was in this competition – in its 'Carling Cup' guise – that the last significant piece of football hooligan violence occurred at Upton Park.

The match against our most-hated rivals Millwall resulted in a 44 year old Millwall fan being stabbed in the chest and a remarkable **five hours** of fighting between the two sets of fans and the police!

It was also noted that the vast majority of those involved in the fighting were not teenagers or even men in their twenties, but were middle-aged males. Presumably, the remnants of the I.C.F. – *"We're West Ham and we run from no-one!"* - and the 'Bushwhackers'; taking this rare opportunity to have a reunion?]

The Villa debacle – and the match against Bradford, in the Premiership – summed up West Ham's crazy season.

1-0 down at home to unfancied Bradford, West Ham recovered to lead 2-1, through goals from Sinclair and Moncur. Bradford equalised before half-time and, early into the second half, led the Hammers by 4 goals to 2.

Then, the drama really started, and nothing summed-up the essence of Paolo Di Canio, more than the following: Here is Paolo's own – **[dramatic]** - recollection of his reaction after being denied a penalty. From *'Paolo Di Canio'*:

"I had been battling furiously, scratching and clawing my way for an opening, willing myself to succeed. For my troubles, I had been kicked and shoved, grabbed and gouged, often just a few feet away from the referee Neale Barry. Earlier, I had been felled, in the penalty area, right under Barry's watchful gaze.

Nothing.

Not even an acknowledgement that I had hit the ground.

272

In the 12th minute of the second half it happened again. This time, there was no question about it, **this time,** even if the referee hadn't seen it, he would have felt the force of the blow which caused me to lose my balance and crash to the ground.

Again, there was no call. Again, I had been summarily ignored.

That's when I sunk to my knees. That's when my world caved in.

I had been telling myself over-and-over again that referees are only human, that they are part of the game and that they make mistakes. But this was beyond anything I had ever experienced. This was total and utter humiliation.

I felt a rage well up inside me. I felt the anger of a million injustices, a million wrongs that went unpunished, a million vendettas that went unserved.

I waited for the adrenalin to kick in. I waited for that fire to engulf my body, the passion that had carried me through so many setbacks in the past, the spirit that made me pick myself up and charge back into battle.

But it wasn't coming.

In its place, wave after wave of frustration was rattling my brain. The realisation that the struggle was over, that my enemies had triumphed.

I felt it was time for the warrior to go home and rest.

I rose to one knee and signalled to my manager Harry Redknapp. I motioned to be taken off; to be substituted. Redknapp, perched on the edge of the dugout, looked at me and slowly shook his head. I saw his lips move. Even if the infernal din of Upton Park hadn't drowned out his words, I would not have heard him. But I knew what he was saying.

'Paolo, you're not coming off. Now get back out there and fight!'

Seeing that this man, this middle-aged figure who had faith in me when, to most Britons, I was either a madman or a disease blighting the national sport, still believed in me was the adrenalin injection I craved.

It started slowly and then it all came rushing back.

I was going to be stronger than my enemies. I would continue the struggle, because I was not alone, because I had supporters, teammates, friends who were behind me.

And because there would always be more glory in fighting on and losing than simply walking away."

[*Not really your typical footballer autobiography! But then, Paolo was never your 'typical' footballer. He was touched by God, you see...the Author says in a warm, loving and completely unbiased way.*]

An enraged Di Canio inspired one of the great comebacks, before an enraptured Upton Park crowd.

The referee – *probably realising that there are only a certain amount of times you can act like a bloody idiot before people become suspicious* – finally awarded West Ham a penalty and the Upton Park faithful were 'treated' to the sight of Di Canio and Frank Lampard, wrestling over the ball; loudly arguing over who was going to take the penalty!

You would've needed a shotgun to have won that argument with Paolo, on that day, and Di Canio blasted the ball into the Bradford net and then turned and berated Lampard, all the way back to the centre-circle, for daring to argue with football royalty over 'who should take the penalty'.

[*I fell in love with Paolo that day; though not in a homo-erotic sense! Not since Billy Bonds had I seen*

274

that kind of passion for the claret-and-blue cause. Well, apart from Julian Dicks, but I always had the feeling there that it wasn't necessarily that he 'loved West Ham'; more that he hated the human race, and any member of it that dared to try and run past him, in a pair of shorts.

Often, when my son James and I used to kick a ball around, we'd pretend to be our favourite players. Oh, come on; you've all done it! This was all well-and-good when he was Hartson and I was Brooking, but it became more complicated when we both wanted to be Di Canio.

*Obviously, as the older, more mature figure, I 'did the right thing'. I let James be someone else and **I was Di Canio!**]*

The rapidly emerging young talent Joe Cole scored the equaliser and then Upton Park exploded as Lampard made it 5-4 to West Ham, in the dying moments.

That was certainly the most thrilling game witnessed at Upton Park that season, but the most impressive performance was the 5-0 thrashing of Coventry. However, this was off-set by a 4-0 defeat to Everton and a humiliating 7-1 capitulation at the hands of Manchester United.

The highlight of the campaign, for Hammers fans, though was the incredible goal scored by Di Canio against Wimbledon. With the goals beginning to dry up, Redknapp had purchased French striker Frederic Kanoute, who promptly scored on his debut against the Dons. However, this was overshadowed by Paolo's stunning air-borne volley; which was voted 'Goal of the Season' by *Match of the Day*'s viewers.

As the ever-humble Paolo himself remembers:

275

"Too few people understand that there is a direct correlation between what you do in training and what you can do in matches. You have to approach both in exactly the same way.

I got a lot of praise for the volley I scored against Wimbledon. Sure, it was a spectacular goal. What I did was extremely difficult, because it requires total body control, timing and balance. Compared to a bicycle kick or a scissor-kick it is much more difficult, because in those situations your bodyweight is going backwards, which helps stabilise you. But when I struck the ball against Wimbledon, both feet were in the air; even just making contact with the ball was an achievement.

But goals like that don't come out of thin air. I was able to do it because it was something I had practised for hours and hours in training. I'd attempted it so many times that it became an instinctive gesture. As the cross came in, I didn't even think about what I was going to do. My brain just decided for me; it just happened."

It was no surprise that Di Canio finished the campaign as West Ham's top goalscorer, in their 9th place Premiership finish but, apart from Paolo's virtuoso displays, the emergence of the two 18 year olds – Joe Cole and Michael Carrick – were the main fan talking-points that season.

Certainly, the 'maestro' himself was impressed. From *'Paolo Di Canio'*:

"Michael Carrick is one of my favourite young players. I think originally he was considered a forward. I don't know why, because he is a natural leader in midfield. He is technically sound, very methodical and is a brilliant, creative decision-maker. Most of all, however, he has a winning mentality. You can't teach that, that's something you're born with. He is very strong mentally;

he is the kind of player you build championship sides around…

Joe Cole is one of the greatest talents – not just of his generation – but of the past twenty years…I see him do certain things with the ball and I have no clue how he does them. The way he spins off tackles, the way he dances through defenders, reminds me of a scaled-down Zinedine Zidane. His movements are so natural, feline; he's like a young tiger. He shows you the ball and then makes it disappear, like an illusionist. At the same time, he has the grace and control of a ballet dancer."

Praise indeed! Unfortunately, these two young talents – and others of their ilk – would soon be departing, as West Ham United followed these seasons of promise under Redknapp, with a demoralising decline and mass exodus of our best players.

*

On paper, West Ham appeared to have their best side in years, at the start of the 2000/2001 season. The promise of Cole on the left wing and Carrick in midfield; the continuing development of the ice-cool Ferdinand in defence and the energetic Lampard in midfield, and the strike pairing of Di Canio and Kanoute, all pointed towards European qualification.

Redknapp awarded the inspirational Di Canio the captaincy and Paolo again sweated blood for the Hammers cause; even turning down the opportunity to join the all-conquering Manchester United, and his old friend Gianluca Vialli, who'd taken over as Chelsea manager, just prior to the start of Abramovich's money-laden 'revolution'.

However, most of the other players lacked Paolo's consistency in their own form and West Ham became embroiled – *not for the first time, you may notice* – in a hugely disappointing battle against relegation.

Despite all of this bright young talent on display, the Hammers struggled to string two wins together and our safety was only guaranteed in the penultimate game of a bitterly unsatisfactory season.

Kanoute and Di Canio were the top scorers but goals had once again been hard to come by and the lone highlight of the campaign was the 1-0 FA Cup 4th round victory against Manchester United, at Old Trafford, which went some way to soothing the previous 7-1 humiliation by them.

At this point the talent-rich Man Utd were head-and-shoulders above all other competition and were expected to effortlessly sweep aside the Hammers – probably by an embarrassing amount of goals – but West Ham gave a gritty display that day and refused to bow under United's pressure; winning with a goal which said a lot about both Di Canio and United's goalkeeper Fabien Barthez.

Kanoute played Paolo through and he was one-on-one with the keeper. At this point Barthez stood straight up and raised his arm; signalling to Di Canio that he'd been ruled offside. This ruse failed and as Paolo calmly passed the ball beyond the embarrassed keeper, the travelling fans went into a frenzy of delight.

The main reason United and the likes of Arsenal, Liverpool and – now – Chelsea, were dominating the Premiership was simply because they were so financially superior to all of the other teams. Affording to 'cherry-pick' the best players and assemble squads of internationals, they were simply too strong – over the course of a season – for the chasing pack. Thus, when Redknapp was forced to sell the Premiership's best

278

young centre-back, Rio Ferdinand, for a then British record fee of £18 million, to Leeds, Harry wanted to know what West Ham's intentions were, in the transfer market. [*Ferdinand would subsequently move on to Manchester United for an incredible £30 million.*]

At season's end Harry met with Chairman Terence Brown and this meeting effectively sealed West Ham's fate.

An angry Redknapp demanded that he be allowed to spend the bulk of the Ferdinand fee, in order to buy quality replacements. However, allegedly Brown wasn't happy at how Harry had negotiated the Ferdinand transfer. A 'sell-on' bonus – [increasingly common at the time] - had not been included and thus West Ham missed out on a lucrative slice of Rio's move to Man United. Also, the money was being paid in instalments and had not been given as a lump sum 'upfront,' and Brown felt that Harry was being naive in demanding money for players, which West Ham didn't actually have in their bank.

Plus, apart from occasional buys such as Di Canio and recent acquisition – Scottish defender Christian Dailly – Harry's transfer dealings had been notoriously suspect, and Brown was reluctant to let Redknapp loose with a wad of money he may end up spending on a middle-aged Romanian bus driver who'd been 'recommended' to Harry by his bookmaker.

[*Things were further complicated when it became clear that Harry was friends with the agent of one of the players he was trying to convince the Board to allow him to buy. Indeed, accusations of 'bungs' and financial impropriety would haunt Redknapp over the following years; although he was never actually convicted of any wrong-doing.*]

The two men argued heatedly. Redknapp publicly criticised the Board, for not backing him and for 'not wanting to be a top six side'. He'd gotten away with such critical public outbursts against Peter Storrie, several years previously, but the charismatic Harry was not so lucky this time. The media loved him for his unfettered comments but the Board reacted to his volatile behaviour by sacking him!

[Redknapp would go on to manage Portsmouth and then Spurs; taking Tottenham into Europe before unexpectedly being sacked, despite guiding them to another fourth-placed finish.]

Perhaps unsurprisingly, Harry's assistant Frank Lampard also departed; a move which provoked his son Frank Junior to declare that he too wanted to leave; now that his dad and uncle were no longer associated with the club.

The fans, who had actually begun to lessen their chants and taunting of Lampard and had started to appreciate his burgeoning attacking-midfielder talents, now renewed their venom towards him, as they watched him leave 'the sinking ship' and move to Chelsea for £11 million.

Lampard Junior would become one of the top 'hate figures' at Upton Park thereafter, and took great delight in excessively celebrating any time he scored against his old team; unlike fellow 'leavers' Rio Ferdinand and, later, Joe Cole, who never celebrated their goals at Upton Park, out of respect for the team which had nurtured and developed their young talents. Perhaps because he'd never really been 'loved' by the Upton Park faithful, Lampard took a far more cynical approach to his old team. [*The fat b*****d!*]

Redknapp later admitted that he used to regularly swear at the chairman and berate him, in his time as manager, and so it wasn't a total surprise when Brown finally decided that he'd had enough. Harry reflected upon his dismissal and his thoughts upon the fans treatment of Lampard Junior, in *'Always Managing'*:

"Ultimately the end of my relationship with the chairman wasn't over anything as meaningful as our league position or transfer policy; it was an interview I gave to a West Ham fanzine *Over Land and Sea*. It was run by Gary Firmager, a typical West Ham nut and a bit of a lad. I was probably a bit more open with him than I would have been with a national newspaper journalist...

Gary started quoting some figures given to him by the chairman about the amount of the Ferdinand money that had been spent. I thought they were misleading figures...I didn't think Terry Brown was being fair. I made a flippant comment. 'Calls himself an accountant', I said. 'He can't even f***ing add up'...

When that month's edition of *Over Land and Sea* dropped, with my interview all over it, Terry didn't like some of the language I'd used, and he certainly didn't like being told that he 'couldn't f***ing add up'!

When I walked into his office he had his speech prepared. 'I'm not happy', he said. 'I think it's time you called it a day'.

And that was it. Do I regret giving that interview now? Absolutely. I didn't mean anything by it. I was just defending my corner against what I saw as a rather unfair appraisal of my record in the transfer market. I didn't think Terry would take it so personally, but I think I was most upset when Terry told me that he wanted Frank to leave too. 'What are you talking about?' I asked. 'He's more West Ham than you'll ever be!'"

And on the subject of Lampard Junior, Redknapp comments:

"Frank Lampard Junior's attitude was amazing, the best I have ever seen from a young player. But I know his secret: parental influence. The only professional I have known who came close to his commitment was his dad. 'Like father like son' is genuinely true in this case. If anyone ever marvelled at Frank Junior's dedication, I simply told them what I knew about Frank Senior. In my playing days at West Ham he was the best trainer at the club.

I remember Frank as a 17 year-old left-back with the pace of a three-legged carthorse. He was a lovely footballer, but he couldn't run. One day Ron Greenwood walked into the dressing room and told Frank, in front of everybody, that he had fixed him up with a move to Torquay United.

Frank was adamant. 'I don't want to play for Torquay', he said. 'I want to play for West Ham. What's wrong with me? What do I have to do?'

We were all looking at the floor, because young players just didn't speak to Mr Greenwood like that. There was silence.

'It's your speed', said Ron. 'You're not quick enough Frank.'

'I'll show you,' Frank shot back. 'I ain't going to Torquay. I'll play for West Ham.'

Everyone thought he was mad. Speed was considered a natural attribute in those days. You were born fast – or you just weren't. Nobody was going to get quicker simply by running. Yet Frank showed them all right.

He came back every day after training and would run and run. He'd be out there for hours on his own, working on these short sprints. And gradually he got quicker.

He used to ask me to stay back and help him sometimes, because I was a quick winger. At first, if I pushed the ball past him, I could give him a five yard start and still get it first. Ron was right – he couldn't run! Yet, the more he worked, the quicker he got, and in the end he could take me on in a straight race.

And when he was finished at the training ground, he would go home and run again. He'd put a sweat-suit on and go for a four-mile run. And he never missed a day. He had a determination that was unbelievable. You got in his way and he'd trample all over you. And his boy was exactly the same!

I remember when he came to the club. Just like his dad: technically a good player, but a bit dumpy and not very quick. The next time I saw him he had running shoes on. It was like watching Frank Senior all over again. And what an athlete he became…

Those fans who had it in for Frank hadn't seen how hard his dad worked to get to the top, so didn't know that I had recognised those exact same qualities in his son. By then, we had all noticed how outstanding Frank's attitude was. He loved football, he wanted to be a top player, and he had that essential determination…

I feel very upset about the way Frank is treated by West Ham supporters now. After Joe Cole left he would return to a standing ovation – the same with Rio Ferdinand – but the abuse they give Frank is merciless. I have never understood what he is supposed to have done wrong.

When they got rid of me in 2001, they kicked Frank Senior out as well and, unsurprisingly, having seen his dad and uncle sacked, Frank Junior didn't want to be there anymore.

The club got good money from Chelsea for him, so what's the problem?"

[*Answers on a postcard, Hammers fans. Please address them to: 'Why we hate that arrogant w****r Lampard' competition, Upton Park, E13...Sorry Harry!*]

Actually, despite Lampard probably being unfairly abused during his tenure at Upton Park, there can be little doubt as to *why* West Ham fans hated him afterwards; for Frank made no secret of the fact that he'd felt disrespected by Hammers fans, and consequently took great delight every time he scored against them. [*Which was a little too bloody often, for my liking!*]

Lampard even stated that he would love to score the goal which resulted in West Ham being relegated. [*Hold me back; **hold me back!***]

In his autobiography *'Why I'm a Fat B*****d'* – oh, no, my mistake; it was actually called **'Being Frank'**, - Lampard recalled:

"I remember when Joe Cole first came to Chelsea, he would turn away in disappointment if West Ham lost. I would smile! **That's** how deeply I felt. I **wanted** West Ham to lose".

[*And that, my dear Harry, is why they hate Frank Lampard, Junior!*]

*

Ex-Hammer Alan Curbishley was the favourite to replace Redknapp; having done a sterling job in lifting unfashionable Charlton Athletic into the Premiership and keeping them there. However, Curbishley declared that he 'wasn't interested' in the West Ham vacancy and the Board decided to appoint the man with zero personality; youth team coach Glenn Roeder, to the role. It was like having John Major at the helm; although, to be fair, Major at least had a vague idea about how to run the country. Roeder had **no clue** on 'how to run a football club'. [*Unless 'running it into the ground' counts.*]

Season 2001-2 was always going to be a struggle. With Ferdinand and Lampard gone, and young Cole and Carrick still learning their trade, the last thing West Ham needed was injuries. And thus, striker Freddie Kanoute, and the shining light that was Paolo Di Canio, all spent large chunks of the season out with injuries.

Roeder made two significant purchases though, which helped to bolster West Ham and at least make them harder to beat; defender Tomas Repka, from Fiorentina, and the re-purchase of battling midfielder Don Hutchison.

Demoralising 5-0 and 7-1 defeats to Everton and Blackburn respectively, early in the season, didn't give Hammers fans any reason to change their belief that Roeder was the wrong man for the job and yet, astoundingly, he managed to surprise everyone by marshalling the team of talented but largely 'green' individuals and getting them to work effectively as a solid unit; guiding them to a surprisingly high 7th place finish and thus only narrowly missing out on Europe.

This achievement was undoubtedly helped; both by the flourishing of Joe Cole's creative talents and by the emergence of the exciting young striker Jermain Defoe, who finished second-top scorer behind Kanoute.

But, Roeder flattered to deceive! 2002-3 brought the painful relegation many had anticipated with Roeder's appointment, and another exodus of our best players; as all of our worst fears and suspicions about Glenn were confirmed. He had 'flattered to deceive', and now he took us where we'd always feared he would; into despair.

Despite fielding a team which featured the rapidly-maturing talents of Cole, Carrick and Defoe, and promising young defender Glen Johnson, West Ham again suffered from the extended absences of Kanoute and Di Canio. Most damagingly, though, they suffered from Roeder's tactical ineptness and, – as fast and accurate as Defoe was, – it was far too early in the teenager's career to play him upfront as the lone striker; something which happened often that season.

[It's significant that Di Canio would finish top scorer; even though he missed a substantial portion of the campaign through injury.]

West Ham again made an awful start to the season but, unlike the previous year, failed to recover from it.

The fans quickly grew restless, as the Hammers languished at the bottom of the table and Roeder seemed helpless to prevent the team's decline. The combination of the embarrassing 6-0 thrashing by Manchester United, in the FA Cup and the **ridiculous** decision not to play a fit-again Paolo Di Canio – [who'd been vocal in his criticism of Roeder's management skills] – led the fans to chant for Roeder's head on a plate.

Strangely, God was listening and attempted to appease the Hammers fans by giving the manager a brain haemorrhage! Roeder collapsed with just three games of the season remaining and the old maestro Trevor Brooking – who had never lost his love for the club -

stepped forward and almost produced the miracle the Upton Park faithful were praying for.

Brooking unsurprisingly reinstated Di Canio and the old master and the current 'magician' worked their magic together to try and save their beloved West Ham.

Amazingly, West Ham beat both Manchester City and Chelsea, before drawing their final game with Birmingham. It wasn't **quite** enough, and a team which both Billy Bonds and Harry Redknapp described as 'West Ham's greatest ever squad of players', were relegated because of the manager's ineptness.

[I can say all of this with a clear conscience because Roeder didn't die. However, following his illness a fund was started by the club, in order to buy him a personality.]

One of the few highlights of the season had been the incredible ball-dribbling performances by Joe Cole; which had earned him the *'Hammer of the Year'* Award, from the appreciative fans. Unfortunately, it also earned him a transfer to big-spending Chelski; along with full-back prospect Glenn Johnson.

From *'Bring Me The Head of Trevor Brooking'*:

"Attacking football, played in a positive spirit, as a form of entertainment. If that has more-or-less been the West Ham Academy playing ethos down the years, then Joe Cole embodies those qualities better than any other Academician.

Cole's Hammers career was always going to be a relatively short one: salivating 'big club' suitors, the Hammers' financial constraints, and the player's own ambitions always made sure of that. Yet, while he went on to achieve great things with Chelsea before joining Liverpool in 2010, there is a school of thought that suggests it was East London – not West – where Cole

287

came closest to fulfilling the extraordinary levels of hype foisted on his shoulders.

Most of the early headlines centred on the amazing things he could do with a ball at his feet, and during Cole's four years as a first-teamer at Upton Park, he was plucky enough, naive enough and audaciously talented enough to want to dip into his bag of tricks as often as possible. For the large part, his adoring East End public were treated to Cole 'the free spirit', unfettered by militaristically defined responsibilities; unconstrained by a requirement to ceaselessly put graft before craft.

Like his team-mate Paolo Di Canio and his hero Zinedine Zidane, Cole was a team man by virtue of being able to 'turn' a game, but most of all he was loved for his unquenchable thirst for attempting the impossible and, very often, pulling it off."

Harry Redknapp felt that the teenage Cole was 'the best young prospect he'd ever seen' and had battled hard to convince the schoolboy to come to West Ham; especially in light of interest in him from Manchester United.

Remembers Redknapp: "I first saw Joe Cole when he was 12. The daftest bloke in the world could have spotted Joe was a star in the making. I remember standing there with Frank Lampard and we hadn't seen a kid like it in our lives. It must have been like watching Lionel Messi for the first time at that age. He was younger than all the other kids, the smallest one on the pitch, all these big teenage lads towering over him, and he was getting the ball, spinning away from them, beating three or four of them at a time and – goal. Then he'd do it again."

However, like Martin Peters before him, Joe seemed unable to convince both Redknapp and Roeder **where** exactly his best position was, and was played on the left wing, central midfield and in a roving position behind the strikers. Perhaps the truth was that – like Peters – Cole just needed to be given free rein to express himself on a football pitch and not be 'labelled' as a winger or midfielder.

Along with Cole and Johnson's departures to Chelsea, Sinclair left for Manchester City and Kanoute departed to Spurs. Most agonisingly, though, it was the end of the West Ham United adventure for Paolo Di Canio.

Rarely had a player given so much of himself on the field as Di Canio had for the Hammers and a saddened Paolo declared: "My four years at West Ham is an experience I will hold in my heart forever."

My feelings for Paolo were echoed by a reminiscence from comedian and actor – and West Ham obsessed – Russell Brand, in 2008:

"At full-time I was approached by a club official, who informed me that Paolo Di Canio was present and had asked to meet me. Through the vestibules and corridors of Upton Park I sweated and fretted the anxious journey that would lead to an audience with an icon.

In the flesh – though flesh seems inaccurate, as he is all sinew, muscle and passion – Di Canio is a force. Forever on the precipice of declarations and tears, he converses how he played; with captivating intensity and awesome commitment. He spoke of West Ham with such love and respect that I quite forgot myself.

At one point I touched his shoulder with my hand and it as if it were connected to the Earth's core, such was the throb of innate potency.

He referred to me and West Ham as 'You', e.g. 'You are a great club'; 'You deserve the best', and when he looked into my eyes it was as touching and as visceral as his volley against Chelsea or when he caught the ball to allow Everton goalkeeper Paul Gerrard to receive treatment, rather than score. The feelings were all too powerful.

'He's so passionate', I thought. I wanted to join in. 'I'm going to say something passionate too.'

After the umpteenth agonisingly sincere handshake I blurted: 'I want to thank you for all that you gave to this club'. I nearly wept.

'No. Thank **you**', retorted Paolo, far more at ease with this manner of discourse.

When he departed I reflected, with some relief, that no one who saw me watching Di Canio leave the room could ever seriously think I'd be interested in their girlfriend. My heart belongs to Di Canio."

Perhaps fittingly, Paolo returned to his first club Lazio, in Italy, but although the fans welcomed him back, the media and hierarchy criticised Di Canio's highly visual embracing of fascism, - [his fascist salutes to fans earning him a fine from the Italian FA] - and verbal admiration for the disgraced fascist dictator Benito Mussolini.

Because of his uncompromising and unpopular political stance, Paolo's contract with Lazio was not renewed, and instead of finishing his career with the club he'd supported as a boy, Paolo's career petered out with lower division Cisco Roma, in 2008.

In July 2010, West Ham United announced the opening of the Paolo Di Canio Lounge, in the Boleyn Ground's West Stand, in appreciation for the magnificent performances he had graced the Upton Park pitch with in his time there.

An emotional Di Canio declared that it was 'his destiny to one day return and manage West Ham United', but it was League Two's Swindon Town who gave him his first chance at a managerial career, and he rewarded them for their belief in his potential by gaining them promotion to League One in his first season.

However, controversy and Paolo Di Canio could not be separated for too long, and he resigned mid-way through the following season, unhappy at the financial constraints imposed on him by the cash-strapped club.

Premier League strugglers Sunderland then offered Di Canio a seemingly thankless opportunity to try and save them from relegation. Paolo duly obliged, and was rewarded for his efforts with the sack at the start of the following season; a group of Sunderland players complaining to the club's Board that Di Canio was 'brutal and vitriolic' in his criticism of them. [*They didn't deserve his talent and passion, the pathetic little Northern cry-baby's.*]

Di Canio meanwhile, proudly displaying the West Ham tattoo he had engraved upon his arm, continues to insist that he will lead the Hammers once more.

*

'London's Curry Capital!'

By 1999, 29% of London's population were from ethnic minorities; compared to just 9% in Great Britain as a whole. The Capital City was proud of this fact and celebrated its ethnic diversity; although not everyone was pleased, and deranged nail-bomber David Copeland targeted both a gay bar in Soho and East London's Brick Lane; nicknamed 'Bangla Town' and

'London's Curry Capital', because of its large Asian – particularly Bangladeshi – community.

[Pola Uddin – now Baroness Uddin – of Bethnal Green, became the first Bangladeshi to enter the House of Lords, in 1998, and thus also became the first Muslim peer.]

In fact, as the decades progressed, the East London Borough of Newham possessed the second-largest population of Muslims in England – around 25% - compared to approximately 45% of Christian residents.

This brought its own problems, though, after the terrorist bombings in Central London, of July 2005, in which 54 people were killed – including the Islamist extremist suicide bombers – and around 750 injured; and racial / religious tension was palpable in East London.

Seizing the opportunity, the successors to the National Front / British Movement; the British National Party [BNP] began vigorously campaigning in the East London and Essex areas; risking the ire of the ethnic communities and playing upon the unease felt by the White British residents. Indeed, the success they enjoyed in some areas was explained by white resentment towards African and Eastern European immigrants, who were perceived to be 'jumping the queue', regarding the offers of jobs and council accommodation.

Newham possessed a significant influx of Eastern Europeans and a 2001 census stated that Newham was 'the most ethnically diverse Borough in England' and, by 2004, Newham's ethnic minorities actually comprised over 50% of the inhabitants. [The only other London Borough to have a less-than-50% White British population was Brent.]

From 2000 onwards multi-racial street gangs proliferated in East London and over a dozen teenagers died because of gang-related violence. Older men, too, died over the course of the decade, as robberies and violence increased, largely due to the on-going battles over control of the drug trade.

Yardie-style contract killings, knife and gun crime and urban music festival gang violence became common-place in the East End; reflecting the larger problems nationally, which resulted in the awful riots of 2011, which devastated many major cities and towns and which placed a large question mark against Britain's ability to safely host the forthcoming Olympics.

Rap music had been under scrutiny for years, due to its alleged provocation of acts of violence and encouragement of negative stereotypes regarding women and gays; as well as glorifying the 'gangsta' lifestyle; sexual conquests; gang rivalries; drug use and even murder.

British youth had adopted the urban black culture of America's ghettos and the music and fashion of the U.S. streets was absorbed by Britain's teenagers; along with all of the positive and negative elements associated with this previously 'underground' music.

The violence around 'urban music' events was thus often linked to some of the lyrics of the compositions, and the new 'Grime' Music – a Bow, East London-born variation on UK Garage, British Hip-Hop and Dancehall – was widely condemned by some observers, for 'promoting killings and violence' through its often aggressive lyrics.

Originating in the late 1990's and gradually gaining in popularity via local East London pirate radio stations, 'Grime' would explode nationally in 2003, with the huge success engendered by one of its primary exponents, Bow-born Dizzee Rascal – real name Dylan Mills – and his hit *'Fix Up, Look Sharp'*; which would be followed by the likes of *'Dance Wiv Me'* and the annoyingly catchy *'Bonkers'*.

Rascal wasn't the only East London born musical artist to achieve national prominence around this time. Back in the late 1980's Whitechapel-born, Leytonstone-raised Damon Albarn had commenced his professional music career; finally achieving the success he'd desired in the mid-90's, as front-man and songwriter for the massive Brit-Pop band Blur.

Post-Dizzee Rascal, came the Forest Gate born rapper-singer, turned actor, Ben Drew – better known as Plan B – whose *'The Defamation of Strickland Banks'* CD dominated the charts in 2010.

*

It's dizzy, on the manager-go-round! [Featuring special guest: Avram Grant as 'The Undertaker'.]
Following the heartbreak of relegation, the fans all wanted Trevor Brooking to remain at the helm and guide West Ham straight back into the Premiership but Trevor had never intended to stay on as manager and so the Board cast their attention elsewhere.

[In 2009, the club would re-name The Centenary Stand, the Sir Trevor Brooking Stand, in honour of the midfielder's marvellous contributions to the team.]

Alan Curbishley still wasn't interested in the role – [perhaps he **still** didn't want to 'be in Brooking's shadow'?] – and so the Board recruited fellow-Championship side Reading's manager Alan Pardew; who was considered one of the best young managers in the game and was certainly tactically more astute than

294

Roeder. [*But, then, so were Noddy and any one of the Teletubbies!*].

The losses of most of our star names meant that it was a severely weakened West Ham team which Pardew inherited and he set about replacing them with the limited funds he had; although the task of supplanting the likes of Cole and Di Canio was an impossible one.

Jermain Defoe had chosen to become the latest Hammer to be the object of the fans hatred. He, too, had tried to leave at the end of the previous season but the Board angrily refused to accede to his written transfer request; insensitively handed in **immediately** following West Ham's relegation.

The ever-tactful Brooking described the act as 'bad timing', but Billy Bonds and Julian Dicks were more brutal; saying respectively, that it was 'a terrible thing to do' and was 'nothing short of disgraceful.' Dicks continued: "The fans are really hurting and this is a real kick in the teeth."

For now Defoe would remain but, in the January transfer window, the Board finally agreed to let Defoe go to Spurs for £7 million, plus striker Bobby Zamora in exchange.

The diminutive Jermain was taunted throughout his final games by chants of '*You're just a short Paul Ince*', and would be roundly jeered every time he appeared at Upton Park thereafter.

[To his credit, despite having his transfer request refused, Defoe scored 15 goals in 22 games before his eventual departure. However, the taunting of the fans began to have an effect and Defoe was sent off three times for ridiculously rash challenges, which perhaps reflected his unhappy state of mind. *The sulking little brat.*]

295

Apart from the arrival of the talented Zamora, Pardew also purchased fellow striker Marlon Harewood; whose lively, aggressive style of play brought him a commendable 26 goals that season.

Michael Carrick too would leave for Spurs, for a seemingly miserly £2.75 million. Not long afterwards he would move on to Manchester United for a far more realistic price tag of £18.5 million; Pardew attempting to replace him with a similar commanding midfield figure, in the shape of the young Nigel Reo-Coker.

Flying winger Matthew Etherington was also added to the side but it was perhaps expecting too much for the manager to be able to produce a cohesive team and garner instant promotion, when so many of the personnel were new and needed time to gel.

After a good start – and despite Harewood's healthy goal-tally – the Hammers form became erratic and they slumped from 2nd to 8th place. However, a good run of form towards the end of the season saw them climb back up to 4th and into the Play-offs; where they defeated Ipswich in the semi-finals; but then came the heartbreak of a 1-0 Play-Off Final defeat to South London rivals Crystal Palace, who had actually finished below us in 6th place.

Despite West Ham being favourites to win, they were disappointing on the day and missed several good chances to score. There would be no 'instant return' to the Premiership.

Nevertheless, despite the bitter disappointment of the Play-Off defeat, most fans believed that Pardew was 'the right man for the job' and just needed a bit more time to shape the side into the way he wanted them to perform.

This belief was sorely tested in the 2004-5 campaign!

Pardew made the all-action Reo-Coker captain; thus becoming West Ham's youngest-ever skipper, at the age of 20, and Alan took a bigger gamble when recruiting the 38 year old former Spurs and Man Utd striker Teddy Sheringham, to join the strike pairing of Harewood and Zamora. [Harewood again being the club's top scorer, although with a slightly less impressive 17 goals.]

West Ham's form that season was best described as 'solid' but they were certainly less-than-devastating and it was far from guaranteed that they would even finish in the play-off places.

A final day 2-1 win against Watford thankfully secured 6th place but, in the Play-Off semi-final first leg with Ipswich, West Ham could only manage a 2-2 draw at Upton Park. Ipswich thus became firm favourites to progress to the Final but the Hammers finally hit top form in the away leg; winning 2-0 and then deservedly beating Preston in the Millennium Stadium Play-Off Final, 1-0, thanks to a Bobby Zamora goal.

We were back in the top flight but, unless some major purchases were made, or Pardew turned out to be the most inspirational manager since Brian Clough, it seemed highly unlikely that **this** West Ham side would be challenging for Europe or silverware.

[*What the Hell do I know?!*]

*

2005-6 turned out to be a magnificent but, ultimately, heart-breaking season, but one which at least provided far more drama and attractive football than the previous two campaigns in the hated Championship.

It was strange that – considering how West Ham had mightily struggled to escape the cloying clutches of the lower division – they had such a solid season in the

Premiership, against much better teams than they had been forced to scrap with in the Championship.

Maybe it was merely a case of Alan Pardew having finally organised a style of play which all of his players felt comfortable with. Equally, it could have been that the likes of Reo-Coker and Rio Ferdinand's younger brother Anton – who had established himself in the centre of the Hammer's defence - had sufficiently matured, and that the players relished the chance to compete at the highest level and thus 'raised their game'.

Certainly, one of the most significant factors was the club record £7 million purchase of one of the country's top young strikers, from Norwich City. Dean Ashton was a Geoff Hurst-style centre-forward; an imposing physical presence, who was great in the air, had a powerful shot, and who could pull defenders out of position and lay off balls for his fellow strikers to latch on to. The fact that the England manager was also a fan of Ashton boded well. [???]

The goals that season were fairly evenly divided but Harewood again topped the list. West Ham finished a creditable 9th place but, for most of the Upton Park fans, the biggest delight of the season came in the final match against Spurs.

Tottenham were just one victory away from 4th place and guaranteed Champions League football. The evening before the game, however, many of the Spurs squad were taken ill with a mystery virus and it was a physically weakened side that took to the field in front of thousands of baying Hammers fans; who cared not that Tottenham's European dream may be shattered by illness. They were only concerned that West Ham bested their hated rivals; especially with the presence of the despised Defoe in their team.

West Ham took the lead but the reviled dwarf Defoe equalised. Former Spurs hero Sheringham then missed a penalty for the Hammers and it seemed that fate was smiling upon Tottenham. Until skilful Israeli international midfielder Yossi Benayoun stunned the visiting fans with a dramatic late winner for West Ham.

The real excitement that season though, - [*for everyone who wasn't a Spurs-hater*] - came in the FA Cup.

Norwich were beaten 2-1 in the 3rd round, thanks to goals from midfielder Hayden Mullins and Zamora, and then Blackburn were impressively dispatched 4-2, via Sheringham, Etherington, Zamora and an own goal.

After defeating Blackburn, though, it took an injury-time winner from Marlon Harewood to give the Hammers a hard-fought 2-1 victory over Bolton in the 5th round, and this scoreline was repeated in the quarter-final win against Manchester City; both goals courtesy of Dean Ashton.

A tight semi-final encounter with Middlesbrough was decided by a lone Harewood goal and, 26 years after their last Cup Final appearance, West Ham United prepared to face the most formidable of foes; as reigning European Champions Liverpool had won the other semi-final.

The boys in claret-and-blue had been the underdogs in their last FA Cup Final but had triumphed against North London neighbours Arsenal. Now, we just had to believe that we could repeat that victory against the multiple European Champions.

Disappointingly, the Final wasn't held at Wembley, as the once-magisterial old stadium had become something of a crumbling relic and was being completely redesigned in order to be a fitting base for the England football team, and as a host venue for major cup competitions. Thus, the two teams travelled to the Millennium Stadium, in Cardiff; the scene of both bitter disappointment and unbridled joy, for West Ham, in two consecutive Play-Off Finals.

[Also, disappointingly, the Hammers wore their uninteresting all-white Away strip; although this had proven fortuitous the last time they'd reached a major Final, against the Gunners. *Don't look for omens; they exist in the same place as leprechauns and the belief that your favourite player really means it when he kisses the badge.*]

My mum came 'round to my place to watch the game with me; a decision she would live to regret. Even though she'd been married to a Docker and thus was no stranger to swearing, the abuse and vitriol I hurled at the TV screen that day would've made Roy 'Chubby' Brown blush.

Hindsight has made me appreciate the game more and I feel proud that West Ham competed in what has been described by many learned observers as 'the greatest FA Cup Final of all-time'.

However, at that moment, all I could think about was my gut-wrenching disappointment and my desire to inject Steven Gerrard with a slow-release venom, and make him listen to Cilla 'I'm-an—annoying-ginger-Liverpudlian' Black CD's until he slipped into blessed unconsciousness.

Rarely have I hated a team more than I hate Chelsea but, that year, Liverpool became the object of my most heated animosity. Let me explain to you, dear reader, why they deserve to have their genitals run along a cheese-grater.

300

West Ham United came flying out of the blocks like a team possessed and raced into an incredible 2-0 lead, thanks to a fluky cross-shot from Argentinian defender Lionel Scaloni – which the defence should have dealt with – and a tap-in from Dean Ashton.

I was ecstatic but then Liverpool pulled one back and the game became an extended period of agony, as I prayed for either a third goal or the final whistle.

Gerrard slammed the ball home to equalise but then West Ham enjoyed another moment of good fortune, when full-back Paul Konchesky's cross sailed over the keeper's head and nestled into the net.

I was filled with God's love for all furry creatures but then came the moment of sheer 'foul play' that condemned Liverpool to be the new focus of my loathing.

With just seconds to go, West Ham defender Scaloni sportingly kicked the ball out to allow for an injured Liverpool player to be treated.

In such circumstances – normally – the opposition will then throw the ball back to their opponents; instead of which, the cheating, loathsome piece of flesh in a blood-red shirt – [*and I'm being kind to him here*] – threw the ball **at** Scaloni, at approximately 90 miles per hour. You'd have needed to have been the love-child of Diego Maradona and Pele to have been able to control that ball. Scaloni certainly wasn't that – [*I've seen his birth certificate*] – and the pressured full-back made a hash of his rushed clearance; giving the ball away. It was quickly played to Gerrard, who smashed an unstoppable shot past Shaka Hislop.

[*The Scouse w****r. Funny that he can never play that well for England! But then, neither does Lampard,*

Defoe or any of the other pond-dwellers that exist just to spite West Ham.]

The final whistle went and the only reason my TV screen stayed intact was that there was still hope that West Ham could rescue victory again in extra-time. They had played **so well** and surely they deserved their moment of unfettered happiness, in a season which had seen the sad demise of legendary figures Ron Greenwood and John Lyall.

[Greenwood had died aged 84, suffering from Alzheimer's, and his protégé Lyall surprisingly followed, just two months later, aged 66, from a heart attack. In 2008 the club named its entrance portals 'The John Lyall Gates', in recognition of his contribution to the Boleyn Ground's history.]

This incredible match, of end-to-end attacking football went to penalties, and like my dreams, West Ham's hopes of against-all-odds glory, faded and died. Never have the words of *'Bubbles'* been more agonisingly appropriate.

A stiff-upper-lipped Alan Pardew commented: "I'm so proud of my team. We played our part in one of the greatest FA Cup Finals ever. It was a fantastic spectacle for English football."

Courtesy of Liverpool having already qualified for the Champions League, West Ham – despite this defeat – had qualified for the following season's UEFA Cup. This, coupled with their solid Premiership season and fantastic cup run, suggested that there were 'big things' ahead for the Hammers.

[*For those of you who have been reading this book carefully...you know what's coming! Gerrard's father Lucifer was waiting with his pin; ready to pop our hopeful little bubbles.*]

*

Things went wrong immediately. Prior to the start of the 2006-7 campaign Dean Ashton broke his ankle, when in a training camp with the England squad. Nobody could have realised that this innocuous-seeming injury would eventually contribute to the finish of the promising young striker's career. Sadly, Ashton never fully recovered from the knock.

Shockingly, two world-class players then arrived at Upton Park! The Hammers had often nurtured young talent into **becoming** world-class, but they'd never previously had the finances to **buy** that level of talent. [*Little did we realise that we **hadn't**.*]

The fans were thus happily bemused at the dual arrival of 22 year old Argentinian World Cup stars; midfielder Javier Mascherano and striker Carlos Tevez, but the two men initially struggled to acclimate to the English Premiership, and Mascherano soon moved on to Liverpool. [*Home of everything foul and demonic.*]

By the time Tevez finally found the net and began his one-man crusade to save the Hammers from relegation, boss Alan Pardew was gone!

A first round exit, in the UEFA Cup, to Palermo of Italy, summed up West Ham's disastrous start to the season. [The second leg of which featured the first bout of serious crowd violence in years, with 26 West Ham 'fans' arrested.]

With Ashton out and Harewood, Zamora and the aging Sheringham all misfiring in front of goal, West Ham slumped to a series of demoralising defeats and, as Christmas neared, it became obvious that Pardew needed to find a way to reinvigorate a team which were playing with no visible confidence.

There could be no doubting Pardew's passion; evidenced in his ecstatic touchline celebrations when West Ham scored a last-minute winner – via Harewood - against Arsenal, and which prompted the normally placid Gunners boss Arsene Wenger to want to 'square-up' to him. [*The French fool; he'd left his hand-bag in the dressing room.*]

However, when West Ham United were shockingly 'taken over' by an Icelandic Corporation, who spent £85 million to gain control of the EastEnders, the first thing the new Board did was to sack the beleaguered manager.

Announcing that they intended to 'make West Ham a top four club', the new owners quickly appointed the oft-linked Alan Curbishley, with the promise of money to be invested in new players **if** he managed to keep the Hammers in the top flight.

It all started perfectly for 'Curbs', with a surprise 1-0 victory against title-chasing Manchester United but this was followed by a succession of disastrous performances, in the New Year; including 6-0 and 4-0 defeats to Reading and Charlton, which prompted Curbishley to criticise his players lack of desire and 'hunger', and to purchase hard-man defender Lucas Neill from Blackburn, along with the more cultured central defender Matthew Upson, in order to try and bolster the Hammer's sieve-like defence.

[Although rumours abounded that several of the players disliked Curbishley's management style and tactics, and were vocally rebelling.]

The most amazing game of the season then occurred at Upton Park, against arch-rivals Tottenham, and I nearly had a heart attack that evening.

Local lad and touted prospect Mark Noble scored on his full Hammers debut, but it was West Ham's second goal that brought the stadium to its feet.

Despite his lack of goals, Carlos Tevez had endeared himself to the Upton Park faithful with his committed performances and unceasing work-rate; whilst other around him seemed disinterested, or – as Yossi Benayoun described – were 'playing like a bunch of drunks'.

As Tevez's curling strike glanced in off the underside of the cross-bar, 30,000 East Enders experienced an orgasmic joy. [*Though the cleaning bill afterwards was horrendous.*]

That lovely little chap Defoe pulled one back for Spurs and then Upton Park fell silent as the equaliser went in. With five minutes remaining Zamora headed West Ham back in front and yet, they somehow contrived to throw away these three valuable points, by conceding two heart-breaking goals in the final minutes.

At this point relegation appeared a certainty, with West Ham firmly rooted to the bottom of the table. It thus seems incredible – nay, **miraculous** – that a Tevez-inspired Hammers won seven of their remaining nine games to produce one of the greatest escapes in football history!

Tevez and Zamora were the goalscorers in the 2-1 and 2-0 victories over Blackburn and Middlesbrough and then fortune favoured the Hammers, as they were completely dominated by a rampant Arsenal side and yet walked away from the new Emirates Stadium with an unlikely three points, courtesy of another Zamora strike.

Disappointingly, this was followed by a 3-0 defeat to our principal relegation rivals Sheffield United and a 4-1 loss to the arch-stealers of West Ham talent Chelski.

Nevertheless, Zamora – who, like Tevez, had left it late in the season to discover his shooting boots; *they were under his bed all along* – scored the winner against Everton, and this hard-fought victory was followed by a 3-0 romp against fellow relegation candidates Wigan and a 3-1 success against Bolton.

Remarkably, West Ham could possibly stay up if they could just win their final game of the season. The remaining relegation spot was between the Hammers, Sheffield United and Wigan. All we had to do was hope for the best, regarding other results, **and** beat champions Manchester United!

But before we get to the thrilling finale, let's take a small step back and revisit the other drama that was dominating the headlines and causing Hammers fans to have palpitations.

*

It had appeared too good to be true when West Ham United inherited the talented Tevez and Mascherano. And so it proved. When Javier moved to Liverpool, it became glaringly apparent that the Hammers didn't receive significant compensation for his loss. This alerted other clubs that there may be a breach of Premier League rules here, regarding 'third party ownership' of players, as it was Mascherano's **agent** that received a hefty fee.

This must mean that Carlos, too, was not actually 'owned' by West Ham, and so it transpired. As the season progressed and Tevez began to find his goalscoring form, the issue took on greater significance for the clubs in direct competition with the Hammers, at the foot of the table.

Wigan chairman Dave Whelan and Sheffield United manager Neil Warnock became particularly vocal in their belief that West Ham were 'cheating their way out of trouble' and were 'getting away with murder', and the Premier League began an investigation into the potential impropriety.

If West Ham United were found 'guilty' it would mean a hefty points deduction and, thus, condemn us to certain relegation.

Thankfully, the Hammers were eventually cleared of serious wrongdoing, as both players **had** been registered with the Premier League, as 'West Ham United' players.

However, the issue of 'third party ownership' was a thorny one. Whilst not illegal in itself, the breach of rules regarded the ability of that 'third party' to influence the course of a club's season. Ironically, then, it wasn't really the presence of Tevez which was the problem – [despite his being the constant target of Whelan and Warnock's ire] – it was the move of Mascherano halfway through the campaign, which could have contributed to altering the final Premiership standings. For this – and for not revealing the clauses in both players contracts, which allowed them to leave if their agent so desired - West Ham were ordered to pay a £5.5 million fine.

*

And so, to that fateful final day of the season. From *'Bring Me The Head of Trevor Brooking'*:

"West Ham were out of the drop-zone for the first time in five long months and could not have hoped for a better scenario for their final-day visit to Manchester

United. With the Premier League title already won, it was a meaningless game for the Red Devils, who were expected to rest key players in preparation for the following weekend's FA Cup Final against Chelsea; although manager Sir Alex Ferguson pledged to name a 'strong' side.

The Hammers could afford to lose at Old Trafford, as long as Wigan – three points behind them – failed to win at Sheffield United but, with both Northern clubs feeling a sense of injustice over the Tevez affair, the conspiracy theories began to circulate before the big day. If West Ham were losing heavily, Sheffield United could afford a modest defeat in the knowledge that both they and Wigan would survive.

Curbishley dismissed such ideas, insisting: 'I don't see any other outcome than everybody trying their hardest to win'…

A skip-load of rubbish has since been written about the team Ferguson named to face West Ham, with one *News of the World* columnist, in 2010, remembering it as 'a second-string line-up', when it was nothing of the sort. Indeed, Edwin Van der Saar, Wayne Rooney and Michael Carrick were actually restored to the side that had played out a goalless draw at Chelsea in mid-week; although Hammers fans were naturally pleased to see that Christiano Ronaldo, Ryan Giggs and Paul Scholes were only on the bench. If anything, it was the less established players who provided most commitment during the game; while Rooney shrugged off wayward shots with uncharacteristic good humour…

After a quarter of an hour, it came through that Wigan had gone in front – at which point Sheffield United were in the bottom three – although it would only take a Manchester United goal to put West Ham there instead.

And they had their chances, with Alan Smith and Kieron Richardson being denied by Yossi Benayoun on the line, as the home fans chanted; 'Send them down! Send them down!'

'Staying up! Staying up!' came the reply from the visitors end when it was discovered that Sheffield United had levelled ten minutes before the break, to restore the table to its earlier order. That belief solidified when Tevez put the Hammers ahead in first-half stoppage-time, with his seventh goal in the last ten games and – surely – his most memorable.

The Argentinian played the ball to Zamora and then bulldozed his way through the home defence to collect the return as it dropped, before slotting home from a tight angle.

Yet Curbishley was brought quickly back down to earth when he returned to the dressing-room to discover that Wigan had gone in front again…

Ronaldo, Giggs and Scholes were all brought on with half-an-hour still to play and United duly stepped up a gear, with Robert Green being forced to make several good saves in the latter stages of the game…when the final whistle blew, the Old Trafford party began – with both sets of fans among the 75,927 crowd, trying to out-celebrate each other. In financial terms, however, West Ham's survival was worth far more than Manchester United's title triumph…

Meanwhile, relegated Warnock complained that he'd been 'sold a dummy' by Ferguson, who naturally defended his team selection. 'I feel for Sheffield United', he said, 'but I think I played the right team. West Ham have been in championship-winning form lately!'

It wasn't the fault of Ferguson – or Tevez, for that matter – that the Blades couldn't even force a draw against 10-man Wigan."

Subsequently, Whelan stated that he'd 'support Sheffield United's cause,' and the relegated sore-losers took West Ham to court, to try and over-turn the decision not to deduct the Hammers points for the 'third party ownership' charade. This bid failed but a separate one – for financial compensation, for being relegated – amazingly succeeded and West Ham were forced to pay the Yorkshire club a sizeable amount of cash.

[*How I feel about Dave Whelan and Neil Warnock can be summed-up by stating that I'd rather have dinner and a big French kiss afterwards with Steven Gerrard and the entire Chelsea team, than to have to listen to their pathetic whingeing Northern twangs, moaning that 'Tevez sent the Blades down'.*

There's a very simple reason that Sheffield United were relegated that season. They were CRAP!

It's not anyone's fault but their own that Whelan and Warnock have both chosen to live in several of the most God-forsaken parts of the country. No wonder they're so unhappy, the miserable saps!

As for that ungracious loser Warnock, he ultimately got what a man like that deserves – Leeds United. Now there's a match made in Hell.]

*

Unsurprisingly, considering his marvellous performances in helping the Hammers retain their Premiership status, hot property Carlos Tevez was ushered over to the champions Manchester United, by his agent, for a paltry token gesture fee.

Nevertheless, to Hammers fans, Carlos was worth his weight in gold and Tevez was received warmly whenever he returned to Upton Park; achieving a hero's status with his valiant displays over the last half of that 2006-7 season.

Someone not received as warmly – and certainly **not** leaving the club with a 'hero's status' - was want-away skipper Nigel Reo-Coker.

Reo-Coker had been one of the players who had under-performed all season and became visibly dispirited at both the team's displays and the crowd's reaction to his own lacklustre performances; with chants of '*It's Nigel Mediocre*'. And yet, he had nobody but himself to blame. As captain he should have been setting an example and motivating the other players, not ending up being described as 'moody' and 'sulky' by certain backroom staff; nor bemoaning the fact that the fans were on his back, and then handing in a transfer request. Julian Dicks - never shy to offer an opinion – suggested that the club 'get rid of him' and new Chairman Eggert Magnusson agreed, stating: "We need grown-up men at this club".

West Ham did well to get £8.5 million, from Aston Villa, for Reo-Coker, because Nigel's career was all downhill from there and he never again evidenced the promise he'd shown when he'd arrived at West Ham as a youngster. [Lucas Neill replaced him as the Hammers captain.]

Also sold were Harewood, Benayoun and Konchesky, as Alan Curbishley attempted to put his own stamp upon the side, in his first full season in charge.

Scott Parker was bought for £7 million, as a direct replacement for Reo-Coker in midfield and this would prove to be one of West Ham United's most rewarding signings; the Duracell-powered Parker **never** letting the fans or his team-mates down, as he fought week-in and week-out, with his heart on his sleeve. [*A medical condition completely unheard of prior to his arrival.*]

Also purchased were Liverpool's pacy striker Craig Bellamy and the right-sided Julian Faubert from Bordeaux. It appeared to be good news, too, that Dean Ashton finally returned to action but, after scoring 10 goals and showing glimpses of his previous form, Dean was forced to announce his premature retirement – at the age of 26 – after receiving medical advice that his ankle was not capable of withstanding any more punishment.

From a purely dramatic point of view, 2007-8 was a huge anti-climax after the nerve-shredding relegation battle the previous campaign but, from the Board's viewpoint, the 10th place finish achieved under Curbishley was a definite step in the right direction; although many of the supporters were unhappy with West Ham's performances that season, believing them to have been too negative and defensive-minded. Curbishley defended these criticisms by claiming that tactics had to revolve around the available players, and if the flair / creative talents were injured, then he had little option but to base his strategies around the more 'straightforward' team members.

Little did anyone know at the time but the 'Curbishley revolution' – along with all of the promises of the Icelandic owners – was already nearing the end.

Despite their claim that they 'wanted to make West Ham a top four side', the new Board were hardly inundating Curbishley with money with which to buy top-quality players.

Reflecting this, at the commencement of the 2008-9 season, the Board sold central defender Anton Ferdinand and gritty left-back George McCartney, to

Sunderland, for a combined fee of £14 million. Neither player had actually requested the move and Curbishley was aghast.

Even as the Board claimed that the sales were good commercial sense, Alan Curbishley was walking out of the job, stating that: "The selection of players is critical to the job of the manager and I had an agreement with the club that I alone would determine the composition of the squad. However, the club continued to make significant player decisions without involving me. In the end, such a breach of trust and confidence meant that I had no option but to leave."

Curbishley thus walked; all the way to his lawyer's office, where he instructed a 'constructive dismissal' compensation case be launched against his former employers; resulting – several years later – in a £2.25 million settlement.

The owners then made a bold move, by appointing the unproven ex-Chelsea star Gianfranco Zola as their new manager. Opinion was sharply divided between the likes of myself – *who thought that anyone who had worn the blue of Chelsea should be slowly tortured to within an inch of their miserable lives; preferably on national TV, and certainly not be given such an esteemed position within the world's most fabulous club* – and those who hoped that Zola's creative, attacking style of play as a player himself would be reflected in the brand of entertaining football he could bring to Upton Park. [Especially after the relative dourness of the Curbishley reign.]

The reality was though that the diminutive and constantly grinning Gianfranco had inherited a relatively limited squad of players, some of whom were carrying more problems than solutions, through Upton Park's gates.

The club discovered, to their dismay, the full extent of talented winger Matthew Etherington's gambling problem, when they had to pay £300,000 in order to pay off his debts, before the nice gentlemen he owed the money to removed his testicles as down-payment.

As the news broke in the media, it transpired that West Ham's players would routinely lose thousands of pounds to each other in card games, travelling to-and-from matches, and this could often cause friction if a player lost a considerable amount. Both Pardew and Curbishley had tried in vain to stop the gambling but it was the extent of Etherington's addiction that brought the subject into sharp focus.

Matthew admitted to the press that he'd previously attended an Addiction Clinic. [*He came away with a gambling addiction, only because they'd run out of sex addictions that week.*] And yet, within months, Etherington was gambling again – at one point owing a massive £800,000 – and the decision was taken to sell him, in the January transfer window, to Stoke City, as it was hoped that 'a change of environment' might help him to 'resist temptation'.

Unfortunately, West Ham also lost star striker Craig Bellamy at this point, when newly-minted Manchester City offered £14 million for his services. The money was nice but the Hammers were already struggling for goals and thus became even more reliant upon the tall, young former Chelsea striker Carlton Cole.

It soon appeared to have been a bad move appointing Zola, as West Ham struggled near the foot of the table; looking for all the world like relegation material.

The players seemed ill at ease with Gianfranco's tactics and his aims. Zola was trying to instil a greater patience and fluency to West Ham's passing but it was painful to watch at times and even opposing managers commented at the 'lack of urgency' in West Ham's approach play. It was an almost **obsessively** patient passing-game but, finally, the penny seemed to drop with the players as to what was expected of them and form visibly improved over the second half of the season; leading to an eventual 9th place finish and renewed optimism that Zola would bring success to Upton Park. This optimism came crashing down, along with the Icelandic Bank!

*

There had already been drama before the 2009-10 season even began. In August '09 midfielder Callum Davenport was admitted to hospital, after being stabbed in both legs. Davenport lost 50% of his body's blood and remained in the intensive care ward for almost a week.

The drunken boyfriend of Callum's sister was arrested and charged with the assault but he claimed, in his defence, that he'd reacted angrily to the fact that Callum had physically assaulted his sister.

The recovering Davenport was thus also arrested and – although eventually cleared months later – he had already been quietly 'let go' by West Ham United; who probably decided that the youngster – and the attendant negative publicity he'd brought to the club - was one 'hot potato' they could live without, so soon after the Tevez and Etherington sagas.

As the '09-10 campaign got under way it quickly became obvious that the owners had problems unrelated to drunken knife-wielding chavs or debt-collectors. They were broke; the Iceland Landsbanki which backed them having 'gone bust'. [*So they **might** have a problem with shaven-headed debt-collectors, after all!*]

As they searched desperately for someone to buy West Ham United from them, Gianfranco Zola attempted to operate in the mega-rich Premiership on a shoestring budget.

England's central defender Matthew Upson assumed the captaincy, as Lucas Neil departed, and the Hammers shirt sponsors SBOBET, actually financed the purchase of a striker for Zola, in order that Carlton Cole didn't have to keep banging his head against the wall as the lone recognised quality striker.

Thus, when the tattooed Italian Allesandro Diamanti arrived from Livorno, for £5 million, Hammers fans had every reason to believe that we had found the 'new' Paolo Di Canio. However, it quickly became apparent that this was not the Second Coming of the eccentric legend. Diamanti was a decent player but he was not an out-and-out goalscorer and what West Ham sorely needed was someone with proven quality in simply banging the ball into the back of the net, and not merely a handsome figurehead for the females to admire.

West Ham were in deep trouble, embroiled **yet again** in a fierce fight for Premiership survival and overly-reliant upon the tenacious midfield battling of Scott Parker and Mark Noble. Goals were a rarity and – by season's end – Carlton Cole would be top scorer with a paltry 10; Diamanti second with 7.

It seemed highly unlikely that even the urgings of Parker or the commanding presence in defence of Upson would save us this time. [Although the emergence of talented young centre-half James Tomkins was one of the few bright moments in the season; along with Swiss international midfielder Valon

Behrami's performances; when injury didn't sideline him.]

In January 2010 David Gold and David Sullivan – former owners of Birmingham City – purchased a controlling 50% stake in West Ham United, for £50 million; declaring: "We wouldn't have bought this club if we weren't fans; it's in a serious mess!" [They would later extend their stake by another £16 million, to 60% ownership.]

They certainly appeared genuine. Gold had actually been born in Green Street and Sullivan commented: "The club is back in the hands of East Enders; people who understand the community and its passion for the Hammers."

Revealing that the club was a worrying £110 million in debt, it quickly became obvious that the new owners were not going to be throwing good money after bad. Zola was going to have to save the Hammers from relegation without the aid of a huge cash injection for new players.

However, the pressure upon Gianfranco was added to by the outspoken criticism of the new co-owner; Sullivan commenting after the 3-1 defeat to relegation rivals Wolves: "I was as angry and upset as every supporter at the disorganised way we played; allowing Wolves to look like Manchester United. I apologise to every fan for our pathetic showing. Our recent performance against Bolton was also appalling." [*Which, to be fair, it **was!***]

West Ham had a worrying habit that season of letting a lead slip and, even when 5-0 up against Burnley, were clinging on at the end for a 5-3 victory.

It was no secret that the co-owners doubted Zola's ability as a manager and, despite somehow avoiding

317

relegation, Gianfranco was unsurprisingly sacked. The only reason West Ham United stayed in the Premiership that year was because there were – amazingly – three teams even more inept than the one which Zola sent out each week.

However, it seemed that the Chelsea connection was not ready to end just yet. In a reciprocal relationship between the two London clubs, Chelsea received all of our best young players and we, in turn, received from **them** managers seemingly determined to get us bloody relegated.

*

Sullivan and Gold obviously believed that it was a minor coup when they appointed Avram Grant; having witnessed him take Chelsea to within a whisker of winning the Champions League. However, it's easy to look good when you've got a squad full of Europe's finest internationals; much harder when you've got the likes of Luis Boa Morte staring blankly back at you.

I previously alluded to the financial impact of having a billionaire backer allowing you to purchase the cream of the World's crop but the difference between the top four teams and those trailing in their wake lies deeper than that.

What that kind of financial clout also allows you is the luxury of buying two world-class players in **the same position;** thus being able to rotate your playing staff. This allows for injuries to key players to be less damaging – as they are generally replaced by players of roughly equal calibre – and for managers to 'rest' players who may also be featuring in international matches.

The likes of West Ham United have never been able to enjoy such advantages. The best we can hope for is for a team of 11 men who can compete with the other Premiership sides, on a roughly level basis. When West Ham have an injury to a key player – or worse, player[s] – it is almost certainly going to be the case that they will be replaced by cheaply bought foreign 'talent', who wouldn't otherwise have made the starting line-up; or, by teenage Academy prospects, not yet really ready for the likes of Man Utd or Chelsea, and who would normally be sent out on loan first, to a lower division side, to earn their experience.

Bad enough, then, that injuries or suspension can rob you of potential precious points. Worse still, if a team struggles to comprehend a coach's tactics, or gel with a new manager – as with Zola – and, **worse yet**; if that manager fails to ignite even the merest spark of inspiration under his already low-on-confidence team; a la Avram don't-let-him-scare-the-kids Grant; the only novelty mask ever to come with a breathing body attached.

If the pocket-sized, wispy-haired Zola had cut a somewhat gnome-like appearance on the touchlines, that was nothing compared with the Zombie King, who stared out at the world through sunken dark eyes and ashen complexion. Unfortunately, he also shared another characteristic common to the Un-dead – the lack of a fully-functioning brain.

West Ham United under Avram Grant were probably the worst Hammers team ever to [dis]grace the Upton Park pitch, and season 2010/11 was one long nightmare. [*Appropriately, under Count Grant!*]

The warning signs were there beforehand. Centre-half Matthew Upson and goalkeeper Robert Green had represented England at the 2010 World Cup and thus been part of a sorry spectacle of idealess football, which made me understand why Paolo Di Canio had repeatedly punched Fabio Capello.

England were awful but – even worse – Rob Green was one of the prime reasons behind our becoming an international laughing-stock; allowing a tame shot from USA striker Clint Dempsey, to trickle through his you-wouldn't-believe-they're-not-butter-fingers.

Thus, part of the Hammers pre-season training routine was to abuse Green from the sidelines, so that the keeper became used to the expected verbal abuse from opposing fans and wouldn't let it affect his performances. [*I bet they had people queuing up for miles to help with that idea!*]

Realising that scoring goals was probably West Ham's biggest problem over the preceding few seasons, the Board allowed the purchase of two new strikers - Demba Ba and Frederic Piquionne – who scored a massive 7 and 6 goals respectively. Actually, blame can't be laid at their doorsteps, as both men are decent strikers. It was the general **awfulness** of the team's play that campaign which limited their goalscoring opportunities.

Somehow, they contrived to reach the semi-finals of the League Cup; beating Manchester United 4-0 along the way – [?] – before losing to eventual winners Birmingham.

In the Premiership though, they were 'pants' and propped up the rest of the division throughout, as Grant plotted, schemed, summoned up Demons from the furthest depths of Hell…and then remembered that he had a football match to go to.

West Ham United have rarely looked so completely clueless; playing with absolutely no conviction. I watched our late-season victory against Liverpool in shock. Why couldn't we play like that **every** week?

But, far more tellingly, Carlton Cole announced that the half-time 'pep' talk which Scott Parker had given in the amazing comeback draw against West Brom - when the Hammers had finished 3-3, after trailing 3-0 at half-time - was 'the most inspirational thing he'd ever heard' and 'had nearly brought a tear to his eye'.

Wasn't the bloody manager supposed to be providing that inspiration? Although his tactics certainly brought tears to **my** eyes!

[*Whilst Parker was urging the troops on to battle, Grant was, presumably, solemnly intoning: "Would you like to see the body?" in his hobby as celebrity undertaker.*]

Once again, as poor as we were, there was still a slim chance that we could pull the rabbit from the hat and save ourselves, as the season wound down.

Thus, when 2-0 up against the hated Whelan's Wigan, we contrived to lose 3-2, and were consigned – once more – to the Championship.

Instead of sacking Grant and risking having to pay him compensation, Messrs Gold and Sullivan merely pushed him out into the sunlight instead and then swept his ashes up with a dustpan-and-brush.

*

An Olympian effort at changing the face of the East End.

On 6th July 2005 London's bid to host the 2012 Olympics was surprisingly accepted; beating the favourites Paris. [Birmingham and Manchester had previously failed in bids to host sports most prestigious event. *Largely because they were full of Brummies and Mancs, and not even the most desperate Eastern*

European dissident would want to defect there. They'd be mugged before they could reach the nearest Embassy.]

What was even more shocking, though, was that the London Olympic Committee intended to hold the event in **East** London!

Newham had already been recognised as the poorest Borough in the whole of the Capital; with poverty levels **still** embarrassingly high. 15% of the working-age populace were unemployed and there were a high proportion of un-qualified people too.

Jack Straw MP commented: "The Games will transform one of the poorest and most deprived areas of London. They will create thousands of jobs and homes. They will offer new opportunities for businesses, both in the immediate area and throughout London".

Despite possessing the smallest amount of 'green space' in London, the unused land around Hackney Marshes was considered perfect to site the intended development and the Olympic Park itself was erected on former industrial land around the River Lea; which formed the boundary between East London and Essex.

[Industry had drastically declined in the area, prompting a resultant rise in unemployment. Even the immense Ford car plant in Dagenham had closed, in 2002.]

Remarkably, by the time of completion, Newham would go from 'smallest green space area' in London to being the proud possessor of the largest 'urban park' in Europe!

Once the Olympics were confirmed for East London, house prices rocketed in the immediate area; provoking some concern that it would worsen the divide between the new wealthy residents and those already struggling to get on the housing-ladder; a la the Docklands

Development's division between the inhabitants of the 'affordable housing' complexes and the luxury apartments overlooking the Thames.

Work commenced in July 2007, when 33 disused industrial buildings were demolished and the 'green space' dug-over. By 2011, when it was completed, the Olympic Park – adjacent to the Stratford City Development and renamed the Queen Elizabeth Park, after the event – contained the Olympic Village, the Olympic Stadium and The London Aquatics Centre.

However, the original budget of £2.4 billion came nowhere near the final figure of a massive £9.3 billion.

This was quickly offset when it was announced that, just a year after the Games, £10 billion had been injected via increased trade and investment, and it was projected that as much as £41 billion profit may result from the success of the London Olympics.

10,500 athletes participated in this globally-viewed event, and Great Britain's sportsmen and women responded by producing the third highest medal tally of the Games.

The long-term aim for the area was far more important though than the simple hosting of a large-scale sporting occasion.

The Royal Mail has given the area a postcode, E20 – [*the previously fictional postcode used in the TV series 'EastEnders*] – and the Olympic Village – used to house the world's athletes and coaches – would be converted into around 3,000 apartments; many of them shared ownership, and renamed East Village.

Other new housing would be constructed, as well as East London Tech City; a huge modern technology centre. Added to this will be top-of-the-range sports facilities, available for the use of local residents and

323

these facilities will host the 2017 World Athletics Championship.

So, maybe, with all of the proposed modernisation and job opportunities, East London really **will** be 'wonderful'!

*

False dawn under Fat Sam?

Who next? That was a worrying thought for the West Ham fans that had seen a remarkable amount of managers' come-and-go over the last decade. Surely the Board would get it right this time?

Gold and Sullivan's choice to garner instant promotion was the veteran figure 'Big' Sam Allardyce; who'd formerly managed Bolton, Newcastle and Blackburn.

His stints at the latter two clubs had been unspectacular, but his time at Bolton had created his reputation as a manager who got results via solid defensive performances and from engendering a work ethic in his players. This had helped Bolton to European qualification in 2004-5; Allardyce surprisingly leaving them shortly afterwards because he wanted to go to 'a bigger club, and win some silverware'. He even claimed that, if he were the manager of Chelsea or Manchester United, he would win 'multiple trophies every season'.

[*Hard to judge on that one. After all, Chelsea's numerous internationals had managed to make Avram Grant appear as if he knew what he was doing...until he arrived at Upton Park! And yet, several seasons on, and Alex Ferguson's successor David Moyes proved a complete bust at Old Trafford, despite the plethora of talent available to him at Man Utd.*]

Sam's first job was to rebuild the Hammers team; both in personnel and in confidence.

Scott Parker had won the *'Hammer of the Year'* Award a remarkable three years running, and had also won widespread plaudits for the wonderful consistency of his passionate midfield performances. However, after **finally** forcing his way into the England team, it was no surprise to hear that Scott didn't want to play in the Championship; believing that it would harm his chances of international selection.

Consequently, Parker left for Spurs and Allardyce drafted in the perfect replacement; his former Bolton and Newcastle attacking-midfielder Kevin Nolan; whom he also made captain.

Another welcome sight was the return of left-back George McCartney, from Sunderland and the purchase of highly-rated young striker Ricardo Vaz Te.

Matthew Upson also left but, by this stage, James Tomkins was giving consistently assured performances in central defence and Mark Noble 'upped his game' in the absence of his former midfield partner Parker.

Although some fans criticised Allardyce's sometimes pragmatic-over-entertaining style of football, results mean everything when your overwhelming desire is to escape the Championship, and Sullivan and Gold defended Sam against all criticism of his sometimes 'Route One' style of football.

[Allardyce had been largely unpopular with the Newcastle fans because of his 'unattractive' style of football there, but Sam angrily rejected claims that he'd played boring long-ball football at all of his previous clubs, and promised that he understood "the traditions of West Ham", and would play "attractive football **and** get them back into the Premier League".]

Occupying one of the automatic promotion places for most of the season, West Ham were frustratingly denied

2nd spot by a magnificent late run of wins from Reading and were thus forced to face the dreaded Play-Offs.

However, after thrashing Cardiff 5-0 on aggregate, the Hammers then defeated Blackpool in the Wembley Play-Off Final, thus cementing the third promotion place. [*Which, of course, is where we came in.*]

Despite the critics of Allardyce's style of play, West Ham's top scorers that season were: Vaz Te [*combined total of 20 goals*], Carlton Cole 14, and Nolan 12. Not a bad return for the Board's money and evidence that the Hammers were finally putting the ball into the back of the net again.

Not content with merely being back in the Premiership, co-owners Gold and Sullivan had big plans for the Hammers. They envisaged West Ham United becoming a top-four club over the next few years; largely via their proposed bid to 'inherit' the Olympic Stadium.

Despite the traditionalists, who were appalled at the idea of West Ham leaving the Boleyn Ground and the Upton Park area, and relocating to Stratford, the Board insisted that the only realistic way of 'moving the club forward' was to increase its fan base and, thus, escalate revenue. The Olympic Stadium will allow 60,000 people to attend the Hammers home matches; almost double the Boleyn capacity and, in February 2011, West Ham's bid to be the tenants of the Stadium was accepted by the Olympic Legacy Committee; only to be challenged by Leyton Orient's owner Barry 'would-you-buy-a-used-car-from-this-man' Hearns, who claimed that West Ham's presence so close to Orient's stadium will effectively kill the smaller club. [*Oooh, what a terrible loss to football that would be.*]

Tottenham Hotspur also complained about the legitimacy of West Ham's move to the modern larger-capacity stadium, - *[Why did the chicken cross the road? Because he wanted to get the f**k away from White Hart Lane!...and yes, I know it's a cockerel]* - and an investigation was launched into whether the Hammers Board had correctly followed procedure in their bid to be the tenants.

Eventually, on March 22nd 2013, West Ham United were confirmed as tenants for the Olympic Stadium, at a cost of £2 million a year rent, and £15 million to convert the stadium into a principally-football venue.

*

The erratic Rob Green lost both his England position and his West Ham goalkeeper's jersey, when he opted to sign for Queens Park Rangers, prior to the 2012/13 season. He was handsomely rewarded for this decision...*by relegation, lol*; the Hammers signing veteran Bolton keeper Jussi Jaaskelainen to replace him. Also signed were Wigan's busy midfielder Mohammed Diame, flying winger Matt Jarvis from Wolves for £10.75 million, and dependable Aston Villa central defender James Collins, as Allardyce sought to strengthen his first-team for the Premiership challenges to come.

The biggest welcome from the fans was reserved for the returning Joe Cole. After his Chelsea and Liverpool adventures had run their respective courses Joe returned to the scene of perhaps his finest performances. Sadly, due largely to a series of debilitating injuries in recent years, Joe's once-dazzling ball-dribbling days were behind him, and he would be a peripheral figure over the next couple of years; showing odd snatches of his former glory, but unable to maintain any consistency in his form.

327

The most exciting acquisition though was young Liverpool centre-forward Andy Carroll, on a season-long loan. Unfortunately, Carroll was injured prior to Christmas and missed a substantial portion of the campaign; accounting in large part for West Ham's poor goal tally that season.

[Captain Kevin Nolan was top scorer with a meagre 10 goals, in a season which witnessed both Carlton Cole and Ricardo Vaz Te spectacularly fail in front of goal; both strikers suffering from a visible lack of confidence as the season wore on.]

Fortunately, the solid defensive performances that Allardyce teams were renowned for, compensated that season for our woeful strike rate, and the Hammers finished in a respectable 10th position; although, once again, a section of the crowd were unhappy with the style of football they witnessed; responding to the lofted long-ball style of play with chants of: *'We're West Ham, and we play on the floor'*.

A criticism which Allardyce cynically responded to by suggesting that it had been a long time since West Ham United had played attractive flowing football, and that his remit was simply to consolidate the Hammers Premiership status.

Best wins were 4-1 and 4-2 against Southampton and Reading respectively, and a magnificent come-from-behind 3-1 victory against reigning European champions and title-chasing Chelsea; although this was offset somewhat by a 5-1 drubbing against Arsenal.

[Yvonne and I were due to attend my mate Gary's 50th birthday celebration after the Chelsea match. Due to the emotion of the moment, I neglected to change into my suit-and-tie for the occasion, and attended the event in my West Ham United training jacket; leading the

328

assembled diners in a few verses of 'Bubbles' and 'Oh, East London'...

Which is not strictly true, as all of the other guests were Chelsea fans, and Yvonne and I were the only ones actually singing...to a sea of silent, angry Chelsea faces.

Which is exactly why we did it! *Lol. You have to get your kicks where you can!*

I mean; I was still trying to get over that egotistical p***k John Terry, watching the Champions League Final in his suit, and then dashing off to put his Chelsea kit on and be photographed with the players when they celebrated their win, as if he'd been playing?!

This was only surpassed when he was then pictured swinging semi-naked from a young lady's chandelier, shouting: 'Look at me, I'm Wayne Bridge'.

'Allegedly'; advised my solicitor!]

*

Prior to the 2013/14 season West Ham announced the purchase of Romanian international captain Razvan Rat, Real Betis goalkeeper Adrian, and Liverpool's former England winger Stewart Downing. Only Adrian would prove popular with the fans; the unfortunately-named Rat being a complete waste of space and not lasting the season, - [*ahh, memories of Harry Redknapp's foreign transfer policy*] - and Downing taking most of the campaign to discover his previous form. [*Actually, he pretty much **did** discover his previous form, and thus the reason Liverpool sold him to us!*]

Biggest disappointment – and a major component in West Ham's struggles this season – was the non-event that was the Andy Carroll purchase.

329

Sam Allardyce followed up the previous season's loan deal by breaking the Hammers transfer record; spending £15 million to make Carroll's move permanent. Despite his preceding season's extended injury absence, it was obvious that Sam saw the tall, aggressive and majestic in the air Carroll as the key to a successful campaign; and so, of course, the striker promptly injured himself in training and spent the vast majority of the season as the highest-paid spectator in the Boleyn Ground.

West Ham's continuing inability to put the inflated round object into the huge oblong net was reflected in the end-of-season statistics. Kevin Nolan once again topped the charts, but with a ridiculously low 7 goals; also reflecting the skipper's own less-than-impressive season; which saw him sent off twice for ridiculously petulant challenges. *It was like having Julian Dicks back, although with a better haircut.*

In a ludicrous piece of near-sightedness, Big Sam had allowed the misfiring Carlton Cole to leave on a free transfer, in the belief that Andy Carroll was the Second Coming of Geoff Hurst. When it transpired that Carroll was actually closer to Dean always-on-the-verge-of-a-bloody-comeback-but-ooh-there's-a-nasty-twinge-in-my-ankle-again Ashton, - *and obvious that Ricardo Vaz Te had suddenly inherited the goal-scoring skills of Ian Dowie* – a cash-strapped Allardyce was forced to ask Carlton to reconsider and return to the Hammers. Fortunately for Sam, he wasn't the only one to doubt Cole's goalscoring abilities; for no other club had made a move for the likeable but hardly prolific striker and, although Carlton was hardly Greaves-like in his scoring ratio, he could at least hold the ball up and bring the midfielders into play.

The season actually started reasonably well, then nosedived sharply into a farcical and painful-to-watch relegation battle; despite Allardyce's ridiculous assessment that 'West Ham were never really in danger of relegation'.

How we could be in the bottom three **and** playing atrocious football, and yet **not** be in a relegation battle was something only Fat Sam – *as he was now referred to by his less-than-adoring Hammers supporters* – could even attempt to explain with a straight face.

Allardyce had based his career upon solid defending and yet West Ham were truly appalling at times defensively. The worst moments of what became a dark and depressing campaign, were the 4-1 league defeat to Liverpool, and the embarrassing 5-0 FA Cup defeat to Championship side Nottingham Forest; eclipsed only by the shambolic roll-over-and-play-dead performances in our 9-0 aggregate defeat to Manchester City in the Capital One Cup.

By Christmas the fans were beginning to vent their frustration. Allardyce's sarcastic claim that West Ham 'hadn't played attractive football in years', had not pleased the supporters and – even if that were true – what was stopping Sam from attempting to rectify that situation?

Demoralising defeat followed depressing reverse and the Hammers owners Gold and Sullivan were forced to constantly defend the manager in the media, as Allardyce responded to the fans unrest at the unedifying football they were being forced to view, with reiterations that it 'wasn't long-ball football'; despite all of the sad evidence to the contrary.

Six weeks of football saved West Ham United's season and – in retrospect – Sam Allardyce's job. Following

331

their humiliating capitulation against eventual Premier League champions Manchester City in what was formerly the League Cup, the Hammers surprisingly rebounded with a 2-0 victory away to fellow relegation candidates Cardiff City, and followed this with a dig-deep defensive display against Chelsea, which prompted their manager Jose Mourinho to describe West Ham's tactics as "19th century football".

Allardyce's response to this criticism was: "I couldn't give a s**t", which – whilst mildly amusing – was yet another cause for consternation for Hammers fans; who worried that Sam genuinely **didn't** give a s**t about our style of play.

Nevertheless Andy Carroll had made his belated return in the 2-0 victory against Cardiff, and now provided both of the knockdowns for Kevin Nolan's goals in the 2-0 win over Swansea. Unfortunately, Carroll was then sent off and served a three match ban just as he was re-establishing himself in the side.

Another brace from Nolan helped us defeat Aston Villa and move out of the bottom three. This was followed by wins against Norwich and Southampton and Allardyce began to talk about the possibility of West Ham finishing the season higher than the previous campaign's 10th position. Thus, of course, we commenced another losing run, and the fans intensified their hate campaign against the manager; brandishing *'Fat Sam Out: You're Killing West Ham United'* banners, and even booing the players off the pitch following the 2-1 victory [!] against Hull.

[Nicky, from work, accompanied her boyfriend to this match. When I asked her, the following day, how she had enjoyed her first taste of the Upton Park

atmosphere, she expressed confusion that supporters would boo their own team for winning.

I explained to her about the fan unrest and displeasure at Allardyce's less-than-beautiful style of play, and then asked her how she had found the overall experience.

"Well, I've learnt something new about West Ham", Nicky replied.

"What's that?" I queried.

Nicky paused, cleared her throat, and then sang:
"Well...They hate Millwall and they hate Millwall.

 They hate Millwall and they hate Millwall.

 They hate Millwall and they hate Millwall.

 They are the Millwall haters...apparently."

And that's really all you need to know, dear Nicky!]

The atmosphere of unrest was only halted when West Ham guaranteed their survival, in the penultimate game of the season, with a 2-0 victory against their arch-rivals Tottenham Hotspurs. In fact, for many Hammers supporters – [*interviewee Alan Burgess springs to mind*] – the season **was** a successful one, in that we managed to 'do the treble' over Spurs; inspiring the sarcastic chant on the terraces: "*It's happened again,*

 It's happened again,

 Oh, Tottenham, it's happened again!"

[After beating Spurs 3-0 at White Hart Lane – a victory which included the goal of the season from exciting young prospect Ravel Morrison's mazy dribble through the Spurs defence – West Ham managed to repeat the feat in the Capital One Cup, and then, of course, the storming end-of-season victory at a raucous Upton Park which guaranteed our survival. For many West Ham United fans, this was as good as it gets! Even Sam Allardyce sarcastically reflected: "Tottenham have kept me in a job this season."]

At campaign's end the disgruntled fans demanded Allardyce's removal, but the manager was bullish in response to their loudly-vocalised criticisms, stating: "This is the highest level of football in the world, and I have successfully managed at this level for many, many years. I know how to manage in the Premier League, and I know how to turn teams into better teams than when I first took them over. We have had no real threat of relegation". [?]

The Board, however, listened to the supporters' comments and agreed that a change **was** required, announcing:

"The Board have insisted upon improvement to the playing and the backroom staff, to ensure the team provides more entertainment for the fans. We have a very clear vision of how we want West Ham United to operate under our ownership.

Although not everybody understands 'the West Ham way', **we do** – and Sam has ensured us that he can deliver that ethos".

A suitably chastened Allardyce promised to 'provide more entertainment'. The man who had sarcastically commented that 'it had been a long time since anyone had seen attractive flowing football at Upton Park', now humbly pledged to 'play entertaining football, the West Ham way'.

Skilful former England striker Teddy Sheringham was hired as 'attacking coach', to help the strikers find the net on a more regular basis, and the Board gave Sam £20 million to purchase a quality forward to assist this aim. This all gave the expectant fans renewed hope for a brighter Hammers future.

...And like my dreams?...We'll have to wait and see.

*

INTERLUDE
A WEST HAM FAN'S MEMORIES.   NO. 6

[Author's Note: This interview was slightly different, in that it focused more upon the terraces than on the football pitch.]

Name: Andrew Silver. **Age:** 63. **Profession:** Chef.

Born: Rochford, Essex. [Now living in Basildon, Essex.] **Connection to West Ham:** Fan. (Former member of the notorious **I.C.F.**)

Why do you support West Ham?

"My dad was a season ticket holder and he took me to my first match when I was seven.

For me, it was the crowd that hit me that day. You know; 'Bubbles' ringing out; the singing, the chanting. I was just in awe of the supporters.

*Also, the colour of the shirts - that claret and blue - it just **all** got to me. It did something to me that day and I've supported them ever since".*

Who is your all-time favourite West Ham player and why?

"Bobby Moore is my all-time favourite player. That man had the greatest footballing brain ever. He anticipated things happening.

I also liked Paolo Di Canio, Tony Cottee, Frank McAvennie...all the flair players basically."

Who is your least favourite West Ham player and why?

"Marco Boogers! That man was a total t**t. Played one game for us, against Manchester United, got sent off and then went to live in a caravan in Holland because he went mad!?"

What's your strongest single memory of supporting West Ham United?

"Can that include a time when I was arrested?"

335

[**Author**: "Yea. The book's not just about the football side of West Ham United. It's also incorporating the history of the ICF and East London."]

"Okay. Then it was when I was arrested at Grimsby about fifteen-odd years ago. I was accused of trying to incite a riot by making insulting gestures at the Grimsby fans. Apparently, I was riling up all of the fans in the West Ham supporters' enclosure as well.

Oh, and for being drunk and disorderly.

They threw the book at me. I was fined £1,000; which was a f***ing lot of money, but it was easier to pay the fine than try to fight it in court. They wanted to make an example of someone and, unfortunately, it was me!"

What's the best game you ever saw, or best experience of supporting West Ham?

"I've got so many memories of great games at Upton Park over the years.

Best experience though was when we played Castilla in Spain. It was just a fantastic feeling, following West Ham in Europe. We took such great support out there and the atmosphere was amazing."

[**Author's Note**: This was the notorious European Cup Winner's Cup tie in 1980/81, which saw many Hammers fans arrested in Spain, as the ICF rampaged.

The media reported that the trouble started when Hammers hooligans urinated over the Castilla fans below them on the terraces. However, the truth was that baton-wielding Spanish police had already clashed in bars with West Ham fans and were only too willing to meet the ICF head-on with reciprocal violence.

As the melee spread outside the ground, one West Ham fan was crushed behind a coach as the violence intensified.]

"We had to play the return leg behind closed doors because of the trouble we caused out there. There was a load of nonsense written about that though. They claimed that we'd been urinating over the Spanish supporters, and that that was what had caused all the trouble.

It was all blown up out of proportion. The fighting had already been going on for ages. It was just a massive ruck, all day!

The support we had out there though was unbelievable, and reinforced for me why I loved West Ham."

What was the worst game you ever saw / worst experience?

"Worst league game was when we were 3-0 up at home to Wimbledon and lost 4-3. That was shockingly bad!

It's mainly the cup games though that depressed me. To keep getting beaten by lower league opposition in the cups is just demoralising.

I remember Ian Dowie scoring an own goal against Stockport. That just sums it all up. He couldn't score to save his life in the 'right' end!"

Any non-football pitch related anecdotes around supporting West Ham?

"I've got loads of stories about the ICF. I grew up with Andy Swallow, and so I used to run with the ICF guys. We ruled the terraces!

I know all of the 'top boys': Cass Pennant, John O'Brien, Carlton Leach...

I'll tell you a funny non-ICF story though.

I remember going to a nightclub in Ilford and Julian Dicks was on the dance-floor. I couldn't believe what I was seeing; he was such an awful dancer!"

337

[Laughs.] *"I went up to him and said: 'It's a good job you're a decent footballer, 'cause you sure are a s**t dancer!'*

He took it well though. I speak to Julian all the time now and he still remembers that...

I'll tell you why I still love West Ham so much. Every year, around August 29ᵗʰ, a load of West Ham fans go up to Blackpool for the weekend. It's a massive Hammers meet-up. Fans not just from London, but from all over Britain, Belgium, Holland, everywhere.

We meet at a pub called 'The Laughing Donkey', and it's just a fantastic weekend. A few beers, a few laughs, and talking about West Ham.

For me, that's what West Ham United are all about – the fans!"

Ever had an affinity for another club and / or hated another club, and why?

"I've never liked another club. I hate Tottenham, Millwall and Manchester United, in that order.

Tottenham, particularly, because their fans are just 'glory hunters', living off their past history."

*

Postscript: What of the future?

Johnny Speight's Alf Garnett character once memorably remarked: "Supporting West Ham is like life itself. There's the odd moment of joy down the years, but most of it is bloody misery!"

Certainly many of the recent seasons have been – as Alf described – a 'bloody misery' to endure, and it's hard for even the most dedicated fanatic to see a day when West Ham United will be challenging for the Premiership title, or even for Champions League qualification.

In truth though, we probably never have had realistic title aspirations, and even the magnificent challenge of 1985-6, when we eventually finished third, seemed to take the players by surprise as much as it did the supporters.

Over a decade later, the fifth place finish under Harry Redknapp was considered a marvellous achievement but - as with John Lyall's campaign - was never built upon. Now, when Sam Allardyce considers a tenth place finish to be 'a good season', most West Ham fans are inclined to agree with him. This mentality of being happy with mid-table security must be eradicated if the Hammers are to ever challenge the elite.

Probably the best chance we ever had of consistent success was the Moore – Hurst – Peters era, when West Ham United were blessed with a plethora of talent. However, the Board seemed content with First Division security; never pressuring Ron Greenwood into expectations of title achievement; seemingly content with FA and European Cup-Winner's Cup triumphs.

This mind-set continued through the Redknapp era; when a frustrated Harry complained several times that the Board 'didn't want West Ham to be a top six club'.

Only in recent years have there been murmurings of increased expectation. The Icelandic owners promised to make West Ham a top four club; *shortly before the financial genius bankers lost all their money on a horse at PaddyPower. Well, it had been a good tip…Harry had given it to them!*

Current owners, Davids' - Gold and Sullivan – have made similar proclamations, but are at least attempting to follow through with the move to the bigger stadium and finances for the manager in the transfer market.

Then again, perhaps that's the truest indication of the genuine love the fans have for the Hammers; an acceptance that they're not going to sweep aside all opposition, but an eternal optimism that they'll win more than they lose, and entertain the supporters along the way. [*Billy Bond's realisation, back in the late 1960's, that the fans cared more for entertaining attacking football than for mere victory.*]

The original supporters were the local EastEnders, and even when the nation's glory-hunters began their obsessive quest for success by following whichever was the hottest team of the moment, West Ham United continued to attract those who simply appreciated good football and skilful players who were pleasing to the eye with their audacious talents. The occasional FA Cup win was a mere bonus.

Regardless of the much-hyped relocation of the club to the Olympic Stadium, the Premiership is the toughest league in the world, and the Hammers future will depend largely upon more consistent performances on the pitch and the sustained financial input of the owners, in order that West Ham United can continue to compete at the highest level and perhaps at least win some long-overdue silverware.

I strongly believe that the thing which has kept most supporters loyal over the last few trophy-less decades has been West Ham United's continuing ability to thrill the fans with eye-catching attacking football; and the presence of some truly gifted individual footballers. However, the awful Avram Grant-helmed campaign and the recent struggles under Zola and Allardyce, are worrying indicators of a move away from our thrilling heritage.

In 2013 West Ham inaugurated their Lifetime Achievement Award, to recognise the contribution to the history of the club of its former heroes. The dynamic former captain Billy Bonds was a most deserving initial recipient, and was followed in 2014 by his friend and former team-mate Trevor Brooking.

More importantly for today's fans though; can some **new** legends finally emerge in the claret 'n' blue? Or will we always be looking back to the 1960's, '70's and '80's for our favourite memories?

In 2009 one of the popular West Ham United fan web-sites asked its readers / contributors to vote for the '*Top 100 West Ham Players of All-Time*'.

The results were intriguing and included many players whom you probably wouldn't have expected to see. [Particularly now, 5 years later.] This anomaly can perhaps be explained though by a tendency for the younger supporters to vote for then-current or very recent players. However, by the time the list reached the top 30, it pretty much reflected the best of the best; the only remaining question marks being over the inclusion of Swiss international midfielder Valon Behrami – who didn't actually make that many appearances for the Hammers – and the then-mega-popular Carlos Tevez, who had recently heroically saved the Hammers from relegation.

The top 30 are:

30: Malcolm Allison. 29: Michael Carrick. 28: Eyal Berkovic. 27: Ernie Gregory. 26: Frank Lampard, Snr. 25: Scott Parker. 24: Valon Behrami. 23: Matthew Upson. 22: Ray Stewart. 21: Bryan 'Pop' Robson. 20: Slaven Bilic. 19: Joe Cole. 18: Rio Ferdinand. 17: Johnny Byrne. 16: Vic Keeble. 15: Frank McAvennie. 14: Ludek Miklosko. 13: Alvin Martin. 12: Robert

Green. 11: Tony Cottee. 10: Phil Parkes. 9: Julian Dicks. 8: Martin Peters. 7: Alan Devonshire. 6: Carlos Tevez. 5: Billy Bonds. 4: Geoff Hurst. 3: Paolo Di Canio. 2: Trevor Brooking. 1: Bobby Moore.

The likelihood of West Ham United ever again discovering someone with the sheer class and panache of the exquisite Bobby Moore is extremely unlikely and – perhaps - that is the way it **should** be; in order that we can continue to appreciate and lionise the greatest defender English football has ever produced.

Other legends, such as Geoff Hurst, Martin Peters, Trevor Brooking, Alan Devonshire, Paolo Di Canio, et al, may be almost as hard to replace, but there have been players who approached their capabilities.

Who knows how good Dean Ashton may have become, had his career not been so cruelly curtailed by injury? Would Joe Cole have been better appreciated had he chosen to continue plying his dazzling ball-dribbling trade in front of the Upton Park faithful? Could the ever-dependable midfield battler Scott Parker have retained his England place **and** helped return the Hammers to the Premiership; perhaps achieving an unheard-of four consecutive *'Hammer of the Year'* Awards, in the process? Will combative midfielder Mark Noble, or smooth central defender James Tomkins, live up to their early plaudits and prove to be future Hammers legends themselves? [Noble being voted *Hammer of the Year 2013/14.*]

Young prospect Ravel Morrison has excited the fans with his performances so far, but there have been question marks against his mentality and commitment, and thus the jury remains unconvinced as to his long-term worth to the Hammers.

More significantly for the fans of the Greenwood / Lyall eras of flowing attacking football; will West Ham United ever again find an attack-minded manager to inspire the players to electrify the supporters? Allardyce's spanked chubby bottom and b******ing by the owners, and subsequent promise to 'be more entertaining and exciting' - and the hiring of Sheringham as his striking coach - strongly suggests that attacking football does not come naturally to Sam.

Likewise, will there ever again be a smoothly creative midfielder in the Brooking / Devonshire mould to make the fans purr with delight; or a dynamic Hurst / Pop Robson style goal-hungry forward to excite the passionate EastEnders?

Many fans hope that the aggressive Andy Carroll may become that new goalscoring hero we've longed for; or perhaps it will be the as-yet unsigned striker Allardyce chooses to partner Carroll?

As the cliché goes…only time will tell.

*

Strangely, I find that I'm no longer quite as passionate about the Hammers as I used to be. Oh, I still shout my appreciation and continue to agonise over the scorelines, each Saturday, but I don't feel the same burning excitement whenever I see the players walk out on to the pitch.

I think the constant changes in personnel – particularly during the perplexing Redknapp era – robbed some of the comforting stability of cheering for the same set of players each month. Also, as noted in the Jeff Ives interview earlier in this book; as I age I find that I no longer idolise players who are young enough to still be discovering shaving-cream and yet earn £60,000 per week.

The working-class game has become anything but, and following football these days is an expensive business; made worse by the knowledge that – for some clubs - success is often being bought rather than earned. [Manchester City becoming the latest club to be purchased by billionaires and made successful through massive financial input.]

There will however be an added poignancy for me whenever I view West Ham United in action these days, due to the tragic death of my son James, in 2012.

He lived and breathed the Hammers, and yet never survived to see his beloved West Ham return to the Premiership; dying shortly before the start of the 2012/13 season.

He was fittingly buried in his old West Ham United shirt, and whenever I watch them play now I always imagine his animated reactions – win, lose or draw.

The fervour is certainly contagious and my wife Yvonne went from quietly accepting my obsession to becoming equally engrossed herself; to the extent that when we went to Spain on holiday she commemorated the visit by having *Bubbles* tattooed upon her arm. West Ham have the ability to suck you in like that!

[*Thank God the ICF are now 'retired'. I'm sure she'd be heading all of their terrace charges otherwise...and getting my little head kicked in, in the process!*]

One day, I'm sure, I will simply retreat to my memories and think of that wonderful Christmas in 1968, when I held the claret-and-blue shirt in my six-year old hands and learned to believe in the ultimate beauty of the 'peoples club'; West Ham United.

But, for now, join me in my passion for the Hammers and feel the hairs on the back of your neck rise as *'I'm*

Forever Blowing Bubbles', plaintively cries its tender song of hope-and-heartbreak to the Heavens.

*

INTERLUDE
A WEST HAM FAN'S MEMORIES.   NO.7

Name: Mitch Burgess. **Age:** 21. **Profession:** Engineer. **Born:** Leyton, East London. [Now living in North Weald, Essex.] **Connection to West Ham:** Fan. [Had a Trial with the club, as a schoolboy.]

Why do you support West Ham?

"I support West Ham simply because my dad supported West Ham. When I was younger my dad was always telling me about games he went to before I was born, and **he** *made me interested in them.*

Then, when I started going to a few games with him, I decided that I liked what I was seeing. The fans, also, made me like them. Their fanatical support; all the constant singing; it was just so much more passionate than what I was hearing from any other fans."

Who is your all-time favourite West Ham player and why?

"Paolo Di Canio. Why? Purely for reasons that aren't connected to what happened on a football pitch". [Laughs.] *"I'll tell you about that later!"*

Who is your least favourite West Ham player and why?

"Bobby Zamora. It might seem funny, because I know he got us promoted, but he was terrible normally!

He's actually started scoring goals nowadays but I didn't think that he scored enough goals for us."

[**Author:** Despite all of the goals he scored, alongside Tevez, to save us from relegation, you mean? Just a thought.]

345

"He was always being caught offside and making silly, needless fouls. I just don't think he was good enough to be a main striker." [Laughs.] *"Plus, it probably didn't help that he'd come to us from Tottenham, to be honest".*

What's your strongest single memory of supporting West Ham United?

*"Probably when the keeper saved Frank Lampard's penalty at Stamford Bridge. **All** of my best memories are against teams or players I hate!*

***Or,** maybe when Anton Ferdinand scored a last-minute equaliser at White Hart Lane, to earn us a draw against Tottenham.*

***Or,** when Glenn Roeder got hit in the head with a pie!"* [Laughs.] *"Yea, that's definitely up there."*

What's the best game you ever saw, or best experience of supporting West Ham?

"The best game I ever saw was West Ham at home to Ipswich, in the Play-off semi-final, when we won 2-1.

Even though that was the year we lost to Palace in the Final, that was probably the best experience I've ever had at Upton Park, because of the atmosphere that day.

Obviously, that win was important, as it got us to the Play-off Final in Cardiff, but – more than the fact that we won – it was just the fantastic atmosphere in the ground that day; it was incredible. I'll never forget it!"

What was the worst game you ever saw / worst experience?

"Oh, I've seen some bad games." [Laughs.] *"Some **bad** games!"*

[Pause.] *"Probably as recently as three or four years ago, in a pre-season friendly against Leyton Orient. We were awful!"*

Any non-football pitch related anecdotes around supporting West Ham?

"Here's why I love Paolo Di Canio!
I was in a TESCO car park with my dad".

[Author's quick – but annoying – interruption. The nationwide chain of successful supermarkets were born from a simple market stall in East London's Whitechapel; owned by Jack Cohen, who named his first grocery shop TESCO, after his wife Tess Cohen.

Also, did you know that entrepreneur Alan Sugar started off with a market stall in the East End's thriving Petticoat Lane Market?

I know, I know, but, hey; it's **my** book and I can interrupt whenever I like! I'm feeding you knowledge here people. This could be life-saving information…if a gangsta rapper ever holds a gun to your head and asks you 'what Jack Cohen's wife's name was', you'll know. Not a very likely scenario admittedly…about as believable as the sign that says: *'Welcome to Scotland'*. They **are** welcome to it!

But I digress…back to the Paolo story.]

"I was about 10 years old and I looked up and saw this silver Jaguar pull in to the car park. I said to my dad: 'That's the car I'm gonna have when I'm older'.

Then I saw Paolo Di Canio step out of this lovely silver Jag. I ran up to him, shouting: 'Di Canio; Di Canio; I love you!'

He smiled and said: 'Oh, thanks', and then went in to do his shopping.

I said to my dad: 'That's not good enough. I've got to get his autograph. I need to see him again when he comes out'.

'But I've got frozen food in the car', he complained."
[Laughs.]

"When he came out, I went over to him and asked: 'Mr Di Canio, can I have your autograph?'

He laughed and said: 'You must really like me, to have waited outside all this time'.

I told him that we'd just come back from Bradford and had seen him score his goal. 'Thanks', I said; holding the signed photo he'd given me, and I got back into the car.

All of a sudden, the car door opened again. He'd gone to the boot of his car; got the football shirt out that he'd actually just worn – [it still had the dirt on it; so I know it was genuine] – and he said: 'As you're my favourite fan, I'm going to give you the shirt which I wore when I scored against Bradford', and he handed me the shirt.

[I've framed it but I've not put it up on the wall, because that's the last thing I'd want a burglar to nick!] Then he leaned down and said to me: 'On Saturday, I'm going to score again, and that goal will be just for you!'

The next Saturday we played Watford, at home, and he scored from a free-kick. Can you imagine how I felt? A 10 year old boy, believing that he'd scored that goal just for me".

Ever had an affinity for another club and / or hated another club, and why?

*"There's three teams I hate. Chelsea, Millwall and Tottenham. And that's because...I just **hate** them!"*

[Laughs.] *"No, I hate Millwall and Tottenham simply because **all** West Ham fans hate them, but I hate Chelsea because of their fans. They think they're 'all that', since they've come into Abramovich's money...**and** they've got Lampard in their team; which makes me hate them even more!"*

[**Author:** See? It's not just **me** that hates Chelsea.]

*

BIBLIOGRAPHY

Giles, A. & Pickford, W. *'Association Football'.* [1905] Caxton.

Blows, K & Hogg, T. *'The Essential History of West Ham United'.* [2000] Headline Book Publishing, Swindon.

Allison, M. & Lawson, J. *'The Colours of My Life'.* [1975] Everest Books.

Powell, J. *'Bobby Moore: The Life and Times of a Sporting Hero'.* [1993] Robson Books, London.

Hurst, G. *'1966 And All That'.* [2001] Headline Book Publishing, London.

Peters, M. *'The Ghost of '66'.* [2006] Orion Books Ltd, London.

Greaves, J. *'Greavsie'.* [2003] Time Warner Books, London.

Ward, H & Weeks, D. *'Bullets, Blood and Broken Bodies: The extraordinary criminal career of Buller Ward'.* [2008] New Breed Publishing, Essex.

Lyall, J. *'Just Like My Dreams'.* [1990] Penguin Books.

Redknapp, H. *''Arry'.* [1998] Collins Willow, London.

Redknapp, H. *'Always Managing'.* [2013] Ebury Publishing, Random House, London.

Greenwood, R. *'Yours Sincerely'.* [1984] Willow Books.

Pennant, C. *'Congratulations: You Have Just Met the I.C.F.'* [2003] John Blake Ltd, London.

Leach, C. *'Rise of the Footsoldier'.* [2002 – revised 2008] John Blake Publishing, London.

Bonds, B. *'Bonzo'.* [1988] George Weidenfeld & Nicolson Ltd, London.

Tomas, J. *'The Hammers: West Ham United's Dream Team'*. [1997] Mainstream Publishing Company Ltd, Edinburgh.

Brooking, T. *'Trevor Brooking'*. [1981] Pelham Books Ltd, London.

McDonald, T. & Francis, D. *'The Boys Of '86'*. [2001] Mainstream Publishing Company Ltd, Edinburgh.

McIlvanney, H. *'Heroic Symbol of a Golden Age'*. [1993] *Guardian* newspaper, London.

Lacey, D. *'England's Golden Boy'*. [1993] *Guardian* newspaper, London.

Corbett, J. *'The Last Days of Bobby Moore'*. [2005] *The Observer Sport Monthly,* London.

Di Canio, P. *'Paolo Di Canio'*. [2000] Collins Willow, London.

Blows, K & Sharratt, B. *'Bring Me The Head of Trevor Brooking'*. [2010] Mainstream Publishing Company Ltd, Edinburgh.

Brand, R. *'Articles of Faith'*. [2008] Harper Collins, London.

[Books read, but not directly referenced from, include: *'Fortunes Always Hiding'* by Blows, K, and *'An Irrational Hatred of Luton'* and *'West Ham 'til I Die'*, by Banks, R.]

*

A review of *'And On the 6th Day God Created Bobby Moore'*, by Steve Marsh, Editor of *'They Fly So High'*; West Ham United fan website.

"Growing up through the same period of support as the author David Weeks, I was

taken on a poignant rollercoaster ride through West Ham United's history.

The author successfully charts the social and political climate through his lifetime journey supporting the Hammers; with all of the major highs-and-lows, both at Home and Away, recounted for the reader...

The book was a great read from cover to cover and, for me, a great reminder of why we support the club we do, and what it means to be a West Ham United supporter.

The cup finals, the yo-yo promotion / relegation seasons, even the infamous ICF, all get a mention in this humorous guide to the history of the club.

We are reminded of some of the good and not-so-good managers, and the legends to have pulled on the claret 'n' blue shirt. The book is also interspersed with 'Fans Memories'. Definitely on my list to give as a Christmas present!"

*

ABOUT THE AUTHOR.

David Weeks is a pseudonym.

David is the author of **'Bullets, Blood and Broken Bodies'**, the biography of Kray-era East London villain Henry 'Buller' Ward; available on Kindle and a revised paperback version on Amazon..

[*Excerpt on the following pages.*]

He has also authored **'Essence Of A Man: A Study in Male Violence and the Use of Weapons'**, available via Amazon Books, through Amazon.com. **&** Amazon.uk and also on **Kindle.** ISBN 9781468072815.

This book examines the various theories behind male aggression; ranging from genetics to learned behaviour; whether violent impulses are in-born; whether personal morality is innate or learned; the effect of male role models and stereotypes; our body's natural reaction to fear and aggression; the influence of alcohol, drugs and pornography upon male aggression; the impact of religion upon mass aggression; the reasons behind gang membership and the use of weapons in today's society.

Includes brutally honest interviews with a diverse selection of men; examining their own personal experiences of violence.

Formerly a graphic designer / portrait artist / self-defence instructor, David has also contributed to various publications, including a regular monthly column for *'Combat Magazine'* and *'Martial Arts Illustrated'*; as well as the on-line e-magazine *'Zani'.*

David has worked with children and adults with disabilities, for the last 19 years.

Now living in Wembley, North-West London, with the lovely Yvonne, he has dedicated this book to his first-born son James. David has two other beautiful children; Della and Lukas Wing.

*

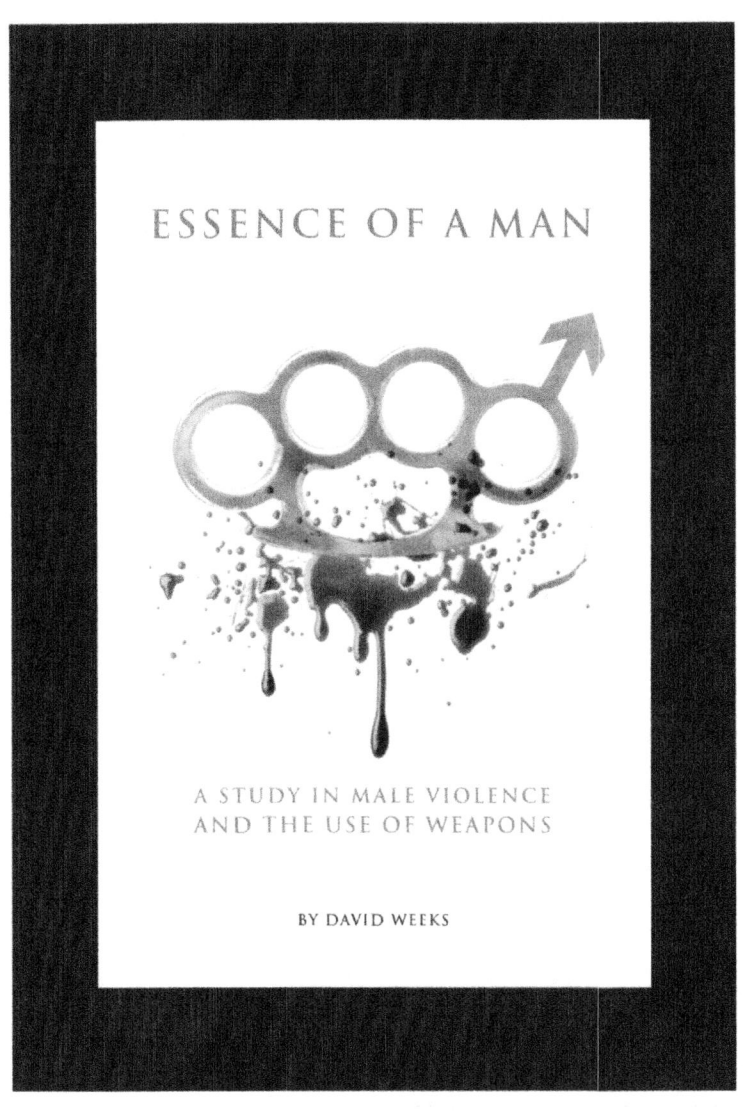

ESSENCE OF A MAN

A STUDY IN MALE VIOLENCE
AND THE USE OF WEAPONS

BY DAVID WEEKS

**Book via Amazon.com or on Kindle. ISBN
9781468072815**

By Henry Ward & David Weeks

The

East

End

Villain

they

couldn'

t kill!

BULLETS, BLOOD AND BROKEN BODIES
THE EXTRAORDINARY CRIMINAL CAREER OF
'BULLER' WARD
BY HENRY WARD & DAVID WEEKS

Now available on Kindle!
Bullets, Blood & Broken Bodies
The extraordinary criminal career of Henry 'Buller' Ward.

Sample Chapter from Buller's book
Introduction – 1967:
'You'll have to do better than that, Reggie boy!'

When Buller saw the Kray twins walk into the Regency Club he knew with an absolute certainty that he would be made to pay a painful price for allying himself with Tony Maffia. He also knew that the value he placed upon friendship demanded that he not stand idly by and allow his friend to suffer a possibly deadly fate at the hands of the increasingly unhinged Kray twins.

Ever since Reggie's wife Frances had committed suicide Reg had become as unpredictable and prone to depression as his heavily-medicated brother and it was common knowledge in London's underworld that the Krays were now totally out of control; using ever more extreme forms of violence and murder, in order to solidify their stranglehold on the capital's more vulnerable and impressionable criminals. In their bid to become all-powerful, the Krays were shedding the last fragile remnants of morality and leaving a trail of broken and bloodied victims in their wake.

'I said to Tony; "We could be in dead trouble here!"
Reggie called me over and asked; "What you doing with Maffia, Buller?"
I said; "He's a pal of mine, you know he is."'
*"Well, we're going to f*****g hurt him! He's going to f*****g pay now for not giving us that money and telling us to 'f**k off'.'*
"Can't you leave him out, for my sake, Reggie?' I asked. 'After all, we're supposed to be friends, aren't we?"
"You're no friend of ours, if you're with him", Kray responded. "You choose; him or us!"
*"F**k it then. I choose him!" I said and straight away I felt my adrenalin rising, as I knew the enormity of my decision.*
I turned and walked over to Maffia and said; 'Right, we'd best have it away on our toes fast.'
He said he needed to use the toilet first but as I turned and looked behind me I could see the Krays and their cohorts

moving across the club towards us and so I shouted; 'For f**k's sake Tone, don't hang about' and he ran out the club. With that Reggie came up to me and snarled; 'You marked his card, Buller'.

"*Course I did. What would <u>you</u> have done, Reg?*"

If I'd expected a reasoned debate well, those days were long gone. No longer was I the older villain who they respected and sought an alliance with. They'd outgrown the need for my protection or help. They feared no-one now.

Reggie lashed out with a right-hander to my jaw but I saw the punch coming and rode it. I smiled derisively and said; "You'll have to do a lot better than that, Reggie boy!"

Then Ronnie stepped forward and threw a punch at me, followed by a quick cluster of blows from Reggie.

To be honest, the twins couldn't fight and I could've smacked the f**k out of both of them in a straightener but they were nasty bastards and didn't fight fair, as I found out when one of their crew cracked me from behind with a cosh.

The pain in my head from that blow, from a cowardly little mug named Ginger, dropped me to my knees and I looked up and saw Harry Abrahams handing the twins some tools.

Although he didn't actually take part in the beating, I held Abrahams just as responsible as the other bastards who were beginning to kick lumps out of me. Cowardly f*****s, all of them!

I lay on the floor and tried to cover up but then I felt something sharp stabbing into my thigh and I saw something glistening in Reggie Kray's hand. He kneeled over me with a crazed look and began slicing away at my face like a maniacal butcher hacking at some tough meat.

I could see my blood pooling around me, as the Krays and their henchmen battered away at me and then Reggie stood up, panting and regarded his handiwork.

'You should've done him with a shooter', observed Ronnie impassively and then the twins walked away, leaving me lying there trying to retain consciousness."

Printed in Great Britain
by Amazon

41529352R00198